SAMEEN RUSHDIE'S INDIAN COOKERY

Sameen Rushdie was born in Bombay but later moved to Pakistan with her family where she practised law before coming to live in London. Brought up in a Muslim – and therefore meat-eating – family, Sameen learned the traditional art of Muslim cookery. Later, in Karachi, she discovered the regional cuisines of Sindh, North-West Frontier Province and Punjab, and her marriage to a Bengali introduced her to *his* culinary traditions also. She now works in the field of adult education.

TO ABDUL MOMEN
But for whom…

SAMEEN RUSHDIE'S INDIAN COOKERY

Sameen Rushdie

ARROW BOOKS

Arrow Books Limited
20 Vauxhall Bridge Road, London SW1V 2SA

An imprint of the Random Century Group

London Melbourne Sydney Auckland Johannesburg
and agencies throughout the world

First published in Great Britain by
Century Hutchinson 1988
Arrow edition 1991

Printed and bound in Great Britain by
The Guernsey Press Co. Ltd
Guernsey, C.I.

ISBN 0 09 974110 5

· CONTENTS ·

· INTRODUCTION ·

The subject of 'Indian' cookery is as vast and varied as the subcontinent itself. When I first became seriously committed to doing this book the difficulty of capturing the essential spirit of all the major regional cuisines, even in microcosm, weighed on me greatly. I wondered whether I knew enough to present the banquet of flavours and experiences necessary to represent the full range of regional dishes and give you the opportunity of becoming acquainted with the incredible diversity that exists in the school of Indian cookery as a whole. I felt it was important to do justice to a cuisine that in the West has been shrouded in mystique and subjected to a mockery which has served to alienate many westerners from Indian food. Then suddenly I realized the trap I was unwittingly falling into was the same one that has historically often worked successfully to undermine the efforts of black people and of women. It could not rationally be my responsibility, even if it were within my power, to wipe the slate clean with a single book or to redress all the wrongs by writing a bigger book than I had experience to draw on.

Once I had reached, albeit by this circuitous route, the only possible conclusion that ever existed, that my book would be about my cooking and the food we eat at home, I felt in control again. But now I was uncertain about what I should call the cuisine . . . Indian, Pakistani or Bangladeshi. One difficulty I have with these nationalist descriptions is that they don't tell you very much about the food. The other, and for me much more real, dilemma has to do with the pattern of my own life, our migration from India to Pakistan, and the influences on me of friends and relatives. It is not irrelevant therefore to tell you that I was born and grew up in Bombay, in a North Indian Muslim family that traces its origins to Delhi, Aligarh and Srinagar. I went to college in Lahore and much of my adult life has been spent in Karachi where my parents live, a city in which there is easy access to a variety of regional cuisines from Sindh, North-West Frontier Province, Punjab and even Uttar Pradesh, on account of the city's large

Muhajjir population that migrated at partition. My exposure to Bengali cuisine came through marriage and was learned in London where I now live. So the cuisine contained in this book doesn't fit neatly into any one slot. Broadly speaking, the recipes you will find here are of a traditional nature and are drawn mainly, though not exclusively, from a North Indian Muslim culture, although I hope they will also reflect the important influences on me of other regional cooking. I believe that this sort of mixture is a more authentic reflection of the cooking you would experience in Indian, Pakistani or Bangladeshi homes where people freely borrow tastes and techniques from other styles of cooking to enhance their own.

In Hindustani, when people pay you a compliment for being a good cook they tell you that 'you have that special taste in your hands'. A person who has this sense of taste in their hands can cook anything and it will be delicious. I do not believe, however, that good cooks are born with some magic gift that sets them above the rest of us. Such myths were probably established by those who did not enjoy cooking and wanted to ensure they would never have to. It also seems likely that men were the original architects of such mythology, cleverly constructed to justify their resistance or refusal to share in the drudge of daily cooking by paying women lavish compliments which praised them for their patience, endurance and delicacy and, finally, endowed them with special powers: taste buds in their hands!

A person whose hands have been blessed with this sense of taste has simply through practice acquired the feel for cooking Indian food. It is similar to learning how to drive a car. You do it by the book to start with but slowly and imperceptibly you do it by reflex and instinct. At this stage of the learning process you can improvise, invent and take short cuts with every confidence that the meal you are about to produce will be no less tasty or authentic for having strayed away from the basic recipe.

There is no law written or unwritten that says to cook well you must be dedicated to the practice of cooking, or indeed even be fond of cooking. Most of us enjoy eating and that is the important thing. I have proof of this. The first time in my life that I ever cooked anything, I found myself in a situation in which I had to cook for my entire family for a whole week. Many years ago my mother suddenly had to rush from Karachi to Islamabad to be with my grandmother who was seriously ill. Throwing me in at the deep end, without a second's thought or hesitation, my mother sat me down an hour before her departure to explain to me how to cook some of those dishes most often eaten in our home. No concessions were made in the selection of dishes nor any allowances given in recognition of my status as a beginner in this field. I had the gravest doubts about whether I would manage to rise to the occasion or bring an acceptable degree of competence to the job and could foresee not only disasters in the kitchen but also my father and sisters refusing to eat anything I cooked. My mother dismissed all my concerns as silliness and insisted that there was nothing to it. She was, of course, right as usual. I produced meal after meal of delicious food and no one's amazement was greater than my own. Yes, it took me much longer than it does now but that was because I was so inept at chopping onions or peeling and crushing garlic; and so spoilt that I had never even washed rice. Her recipes were vague and my lesson went something like this:

HOW TO MAKE ALOO GOSHT

AMMA: Take a few onions and chop them up. Fry about half of them in *ghee* until they are a pinkish-almondy colour.

ME: How many onions? How much *ghee*?

AMMA: Oh, just a few. Maybe two or three, depending on their size.

ME: You still haven't told me how much *ghee*.

AMMA: About one or two cooking spoonfuls. The more *ghee* the tastier the food. If you find at the end that you have too much *ghee* you can always remove some from the top before serving. It's better to use a bit more than a bit less to cook with as it makes the food much tastier.

ME: What do I do next?

AMMA: While half the onions you have chopped are frying in the *ghee*, you should grind the other half and have them ready. When your onions are pinkish . . . and remember not to let them get too dark as the final colour of your dish will depend on the colour of your onions; if you burn them you will have a dark-coloured gravy like they have in roadside cafés; if they are underdone your food will look bland and won't have that pretty, blossomed look. It really is better to get the right colour by doing your onions properly than by trying to make up for it later by the use of too many spices. . . . Oh yes . . . now where was I? . . . Add the crushed garlic and grated ginger to the frying onions.

ME: Amma, you always forget to tell me quantities.

AMMA: About a teaspoon of each should be all right. You shouldn't need more than half a teaspoon of *haldi* and you may like to use two teaspoons of *dhania* powder, as that is what gives it its main taste. It is not essential but if you have some *zeera* powder handy you can throw in a pinch or two. Then just stir-fry the spices together with the browned onions for a few seconds. Be careful not to overdo this or you will find the spices sticking to the bottom of the pan and they may turn bitter and will certainly get too dark. The next thing is to add the remaining ground raw onion and then the meat followed by chopped tomatoes. The tomatoes should give out enough water to enable the lamb to simmer over a low flame. If you think it is necessary, or if the meat is tough from an old animal, you can add some water and let it cook gently. After about half an hour add the diced potatoes and let the food carry on cooking over a low flame until the meat is tender and the potatoes are cooked. You see, there's nothing to it.

I tell you, it worked. Although her recipe was vague when it came to describing quantities, she told me things which otherwise I could have learnt only by trial and error over a long period of time. What it proved to me was that it really is true that anyone can cook.

I have noticed a distinctly different approach to cooking in India and Pakistan to that which I have observed in England where people appear to follow their recipe books as closely as possible. I have never seen an English person cook for a dinner party without a recipe book open by the side of the cooker. It is equally true to say that I have never seen an Indian friend using a recipe book in quite the same way – at least not when cooking Indian food. The reason for this is that right from the beginning such blind dependence on written recipes is not encouraged. We do not have a tradition of learning to cook with the help of cookery books. When you first start to cook you are usually taught by someone in your family. Even later, if you are eating at a friend's house and are served with something that strikes you as unusual or delicious, it would be quite normal to ask how it was made. The recipe would be explained to you quite simply in a few minutes; you would have been told the basic ingredients used and given a short explanation of the method employed. It would be assumed that you had a basic understanding of the principles of Indian cookery, and there are clearly no hard and fast rules about quantities.

Tastes vary enormously and there is room within a single recipe to put one's own mark on a dish. There is, of course, such a thing as too much or too little – but somewhere in between those extremes there is a correct approximation of the *right* quantity. The same is true about the timing of the different stages at which the spices should be added to the cooking and the forms in which they are used. This touch is soon acquired by practice. For those of you who will only cook the occasional Indian meal it will probably be simplest and safest to use the quantities I suggest. If, on the other hand, you are someone who cooks Indian food regularly, you will yourself, I imagine, begin to use these recipes in much the same way as I use other people's recipes, as a source of new ideas. I read through the whole recipe to get a sense of the kind of food that is to be prepared, the method, the ingredients, their suggested quantities and proportion to each other and then I close the book and do it. This is not because I do not trust someone else's recipe but because I cook too much in my life to spend the additional time necessary to follow a recipe accurately – reading, weighing, measuring, and so on. Also it is crucial to remember that, however faithfully you may follow instructions, if you do not stop to think about what you are doing, and why, you will seldom be able to produce a dish of real excellence. This is because the most precise recipes cannot be thought of as scientific formulas programmed so as to be incapable of error. There are too many factors that are unpredictable that could affect the cooking process: the quality of meat, freshness of a vegetable, age of rice, hardness or softness of local water and so on. The best recipes and the best cooks will always make allowances for these variables and the quality of the dishes produced will then be marked by distinction and originality.

There are certain myths about Indian cooking that were developed during the days of the British Raj which have been painstakingly nurtured since. Racism has made the task of perpetuating the commonest of these myths easy. There is the overt and easily recognizable variety which tells us that Indian curries can be smelt a block away, are heavily overspiced, full of chilli and mouth-searingly hot! Haven't we all heard that this food is saturated in grease and so terribly overcooked that all meats and vegetables lose their natural flavour and goodness? Close runners-up are the exotic myths which feast on reminiscences of the days of the Raj and speak of the colourful East with its different alluring smells of intricately blended spices; stories abound of nostalgic memories of *sahibs* and *memsahibs* picnicking on succulent quail and partridge on elephant back, under gaily coloured canopies, while barefoot natives ingeniously serve the meal raised up on the elephants' trunks. We are told of the labour-intensive method of cooking because time is meaningless in India and people come cheap. We must believe that the best cooking is the result of elaborate and lengthy preparations because our finest dishes are handed down to us from kings, queens and *nawabs* whose vast slave kitchens devised dishes that were painstakingly and lovingly prepared: *For best results cook your* biryani *by candlelight*. I must admit that there are those of us who have colluded in spreading some of these messages. It was good business.

The truth is that Indian food does not have to be overspiced or full of chillies. In fact the best cooking always shows restraint in the use of spices and it is commonly known that ordinary cooks will use too many spices in large quantities in an attempt to camouflage an inadequate control over their art. It is also a fact that most of the spices commonly used contain valuable properties, vitamins and minerals and have medicinal qualities that cure or ward off illnesses such as heart disease, gout, ailments of the skin and so on.

I sometimes cannot fully believe how deep-seated is the conviction in those who have never cooked a single Indian meal that it is a hugely complicated business requiring elaborate preparation, endless patience and endurance. Certainly there are dishes that take a lot of fussing over – but so there are in all kinds of cooking. Just as European food has some quickly put together meals and other complicated ones, so do we. There are many wonderful dishes eaten in Indian homes every day that take less than an hour to prepare and cook. It should be remembered that it does not follow that just because these meals are simple and painless to prepare they are any less tasty than those which require a great deal of care and trouble. Dishes which are time-consuming like *Haleem* and *Nihari*, for example, have come to be regarded as special treats. This is not so much because they taste better than 'everyday food' but because they are cooked less often as the process is so slow. For those of you that have a 'slow cooker' or want to invest in one, even these meals become less of a chore. I know that it is commonly believed that cooking a roast or grilling chops is so much quicker and easier than preparing an Indian meal. I have yet to be convinced that this is the case. Another of the great advantages of Indian food is that there are very few dishes for which mealtimes have to be planned precisely. I think this is a big advantage both in daily life and at dinner parties. Food can be cooked well ahead, allowing your family or guests complete flexibility about when to sit down and eat.

On the whole it is now recognized that the word 'curry' is inappropriate and inadequate as a generic description of Indian/Pakistani/Bangladeshi food. It is difficult for me to use the word without hearing and being deeply offended by its racist connotations. In recent years many Indian cookery books published in the West have gone to great pains to explain the simple fact that in the subcontinent there are a wealth of dishes from different regions which are as unlike one another as the languages, customs and religions of the people who cook and eat them.

Britain now has large Asian communities who have brought with them the knowledge of traditional cooking methods and food habits of their families back in the subcontinent. Indian food is therefore eaten in thousands of British homes every day. I think it is important to understand the impact this is likely to have on British food as it has been thought of until now. In any case, it is no longer necessary, in my view, to look to India, Pakistan or Bangladesh and to talk about 'regional' foods in that context alone. Within the British Asian community there are Punjabis, Kashmiris, Gujeratis, Bengalis, Sindhis, Tamils, Sinhalese and people from Uttar Pradesh, Maharashtra and Hyderabad who may be Hindu, Muslim, Sikh, Parsee or Christian. There are also British-born Asians who, having been raised on Indian food, eat it every day although they may never have visited the subcontinent at all.

In those pockets of England where Asian people have settled in large numbers, this has meant that just about every conceivable ingredient needed to cook any Indian dish ever invented is available. In the Greater London area, in places such as Southall, Wembley and Brick Lane, the very atmosphere of a bustling subcontinental-style market where business is brisk, but the pace is leisurely, has been authentically recreated by the shopkeepers and shoppers. Prime specimens of tropical fruit, vegetables and herbs are displayed in abundance. Recently when my husband and I moved to Wembley and visited the Ealing Road market area for the first time, the pitch of excitement in both of us instantly rose to a dangerous level. It was as if we had turned off a busy English high street and arrived round the corner, in a dream, at some place thousands of miles away. Greedily we reached simultaneously for everything we saw, as if afraid that if we didn't hurry we might wake up. Two pairs of hands eagerly scooped up more than we could possibly cook, eat or even carry home . . . tender young okra, Kenyan aubergines, fresh spinach in mid-winter, green papaya and mangoes, fenugreek greens, mustard leaves, *same* and *gwar phalli*, *tinda*, *mooli*, custard apples, *potol*, bitter gourds, lychees, coconut, guavas, *cheeko*, raw sugar cane. The list is endless.

The present situation in inner-city areas generally may not be as glorious, but all the important ingredients necessary to cook Indian food are now widely available. Most districts I can think of have at least one or two shops that stock Indian spices, *daals* and herbs. You never have to travel very far to find a basic selection of imported vegetables which are sought after not only by Asians but also by African, Caribbean and Chinese communities. Supermarkets are beginning to accept that there is a rapidly growing market for such food, and all kinds of *daals*, rice, both fresh and ground spices, Indian fruit and vegetables are increasingly visible on their shelves side by side with the more conventional items. But although it is good news that some of the popular fresh produce from the tropics is being imported, if you have a taste for the 'exotic' it still remains an expensive choice compared with more common vegetables and fruit. I hope it will not be much longer before the demand grows sufficiently either to allow local cultivation to cater for changing tastes or to enable imports on a large enough scale to make such produce less of a luxury and more accessible to all.

AT HOME IN AN INDIAN KITCHEN

THE VALUE OF SPICES

The realm of Indian cookery is inhabited by such a wealth of herbs, spices and seasonings that it may at first glance be quite bewildering to the uninitiated cook. The sheer excitement and challenge of being admitted to a culture worlds away from one's own, through a true appreciation of its culinary traditions, is a sensation that carries most of us quite a long way forward when trying to grapple with an entirely new cuisine. In order to prevent this pleasure and exhilaration being dampened by a feeling of being overwhelmed by it all, it is important to know and be familiar with the spices and seasonings that create the essential quality of different Indian dishes. And in doing so, you will have understood the intrinsically simple genius of the cookery of the subcontinent.

Spices are used primarily as appetizers to infuse different dishes with exciting flavours designed to tempt our palates. But apart from the obvious importance of Indian spices as seasoning for foods, they have significant medicinal value and can greatly influence our health. Spices are also used more directly in the preparation of medicines. Traditional wisdom and knowledge of herbal remedies and home-made medicinal potions continue to be passed down through communities and families as a matter of course. Much of the indigenous medical treatment has proved over time to be effective in curing a whole series of common ailments. Spices may act as appetite stimulants, cure dysentery, diarrhoea and other stomach ailments, provide relief from nausea, act as tonics to the heart and liver, be carminative or aphrodisiac, and so on. For example, garlic is used to ease flatulence and aids in the digestion of food; turmeric is an important ingredient in skin ointments and is a tonic and blood purifier; a daily gargle with cardamom seeds is supposed to ward off colds and flu.

Amongst the many spices that are used in Indian cookery some are more common than others and appear repeatedly in several recipes in varying quantities, in different combinations and in many forms – whole, ground, fried or roasted. A broad classification of spices into common and uncommon would also vary to some extent, depending on the regional cooking in question.

Within the long list of spices there are several groupings and families of spices which are traditionally regarded, for different purposes, as belonging together. Although it broadens our understanding of Indian cookery to locate these spices firmly within their families, it is important to remember that they are by no means locked into these groupings or bonded together in exclusive or monogamous relationships. They all retain clear identities of their own and are capable of forming alliances in any number of variations. At one time a certain spice may dominate the flavour of a particular dish, but at another simply provide a discreet background against which other spices may be shown off to better advantage.

One such group is called *haldi kay masalay*, which would be literally translated as 'turmeric spices'. It is something of a misnomer, as this group includes several spices in addition to turmeric, but there is nevertheless a certain logic behind their being grouped together, namely that they broadly constitute a very basic prescription handy for many dishes. Belonging to this group are: *lehsun* (garlic), *adrak* (ginger), *dhania* (ground coriander), *lal mirch* (red chilli powder), and *haldi* (turmeric).

Another well recognized grouping is that of the *garam masala* spices. Members of this family are *choti elaichee* (small cardamoms), *bari elaichee* (large cardamoms), *kala zeera* (black cumin seeds), *dalchini* (cinnamon), *kali mirch* (black pepper), *laung* (cloves), *tejpatta* (bay leaves), *jaiphul* (nutmeg) and *jaivitri* (mace).

Garam masala mixtures may be used whole or ground. Ground *garam masala* is best when freshly prepared at home, and I find the ready-made, commercially available, ground mixtures quite unpalatable. They economize on the use of the more expensive spices such as cardamoms, black cumin and cloves to keep their cost price down, and in doing so disturb its balance and all but eliminate the most highly prized aromas which are its hallmark. Although the basic ingredients of all home-made ground *garam masalas* and the proportions in which they are used remain substantially the same, every person's concoction varies a little. Individuals are influenced by their own tastes and preferences to add a little more cardamom, use a little less cumin, or whatever.

Garam Masala

Take the following whole spices and using a coffee grinder make a fine powder. (The * sign indicates those spices which are essential for any *garam masala* mixture.)

* *choti elaichee* (small cardamoms)   12–14
* *bari elaichee* (large cardamoms)   4–5
* *kala zeera* (black cumin seeds)   1 tsp
* *dalchini* (cinnamon)   1½ in./3·8 cm stick
* *kali mirch* (black pepper)   1 tsp
* *laung* (cloves)   8
* *tejpatta* (bay leaves)   2
   jaiphul (nutmeg)   ¼ tsp (ground)
   jaivitri (mace)   ¼ tsp (ground)

A third group you may hear mentioned is that of *harey masalay* or 'green spices', which include *hari mirch* (fresh green chillies), *hara dhania* (fresh coriander leaves) and *pudeena* (fresh mint leaves); *adrak* or fresh ginger is also in this context one of the family. *Hari pyaz* or green onions – spring onions – are not immediate family members and would not therefore be automatically included, but would certainly count as close relatives.

In Bengal a popular mixture comprising equal quantities of five whole spices called *panchphoran* is made with *sabut safeid zeera* (white cumin seeds), *methi dana* (fenugreek seeds), *rai* (mustard seeds), *sonf* (fennel seeds) and *kalonji* (nigella seeds), and is used in many vegetable and fish dishes.

Then there are some herbs and spices that are always thought of in pairs such as *dhania/pudeena* (fresh coriander and mint leaves), *lehsun/adrak* (garlic and ginger), *dhania/zeera* (ground coriander and cumin), *jaiphul/jaivitri* (nutmeg and mace) and, of course, the two *elaichees*, *choti* and *bari*, (small and large cardamoms).

I am now going to look one by one at some of the spices you will encounter most often in my recipes.

Lehsun (Garlic)

Garlic is an important spice in Indian cookery. It needs little introduction as it is used widely in many cuisines all over the world. Make every effort when cooking Indian food to use fresh garlic in preference to garlic powder or salt. It is well worth the small amount of additional effort as the food you are cooking will clearly reflect the difference and be infinitely improved by the real flavour of fresh garlic.

The sort of garlic which has large cloves and has been allowed to fully mature before being harvested can be peeled very easily as the skin comes away with only a little more trouble than if it were wrapping paper. Younger cloves have fine sticky skins that tend to cling to your fingers which can make them a nuisance to peel – especially as the cloves themselves are usually quite tiny which means you are likely to need many more. If you inadvertently find yourself with this variety, then slice off both ends of each garlic clove, as you would normally do, and then soak them in water for about 15–30 minutes, by which time the skins should come away without any fuss.

I tend to peel and crush my garlic in a garlic press, using only as much at one time as the particular recipe I am cooking calls for. Fresh garlic can be stored successfully for quite long periods when placed in a sealed polythene bag in the fridge. And as garlic can be frozen extremely successfully, you can in fact make a paste of a fairly large quantity in an electric blender all at once and freeze it in cubes of a tablespoon measure for future convenience.

Adrak (Ginger)

This is a major spice in Indian cookery and has been one of its essential ingredients from the earliest times. Ginger is the rhizome of a herbaceous plant, which has a thin brown outer skin and is a moist, pale, greenish-yellow inside. It is sometimes bleached with lime to lighten the colour of its outer coating; this has no real advantage, and is apparently done purely for cosmetic reasons. Fresh ginger is graded by the number of fingers on the rhizome as well as its degree of fibrousness. Jamaica and India are considered to be producers of the best quality ginger, with the highest pungency and the best developed aroma.

If a recipe calls for ginger it is important to use it fresh whenever possible. Peel it as you would an apple or a potato, and finely grate or blend the flesh into a paste as required. Although fresh ginger can be stored fairly safely in a cool, well-aired place, it will keep moist and fresh much longer if you put it in the vegetable compartment of your fridge. Ginger freezes well, too, and you can peel and blend larger quantities to store in your freezer for long-term convenience.

Dried and powdered ginger is also used in certain Indian dishes, but as its taste alters so dramatically in this form it is given another name altogether, *sonth*.

Haldi (Turmeric)

This spice is derived from cured, ginger-like rhizomes of a herbaceous perennial plant that is native to India and China. It is normally only seen in western countries in the form of a bright golden yellow powder, obtained after the rhizomes have been thoroughly boiled, dried in the hot tropical sun then cleaned and polished. A proper curing of the raw rhizome is vital in order to enable the characteristic turmeric colour and aroma to develop fully.

Haldi is widely used in many Indian dishes, though only in small quantities; it is carminative, and is good for the digestion. It is known to have certain antiseptic properties which is probably why it is customary to rub raw fish with turmeric or to wash it in turmeric flavoured water before it is cooked.

Turmeric is a useful ingredient in indigenous medicinal preparations such as oils, ointments and poultices, and is a natural toner, conditioner and cleanser for the skin. Apart from its many uses in medicine, *haldi* is an important and versatile vegetable dye, and has been used for centuries in India as food colouring, as a dye for cotton, and even in paints and varnishes. In Hinduism, *haldi* has a religious significance and is employed in certain devotional ceremonies and rituals.

Although it is sometimes called the 'poor man's saffron', any resemblance is only the most fleeting and superficial. It shares little with that highly prized stigma of the crocus flower, other than an ability to impart a yellow colour to the food with which it is cooked. Turmeric is an important spice in Indian cookery when used in its own right, but there is no doubt in my mind that it is a very sorry substitute for saffron. So entirely different are they in aroma, flavour and colour that it does not take even an inexperienced eye a moment to detect the difference between a dish falsely embellished with a turmeric yellow and one that has been treated to the golden sunset hues of true saffron.

Lal Mirch (Red Chillies, Whole and Ground)

It is interesting to note that although red chillies are virtually indispensable in Indian cookery, this was not always the case. They were introduced to the subcontinent only comparatively recently, by the Portuguese some 400 years ago. Red chillies were originally native to South America, but different varieties are now grown all over the subcontinent.

Chillies are graded by their size, colour and potency. Commercially, red chillies are available dried, either whole or ground. Ground red chilli powders sold in packets may contain several different sorts of chillies, and there can therefore be enormous variations from one packet to another in potency and colour. It is wise to be cautious when opening a new packet of chilli powder, at least until you become familiar with its strength. Store chillies, whether whole or ground, in an airtight, cool, dry, dark place, as exposure to light can bleach their colour. Over a period of time the intensity of the chilli will also diminish so, unless you are intending to cook frequently with red chillies, it's best not to buy a very large quantity all at once.

Whole red chillies may be round, about the size of a large marble; the other common varieties are long, though they come in all sizes ranging from very small, to medium, about 1 inch/2·5 cm, and large, around 2 inches/5 cm or more. The medium and large ones are best for those recipes which call for crushed or broken chillies. When they are used whole, to flavour a dish, they are generally not supposed to be eaten and, unless someone knows what they are doing and consciously *chooses* to eat a chilli, they are usually left to the side of the plate. The tiny chillies give an excellent flavour when used in a *bhagar* on a *daal* and also look appetizingly decorative in the dish. Once again they are generally not eaten but put to one side.

Personal tastes and tolerance for chilli can vary a great deal, which is why in most of my recipes I have not stipulated any precise quantities. Even where I have, you should treat it merely as a suggestion, and it is offered simply as a tentative guide for those of you who may find it useful – if only to know how far you prefer to deviate from it. It seems to me that chillies can add to or detract from the taste of a dish in much the same way as salt – a moderate amount stimulates the taste buds and serves to bring out the other flavours, but in excess it can ruin the taste of even the finest dish by numbing our appreciation of its subtler aspects.

Dhania (Coriander, the Herb and the Spice)

Practically every part of this herbaceous plant of the umbellifer family, *Coriandrum sativum*, is used in Indian cookery. It seems like yesterday, when I was young and the best things in life still came free, that there was a convention in the vegetable markets of the subcontinent to throw in a complimentary bunch of fresh coriander and a handful of fresh green chillies with the purchases of every customer who bought a reasonable quantity of vegetables. When this practice was abandoned, our craving for the weed remained, though it took some mental adjustment to begin thinking of fresh coriander as something you now had to pay for.

In England, fresh coriander is easily available in shops specializing in Indian, Chinese, Cypriot, African or Caribbean foods; it is also finding its way on to more and more supermarket shelves. Fresh coriander is usually sold by the bunch intact with stem and roots. I have found that it keeps fresh longest if you wash it well and then stand the whole bunch in a glass or jam jar of water, as you would flowers in a vase, and place it in your fridge. Fresh coriander leaves, immensely rich in Vitamin C, are almost a standard garnish for many dishes. The tender young stems and leaves are also ground into delicious fresh chutneys, either simply on their own or else blended with other herbs such as mint. There are many variations of the popular green chutney which can also be prepared in combination with green chillies, coconut, tomatoes or ginger.

The round, light brown coriander seeds are one of the most frequently used spices in an Indian kitchen. Ground coriander is the form in which the spice is most commonly employed, although certain recipes require the seeds to be used whole or just lightly crushed rather than finely ground. Roasting the seeds brings out their flavour more strongly, although care needs to be taken not to overdo this process: the natural colour and flavour could be greatly altered to the detriment of the dish being cooked. Coriander seeds are sold both whole and ready ground. If stored in a tightly sealed jar the spice should retain its characteristic aromatic quality for a fair length of time.

But no spice will remain in pristine condition indefinitely, and *dhania* is no exception. If stored badly or for too long a period it will eventually taste little better than sawdust.

Zeera, Kala aur Safeid (Cumin, Black and White, Whole and Ground)

Cumin seeds are the aromatic fruit of an annual herb of the same family as coriander. They bear some resemblance to caraway seeds but should not be confused with the latter or used as a substitute as they are very dissimilar in aroma and flavour.

Kala zeera, also called *shah zeera* – black cumin seeds – belong to the *garam masala* group of spices. They are in a sense the 'true' cumin and are both rarer and the more expensive of the two kinds. *Kala zeera* seeds are smaller, darker and finer in appearance than the more common *safeid zeera*. They should be used only in tiny quantities and with much greater restraint than the white cumin seeds as they are much more potent and strongly flavoured. Black cumin seeds are seldom used ground, except when preparing a ground *garam masala* mixture when it would be considered one of the more important ingredients. *Kala zeera* is traditionally used whole when preparing rich rice dishes such as *pullaos* and *biryanis*, which are enormously improved by its gentle yet distinctive flavour. Black cumin seeds are generally available only at Indian spice stockists, and have not as yet found their way on to the shelves of supermarkets, high-street stores and corner grocery shops.

Safeid zeera – white cumin seeds – are regularly used both whole as well as ground, and I would find it hard, if asked, to say which form was more popular or common. In my own kitchen, I think that there is little doubt that whole cumin seeds disappear the faster of the two. Ground cumin is often used with the *haldi kay masalay* group of spices, and also goes extremely well with fish. White cumin seeds have strong associations in my mind with potato dishes and also with aubergines and other vegetable dishes; *safeid zeera* can be used as one of the simplest and most delicious of the hot oil seasonings poured over *daals*. Sometimes whole white cumin seeds are lightly dry roasted and then ground – when used as a garnish sprinkled over a yoghurt *raita*, for instance.

Bari Elaichee (Large Cardamom)

The big, brown, coarsely textured cardamoms remind me of an ugly bug-like thing that probably exists only in my imagination. They are cheaper to buy than the small 'true' cardamoms, and are therefore sometimes used as substitutes for the 'real' thing. Yet it has become traditional for them to be used in their own right to add flavour to special rice preparations such as *pullaos* and *biryanis* in which they are always used whole. When serving dishes containing whole cardamoms, remember to warn those of your guests who may not know that the spice is not supposed to be eaten, that it is customary to leave them to one side. Some meat and chicken recipes call for these cardamoms to be used ground and they are also considered important in any *garam masala* mixture.

Choti Elaichee (Small Cardamom)

Popularly known as 'small' cardamoms, the characteristic oval-shaped, angular, three-sided pod is the 'true' cardamom, and it is vastly superior to the large cardamom in just about every way. This cardamom is one of the most valued and valuable spices in India and has a more refined and powerful fragrance than the large cardamom. It has a beautiful natural green colour which is highly prized by connoisseurs in the subcontinent. Nevertheless it can be hard to find in its original green state in the West as growers and traders, bowing to foreign demand and preference, often bleach it white for export. This does nothing whatsoever to improve its quality and indeed it somewhat ruins its delicate fragrance and flavour. However, I am informed that this practice is gradually decreasing as appreciation grows for the spice in foreign markets.

The timing of harvesting the fruits is crucial. Ideally the cardamoms should be allowed to grow to their maximum size and achieve full maturity and colour, but must be picked moments before they become fully ripe or else the pods tend to split open at the next stage, while they are being dried. Cardamoms may be sun-dried or kiln-dried depending on the size of the operation and the resources of the farmer. The green colour of the pods is an indication of freshness, but the real calibre of the cardamom is determined by the quality of its seeds. In high-grade cardamoms the pods will be safely sealed and should be bursting full of dark brown, highly aromatic seeds.

Small cardamoms are employed in Indian meat, chicken, fish and rice cookery for which purpose they may be used whole, lightly bruised, crushed or finely ground. They have an important role in the preparation of Indian sweets and sweet dishes, where the large cardamoms would not be appropriate and are seldom, if ever, used. Small cardamoms are an essential part of every *garam masala* mixture, whether whole or freshly ground.

People will tell you that the proper way to use small cardamoms, in such recipes as require them to be crushed or ground, is to remove the seeds and discard the husk. This is rather tedious and time-consuming and I never do it (as, I'm sure, if the truth were told, few people actually do). Just crush or finely grind the entire pod in an electric coffee grinder.

Ground cardamom seeds (to which you can add a little cinnamon and a clove or two, if you like) make a delicious tea which is also a terrific pick-me-up in moments of fatigue or depression. It is said to be good for stomach ailments such as dysentery and diarrhoea, too, and provides relief from nausea. A daily dose of crushed cardamom seeds and honey (here you may like to discard the pod) is supposed to be beneficial for the eyesight and good health in general. A few cardamom seeds are also delicious when used to flavour a pot of regular tea. It is a popular habit amongst North Indians to chew the small cardamom as a mouth freshener, and it is therefore customary to serve these cardamoms, perhaps with fennel seeds, at the end of a meal. Heavy smokers also like to use small cardamoms for the same purpose.

Dalchini (Cinnamon)

Cinnamon is a spice derived from the inner layers of bark of the branches and young shoots of the cinnamon tree. Sticks of cinnamon bark are graded according to their length, breadth and thickness.

For Indian cookery it is best to buy whole cinnamon in sticks rather than powdered. It has a warm fragrance and is used whole in making some rice and meat dishes. It belongs to the *garam masala* group of spices and in Indian cooking is probably encountered most often in its ground form only as part of a *garam masala* mixture.

Kali Mirch (Black Pepper)

Black pepper must be one of the most widely used spices in the world, and the story of the almost universal taste for pepper is intimately linked with the history of India's colonization.

For a real appreciation of its taste, always buy whole peppercorns. Black pepper is another member of the *garam masala* family and is used whole as well as freshly ground.

Laung (Cloves)

Cloves are classified in Indian cookery as one of the 'heat-giving spices' and are therefore placed within the *garam masala* group. They are used whole to flavour rice dishes and certain meat dishes and are also ground with other spices to form a *garam masala*.

Cloves are shaped like small nails and are the fully grown but unopened flower buds of an evergreen tree found in the south of India. They are picked while still green and are dried in the open air and the hot sun until they turn the very dark shade of brown that we all recognize. Although cloves have been cultivated in India for almost 200 years – since they were first introduced by the East India Company – much of the demand is still met through a large-scale import of the spice (Zanzibar being the most famous clove island).

Oil of cloves has antiseptic and antibiotic properties and is well-known as one of the most miraculous pain relievers for toothache. If it is not possible to find any, then strategically place a clove or two over the painful tooth or inflamed gum area and it will soothe the persistent pain.

Tejpatta (Bay Leaf)

Tejpatta is the aromatic leaf of the evergreen *cassia* tree found in the subcontinent. It is dried and used as a flavouring in Indian cookery. The closest western equivalent is the bay leaf which serves perfectly adequately as a substitute. *Tejpatta* is chiefly used together with other whole *garam masala* spices to flavour rice dishes such as *pullaos*.

Jaiphul aur Jaivitri (Nutmeg and Mace)

Nutmeg and mace are two distinct spices originating from the same fruit of the nutmeg tree. When fully ripe this fruit, similar to an apricot or peach, bursts open and splits into two to disclose mace, which is the scarlet outer cage-like covering of the brown nutmeg seed. The mace is carefully removed and dried, whereupon it turns a yellowish brown or tan colour, and is commercially available whole, broken or ground. Nutmeg can also be bought whole or ground, although its flavour is undoubtedly better if freshly ground.

In the subcontinent both are used far more medicinally than in the kitchen. When used as a condiment only tiny quantities are needed. The flavour of both is similar, but that of mace is more refined (which is why it's more expensive). *Jaiphul* and *jaivitri* are added to some rich *garam masala* mixtures. The rinds of the ripe fruit are also used in making pickles.

Methi Dana aur Methi ka Saag (Fenugreek Seeds and Fenugreek Greens)

Fenugreek seeds are the dried ripe seeds from the slender curved pods of an annual herb. Yellow ochre in colour, they are small and rectangular in shape, each one marked by a tiny groove. The seeds have a mild, pleasantly bitter taste and are only ever used in small quantities. Care should be taken not to allow them to burn while cooking or their bitterness can be greatly accentuated.

The fresh tender leaves and shoots of the herb have a powerful aroma and a distinctive taste. They are used to flavour meat and vegetable dishes and are also cooked as a green spinach-like vegetable. Fenugreek greens are rich in Vitamins A and C, and they contain iron and calcium.

Kalonji (Nigella Seeds)

These tiny Paisley-shaped, jet-black seeds are nearly always used whole in Indian cooking. *Kalonji* has particularly strong associations with the regional cookery of Bengal and Hyderabad, although several North Indian recipes also rely on it. Nigella seeds complement vegetable and fish dishes, but can also be used to great advantage in some chicken and meat dishes. They are a popular pickling ingredient, and many different kinds of pickles owe their success to nigella seeds.

Sonf (Fennel)

Fennel seeds are small and ridged, with an elongated shape which may be straight or slightly curved. They resemble cumin seeds a little, but are much plumper and a pale greenish yellow in colour. All parts of the fennel plant are aromatic, the seed particularly so as it has the largest concentration of oil. Fennel seeds also resemble anise seeds and the two are often confused, although there are distinct differences in their taste and aroma.

Apart from its culinary value, fennel has an important social place in the subcontinent and particularly amongst North Indians. *Sonf* is served at the end of a meal both to cleanse the palate and for its carminative quality, which is supposed to facilitate digestion. Smokers trying to rid themselves of the habit turn to fennel seeds in much the same way as a westerner might chew gum. Sugar-coated *sonf* sweets are a favourite with children and I can still remember not being able to resist the brightly coloured grains that filled the bell jar at the sweet shop where we used to wait for our school bus.

Til (Sesame Seeds)

Sesame seeds are obtained from a tropical herbaceous plant cultivated in India. They are not used as commonly as some other spices in Indian cooking, but the delicate nutty taste of the hulled, oval-shaped, creamy white seeds is distinctly delicious when stir-fried with potatoes or cauliflower. All sorts of *naan* and other Indian breads are traditionally baked with a surface sprinkling of sesame seeds.

Khas Khas (Poppy Seeds)

The poppy plant, *Papaver somniferum*, is the opium poppy, and in India a variety which yields white seeds is cultivated for use in cooking. In Europe a poppy which produces darker, slate-coloured seeds (known as *maw maw*) is more commonly cultivated. Buy your *white* poppy seeds at Indian spice stores – the other variety is not a suitable substitute. I am told that white poppy seeds are the most nutritious and contain the finest oil, similar to olive oil which is used for culinary purposes. Both the seed and the oil extracted from it are quite free of any narcotic effects.

Poppy seeds are usually ground before use in cooking Indian food, and are also sometimes lightly roasted before being ground.

Rai (Mustard Seeds)

There are three different kinds of mustard seed. The yellow mustard seed is not really used at all in Indian cookery; the black mustard seed and the Indian mustard or *rai*, a dark reddish brown colour, are both suitable for use in a variety of different dishes as well as pickles. Mustard seeds may be used whole as well as ground and are outstandingly delicious when used in Indian vegetable and fish dishes, where they are sometimes perfectly complemented by the use of mustard oil. Mustard seeds, whether used whole or ground, have a distinctly different taste in Indian cookery to the mustard preparations westerners are most familiar with. Both the black and reddish brown mustard seeds are available at Indian spice stockists.

Karri Patta (*Karri* Leaves)

There is no western equivalent or other substitute for the Indian *karri patta*. The aromatic leaves of this deciduous ornamental shrub or small tree have always been used as a flavouring in South Indian dishes and chutneys. They are available at Indian shops both fresh and dried. It's harder to find them fresh, but well worth it if you do as the flavour and aroma are largely lost in the dried leaves.

Zafran (Saffron)

The saffron crocus is a bulbous perennial plant with purple coloured flowers, and it is the stigmas of these flowers that are the spice we know as saffron. Harvesting the saffron is a very labour-intensive business as each flower yields only three precious stigmas and the work of separating stigma from flower must all be done by hand (there is no mechanical device suited to the purpose). In Kashmir – famous for its fields of saffron – there are large posters which tell you that it takes 75,000 flowers to produce 1 lb/450 g of saffron. Little wonder, then, that its price is so high!

Spain, Iran and Kashmir are all important growers of saffron and inevitably therefore saffron forms an important part of their culinary traditions. I have used all three kinds of saffron and can say without a moment's hesitation or bias that the first-grade Kashmiri saffron is by far the best. *Shahi zafran*, or royal saffron, is the first-grade saffron and consists purely of the sun-dried stigmas of the saffron crocus. Other parts of the flower are also aromatic, although much less so. Once the stigmas are removed the flowers themselves are then dried and after being lightly beaten with a stick are strained through a coarse sieve over a container of water. Those bits that sink to the bottom are dried once again in the sun and are sold as a lower-grade saffron.

Saffron is used in Indian cooking to enhance the flavour of *qormas*, *biryanis*, sweet dishes and so on. Its wonderful golden red colour adds to the rich appearance of the food.

Saffron also plays a part in some traditional and religious rituals; one such example is the custom of placing a mark of saffron paste in the centre of a person's forehead as a symbol of good luck.

To get the most value out of the least weight of saffron, first lightly roast the threads in a heavy cast-iron or other non-stick frying pan and then crumble them either directly over the food or into a little hot milk which, once it is infused with the saffron, can be poured over the food as it cooks. Alternatively, soak the saffron in a little warm water or milk and, using the back of a small teaspoon, mash each strand of saffron to extract as much colour from it as you can.

Imli (Tamarind)

Tamarind is obtained from the ripe fruit or pods of the large tamarind tree. It is popular all over the subcontinent and is used to add a much loved sour flavour to many savoury dishes and chutneys. Indian children enjoy sucking the seeded and peeled pulp concentrate as much as western children enjoy sucking sweets. It is paradoxical that while indulgence in large quantities of tamarind can encourage a sore throat, a gargle of tamarind water is known to soothe one.

Tamarind is available in cubes, blocks or slabs in which the pods are tightly compressed, and it is also sold ready seeded and peeled as a pulp concentrate. The pulp ferments rather quickly which is why it is preferable to buy packets of the compressed pods which keep well for much longer. To extract the tamarind pulp simply break off a 4 oz/125 g piece and soak it in boiling water for 10–15 minutes, then break it up with a spoon once it has softened. Pour the thick juice through a fine sieve, pressing through as much of the tamarind as you can. Discard the seeds and remaining bits and pieces of the tamarind pod left in the sieve.

KITCHEN EQUIPMENT AND COOKING UTENSILS

Cooking Indian food in a western kitchen should not present the cook with any special difficulties. All the usual pots and pans are perfectly adequate. I find a large wok extremely useful for several different kinds of dishes, and not just the ones which require stir-frying. I have indicated in individual recipes where I think having a wok is advantageous. Other than that the equipment I rely upon for daily use is a colander for rice cookery, a coffee grinder for grinding whole spices, a blender, a garlic press, a hand grater and several frying pans, both with and without lids. I prefer the wide open shape of a frying pan to make most vegetable dishes in and find those with lids particularly handy. I feel certain that a food processor would be extremely useful, especially for chopping onions when cooking in large quantities, or for dishes like carrot *halwa* which require mountains of grated carrots. So far this energy-saving invention has eluded me and remains a luxury to look forward to in the future. A pressure cooker for those moments of crisis, and a slow cooker when time is no problem, can both be welcome items in a kitchen.

The only articles of Indian origin amongst my kitchen equipment are a *tava* and a *chimta*. A *tava* is a large, round, cast-iron, hot-plate-type of object, modern versions of which are often made with long saucepan-like handles which make lifting and moving them around much easier. A *tava* is especially useful to diffuse the heat under a saucepan of rice in *dum* (or steam) cooking as for *pullaos* and *biryanis*. I have seen an object called a heat diffuser for sale in western shops which may serve the same purpose. A *tava* is also used for making many sorts of Indian bread such as *chapattis* and *parathas*. A heavy-bottomed frying pan can be used as the perfect substitute here. A *chimta* is a pair of tongs traditionally used to handle *chapatti* bread once it comes off the *tava* and is placed directly on the open flame. I am sure you could find a substitute pair of tongs amongst the tools of a barbecue set to fulfil this need.

PLANNING AN INDIAN MEAL

Below are some menu ideas that you may want to cast a glance over while you think about what you feel like cooking and eating. In putting together an Indian meal, leaving aside the minute variations in regional customs, there are just a few well-established traditions that are commonly observed. In the main these arise from certain foods being regarded as going particularly well together and it is worth knowing, for the sake of your own self-confidence, that there is very little that you can do that would be considered entirely wrong if you made a selection of dishes chosen purely for their appeal to you.

I ought to tell you, by way of illustration, of a few of the more important of such conventions. For instance, it is generally accepted that lentils are not an appropriate accompaniment to *biryani* dishes. Knowing this you would be quite wrong, however, if you assumed that *daals* do not go well with rice. Boiled rice and *daal* is an old and accepted partnership and a very popular pair, as is the dish *karhi* (see page 156) which it is thought only ever tastes just right when eaten with plain boiled rice. *Kababs*, especially *shami kababs* with a yoghurt *raita*, would be thought of as the classical accompaniment to a dish of lamb or chicken *biryani*. On the other hand, some people may tell you that rice is an absolute must when serving fish, or that *pooris* are perfect with certain kinds of potato preparations, but many of these statements are merely expressions of regional taste and need not be strictly adhered to.

The important point to remember when planning an Indian meal is that you must always serve some kind of rice or bread or both, as it is inconceivable to eat Indian food without at least one or the other. In most Indian homes you would also be very likely to see a *daal* dish at every meal, but in this case it would be perfectly acceptable if you wanted to give the lentils a miss, and there is no custom, convention or rule in this regard which says you should not do so.

The menus I have drawn up for you to refer to are broadly of four kinds. Those in the first group provide meals for between two to four people and contain a rice dish and/or some bread, a meat, chicken or fish dish, accompanied by a vegetable and/or a *daal* or perhaps a yoghurt *raita*. It is difficult when cooking Indian food to cook just for two in as precise a way as is possible in several western cuisines. A quick adjustment in the quantity of rice according to the number of people present at the meal is all that is needed. It is certainly a more hospitable culture which can extend a welcome to the unexpected guest at mealtimes.

The second group is for those times when you are cooking for about six people. You may prefer simply to choose a menu from the first group but increase the quantity of food in all the dishes or you may prefer, as I have done in these samples, to add an additional item. Remember to cook extra rice in either case.

The third group is for more special occasions and here I have written up some more elaborate menus both for four to six people as well as six to eight people.

The fourth category is that of vegetarian dishes and is again divided according to the numbers being catered for and covers both the ordinary as well as the special occasion.

I have deliberately not specified any sweet dishes with my menus. You may either choose one for yourself from the relevant section in this book or serve fresh seasonal fruit, or even a western-style dessert, at the end of the meal. I sometimes like to offer my dinner-party guests imported tropical fruits, attractively cut and served, as a way of presenting them with something simple, unusual and in keeping with the culture of the cuisine they have just eaten.

In the sample menus I have also omitted in most cases to specify any chutneys, relishes or fresh salad items. Refer to the appropriate chapter and pick out any that take your fancy.

When all your food is cooked and ready, serve it out into dishes and lay them all out together either on the table at which you intend to eat or else display them buffet style. It is customary to allow people to serve themselves and the pleasure of this food lies in being able to dip into different tastes, taking several small helpings almost randomly. However, if you were to serve both rice and some kind of bread, people would probably start with one and finish with another. Also if there were both fish as well as meat it is usual to taste the fish before going on to the meat.

Take care to increase the quantity of food in the different recipes when cooking for large numbers of people.

Sample menus for two to four people:

KHUSHKA
(Plain Boiled Rice)   page 204
and/or
CHAPATTI or **PITTA BREAD**
page 215
**SPICY STIR-FRIED PRAWNS WITH SPRING ONIONS
AND FRESH CORIANDER**
page 196
LAL MASOOR KI DAAL I
(Red *Masoor* Lentils)   page 139
ALOO KA BHURTA
(Spicy Mashed Potatoes)   page 117

———— ● ————

MATAR PULLAO
(Peas *Pullao*)   page 207
LAMB QORMA or **BEEF PASSANDA**
pages 62 and 54
BAINGAN KA BHURTA
(Aubergine *Bhurta*)   page 118
YOGHURT RAITA
pages 249–252

———— ● ————

JHINGAY KA PULLAO
(Prawn *Pullao*)   page 208
ALOO ZEERA
(Sauté Potatoes with Cumin Seeds)   page 110
PYAZ AUR TIMATAR MAIN BHINDI
(Okra with Tomatoes and Onions)   page 125
YOGHURT RAITA
pages 249–252

———— ● ————

TEHRI
(Vegetable *Biryani*)   page 208
**HADDOCK IN A SPICY ONION SAUCE WITH FRESH GREEN CHILLIES
AND CORIANDER**
page 187
BUND GOBI KI TARKARI
(Fried Spicy Cabbage)   page 132
PANCHMEL DAAL
(Five *Daals*)   page 149

MATAR PULLAO
(Peas *Pullao*)   page 207
KHAREY MASALAY KI MURGHI
(Sautéed Chicken in Whole Spices)   page 176
PYAZWALEY KARELAY
(Bitter Gourds with Onions)   page 128
LOKI or SHALJUM BHURTA
(Marrow or Turnip *Bhurta*)   pages 121 and 120

———— ● ————

KHUSHKA
(Plain Boiled Rice)   page 204
and/or
CHAPATTI or PITTA BREAD
page 215
LAMB DOPYAZA
(Lamb with Onions)   page 78
TALI HUI BHINDI
(Deep-fried Crispy Okra)   page 123
HAREY MASALAY KAY ALOO
(Potatoes with Spring Onions and Fresh Coriander)   page 112

———— ● ————

SAADA PULLAO
(Plain *Pullao*)   page 205
SHAMI KABABS
page 92
ALOO GOSHT
(Lamb and Potatoes in Gravy)   page 73
MOONG DAAL AUR METHI KA SAAG
(Yellow Split *Moong* Lentils with Fenugreek Greens)   page 147

———— ● ————

SAADA PULLAO
(Plain *Pullao*)   page 205
or
PARATHA
page 216
DHANIYAY KI MURGHI
(Lemon Coriander Chicken)   page 166
PHOOL GOBI KI BHUJIYA
(Fried Cauliflower with Cumin and Sesame Seeds)   page 130
YOGHURT RAITA
pages 249–252

KHUSHKA
(Plain Boiled Rice)   page 204
and/or
CHAPATTI or PITTA BREAD
page 215
PALAK GOSHT
(Spring Lamb with Spinach)   page 72
PANCHPHORAN ALOO
(Potatoes with Whole Spices)   page 111
BHUNNI HUI DHULLI MOONG
(Spicy Fried Split Yellow *Moong* Lentils)   page 145

●

SAADA PULLAO
(Plain *Pullao*) page 205
or
PARATHA
page 216
MURGH IRANI
(Chicken with Fresh Cream, Saffron and Green Cardamoms)   page 164
ALOO PALAK
(Diced Potatoes and Spinach)   page 115
CHANNA DAAL
(Split Yellow *Channa* Lentils)   page 153

Sample menus for about six people:

KHUSHKA
(Plain Boiled Rice)   page 204
and/or
CHAPATTI or PITTA BREAD
page 215
BAKED TROUT WITH SEASONED YOGHURT
page 192
KARHAI CHICKEN
(Stir-Fried Chicken with Onions, Tomatoes and Peppers)   page 173
HAREY MASALAY KAY ALOO
(Potatoes with Spring Onions and Fresh Coriander)   page 112
LAL MASOOR KI DAAL II
(Red *Masoor* Lentils)   page 140

———— ● ————

SAADA PULLAO
(Plain *Pullao*)   page 205
HYDERABADI MURGH QORMA
(Chicken *Qorma* Hyderabadi Style)   page 168
ALOO QEEMA
(Minced Beef with Diced Potatoes)   page 85
PYAZWALEY KARELAY
(Bitter Gourds with Onions)   page 128
YOGHURT RAITA
pages 249–252

———— ● ————

MATAR PULLAO
(Peas *Pullao*)   page 207
LEMON PEPPER PLAICE IN BREADCRUMBS
page 189
TIMATAR GOSHT
(Lamb in a Rich Tomato Gravy)   page 74
ALOO ZEERA
(Sauté Potatoes with Cumin Seeds)   page 110
CHILKON VALI MOONG AUR DHULLI MOONG
(Split Green and Yellow *Moong* Lentils)   page 148

TEHRI
(Vegetable *Biryani*)   page 208
CHAPLI KABAB
page 94
KALI MIRCH KI MURGHI
(Black Pepper Chicken)   page 167
LAL MASOOR KI DAAL I or II
(Red *Masoor* Lentils)   pages 139 and 140
KACHOOMAR
(Onion, Tomato and Green Chilli Relish)   page 242

———— ● ————

KHUSHKA
(Plain Boiled Rice)   page 215
and/or
CHAPATTI or PITTA BREAD
page 215
SHALJUM GOSHT
(Lamb with Turnips)   page 56
MASALAYDAR GAJAR AUR PALAK
(Spicy Carrots in a Sea of Spinach)   page 131
DHULLI MOONG KI PATLI DAAL
(Split *Moong* Lentils)   page 143
MOOLI KI SABZI
(Diced White Radishes)   page 122

———— ● ————

SAADA PULLAO
(Plain *Pullao*)   page 205
and/or
PARATHA
page 216
BIHARI KABAB
page 97
GOBI GOSHT
(Lamb with Cauliflower)   page 64
ALOO ACHAR
(Diced Potatoes with Lemon or Mango Pickle)   page 113
LAL MASOOR KI DAAL I or II
(Red *Masoor* Lentils)   pages 139 and 140

KHUSHKA
(Plain Boiled Rice)   page 204
CHINGRI ALOO PALONG SHAK
(Prawns with Fresh Spinach and Diced Potatoes)   page 194
DHANIYAY-ZEERAY KI SABUT MURGHI
(Chicken Baked with Roasted Coriander and Cumin)   page 175
HYDERABADI TIMATAR CUT
(Hot and Sour Tomatoes from Hyderabad)   page 129
SPLIT ARHAR KI DAAL
(Split *Arhar* Lentils)   pages 152 and 153

———— ● ————

TEHRI
(Vegetable *Biryani*)   page 208
MASALA FRIED COD
page 191
SABUT RAAN
(Whole Roast Leg of Lamb)   page 66
ALOO TIMATAR PANCHPHORAN
(Potatoes with Whole Spices in a Tomato Sauce)   page 112
YOGHURT RAITA
pages 249–252

———— ● ————

JHINGAY KA PULLAO
(Prawn *Pullao*)   page 208
MASALA FRIED COD
page 191
ACHAR GOSHT
(Lamb in a Pickle Sauce)   page 53
TURAI KI SABZI
(Braised Courgettes with Cumin and Broken Chillies)   page 134
ALOO KA BHURTA
(Spicy Mashed Potato)   page 117

———— ● ————

KHUSHKA
(Plain Boiled Rice)   page 204
KARHI
page 156
HARI MIRCHON KA QEEMA
(Minced Beef with Green Chillies)   page 88
TALI HUI BHINDI
(Deep-fried Crispy Okra)   page 123

Six people at a special occasion

GOSHT KI BIRYANI
(Lamb *Biryani*)   page 211
MASALAYDAR BATTAKH
(Braised Duck in a Rich Spicy Sauce)   page 177
BHAGAREY BAINGAN
(Hyderabadi Style Aubergines)   page 126
HAREY MASALAY KAY ALOO
(Potatoes with Spring Onions and Fresh Coriander)   page 112
SALAD/CHUTNEY/RAITA
pages 242–252

———— ● ————

MATAR PULLAO
(Peas *Pullao*)   page 207
AAM QALIYA
(Lamb with Green Mangoes)   page 65
BRAISED FILLETS OF SOLE WITH MUSHROOMS
page 190
KARHAI BHINDI
(Stir-Fried Okra)   page 124
YOGHURT RAITA
pages 249–252

———— ● ————

JHINGAY KI BIRYANI
(Prawn *Biryani*)   page 210
MURGH FRY
(Fried Chicken)   page 170
or
CHICKEN COCKTAIL SNACKS OR STARTERS
page 174
NARGISSI KOFTA
page 81
TURAI KI SABZI
(Braised Courgettes with Cumin and Broken Chillies)   page 134
YOGHURT RAITA
pages 249–252

HYDERABADI KATCHEY GOSHT KI BIRYANI
(Hyderabadi Lamb *Biryani*)   page 212
HYDERABADI TIMATAR CUT
(Hot and Sour Tomatoes from Hyderabad)   page 129
TEETAR AUR BATAIR
(Partridge and Quail)   page 178
ALOO AUR SIMLA KI MIRCH
(Potatoes with Green Peppers)   page 116
SALAD/CHUTNEY
pages 242–248

•

SAADA PULLAO
(Plain *Pullao*)   page 205
or
PARATHA
page 216
KHATAI KAY KABAB
(*Kababs* in Sour Sauce)   page 96
HYDERABADI MURGH QORMA
(Chicken *Qorma* Hyderabadi Style)   page 168
PHOOL GOBI KI BHUJIYA
(Fried Cauliflower with Cumin and Sesame Seeds)   page 130
YOGHURT RAITA
pages 249–252

Eight people at a special occasion

MATAR PULLAO
(Peas *Pullao*)   page 207
SABUT PAMPLET AUR HARI CHUTNEY
(Whole Pomfret Stuffed with Fresh Mint and Coriander Chutney)   page 188
MARY MANEZES' LAMB IN COCONUT MILK
page 77
MAGHAZ
(Brain *Masala*)   page 101
PHOOL GOBI KI BHUJIYA
(Fried Cauliflower with Cumin and Sesame Seeds)   page 130
BHUNNI HUI DHULLI MOONG
(Spicy Fried Split Yellow *Moong* Lentils)   page 145

———— ● ————

MURGH KI BIRYANI
Chicken *Biryani*   page 211
SEEKH KABAB
page 98
KOFTAY
(Meatballs in Gravy)   page 80
PYAZ AUR TIMATAR MAIN BHINDI
(Okra with Onions and Tomatoes)   page 125
HYDERABADI TIMATAR CUT
(Hot and Sour Tomatoes from Hyderabad)   page 129

———— ● ————

SAADA PULLAO
(Plain *Pullao*)   page 205
HALIBUT SEASONED WITH GROUND MUSTARD IN A RICH GRAVY
page 185
SABUT MURGHI DAHI MAIN
(Whole Chicken in Yoghurt)   page 163
ALOO METHI
(Diced Potatoes with Fenugreek Leaves)   page 114
CHANNA DAAL
(Split Yellow *Channa* Lentils)   page 153
KACHOOMAR
(Onion, Tomato and Green Chilli Relish)   page 242

MATAR PULLAO
(Peas *Pullao*)   page 207
SABUT RAAN
(Whole Roast Leg of Lamb)   page 66
KHAREY MASALAY KI MURGHI
(Sautéed Chicken in Whole Spices)   page 176
BESAN MAIN TALEY HUAY JHINGAY
(Fried Prawns in Gram Flour Batter)   page 197
HAREY MASALAY KAY ALOO
(Potatoes with Spring Onions and Fresh Coriander)   page 112
TURAI KA RAITA
(Courgette and Yoghurt Relish)   page 250

———— ● ————

GOSHT KI BIRYANI
(Lamb *Biryani*)   page 211
MURGHI KA TIKKA
(Grilled or Barbecued Chicken *Tikka*)   page 169
or
SHAMI KABABS
page 92
SHALJUM KA BHURTA
(Turnip *Bhurta*)   page 120
BAINGAN KA RAITA
(Spicy Aubergine in Yoghurt)   page 249

Vegetarian meals for four to six people

When cooking for two people, reduce each menu below by one dish.

TEHRI
(Vegetable *Biryani*)   page 208
PYAZWALEY KARELAY
(Bitter Gourds with Onions)   page 128
MASALAYDAR GAJAR AUR PALAK
(Spicy Carrots in a Sea of Spinach)   page 131
KHEERAY KA RAITA
(Grated Cucumber in Seasoned Yoghurt)   page 249

●

KHUSHKA
(Plain Boiled Rice)   page 204
and/or
CHAPATTI or PITTA BREAD
page 215
LAL MASOOR KI DAAL
(Red *Masoor* Lentils)   pages 139 and 140
ALOO ZEERA
(Sauté Potatoes with Cumin Seeds)   page 110
PYAZ AUR TIMATAR MAIN BHINDI
(Okra with Onions and Tomatoes)   page 125
LOKI KA BHURTA
(Marrow *Bhurta*)   page 121
CHUTNEY/KACHOOMAR
pages 242–248

●

SAADA PULLAO
(Plain *Pullao*)   page 205
or
PARATHA/POORI
pages 216 and 217
PHOOL GOBI KI BHUJIYA
(Fried Cauliflower with Cumin and Sesame Seeds)   page 130
ALOO PALAK
(Diced Potatoes and Spinach)   page 115
MOONG DAAL AUR METHI KA SAAG
(Yellow Split *Moong* Lentils with Fenugreek Greens)   page 147
A RELISH OF YOUR CHOICE
pages 242–252

MATAR PULLAO
(Peas *Pullao*)   page 207
and/or
PARATHA
page 216
BAINGAN KA BHURTA
(Aubergine *Bhurta*)   page 118
BUND GOBI KI TARKARI
(Fried Spicy Cabbage)   page 132
ALOO TIMATAR PANCHPHORAN
(Potatoes with Whole Spices in a Tomato Sauce)   page 112
PALAK KA RAITA
(Spinach and Yoghurt Relish)   page 251

———— ● ————

KHUSHKA
(Plain Boiled Rice)   page 204
and/or
CHAPATTI or **PITTA BREAD**
page 215
KHARI KALI MASOOR KI DAAL
(Whole *Masoor* Lentils)   page 142
ALOO KA BHURTA
(Spicy Mashed Potatoes) page 117
BAVLI HANDYA KI TARKEEB
(A Dish of Mixed Vegetables)   page 133
TURAI KI SABZI
(Braised Courgettes with Cumin and Broken Chillies)   page 134
HARA KACHOOMAR
(Green Salad Relish)   page 242

Menus for vegetarian dinner parties for six to eight people

KHUSHKA
(Plain Boiled Rice)   page 204
KARHI
page 156
TALI HUI BHINDI
(Deep-fried Crispy Okra)   page 123
BAVLI HANDYA KI TARKEEB
(A Dish of Mixed Vegetables)   page 133
HYDERABADI TIMATAR CUT
(Hot and Sour Tomatoes from Hyderabad)   page 129

●

MATAR PULLAO
(Peas *Pullao*)   page 207
and/or
PARATHA
page 216
BHAGAREY BAINGAN
(Hyderabadi Style Aubergines)   page 126
ALOO ZEERA
(Sauté Potatoes with Cumin)   page 110
MOOLI KI SABZI
(Diced White Radishes)   page 122
BHUNNI HUI DHULLI MOONG
(Spicy Fried Split Yellow *Moong* Lentils)   page 145
SALAD KA RAITA
(Yoghurt Salad)   page 252

●

TEHRI
(Vegetable *Biryani*)   page 208
CHANNA DAAL AUR KARALAY
(Split Yellow Chickpeas and Bitter Gourds)   page 155
PYAZ AUR TIMATAR MAIN BHINDI
(Okra with Onions and Tomatoes)   page 125
MOOLI KA BHURTA
(Mashed White Radishes Sautéed with Spices)   page 121
A RELISH OF YOUR CHOICE
pages 242–252

SAADA PULLAO
(Plain *Pullao*)   page 207
and/or
PARATHA
page 216
ALOO ACHAR
(Small Diced Potatoes with Lemon or Mango Pickle)   page 113
BUND GOBI KI TARKARI
(Fried Spicy Cabbage)   page 132
PHOOL GOBI KI BHUJIYA
(Fried Cauliflower with Cumin and Sesame Seeds)   page 130
CHANNA DAAL
(Yellow Split *Channa* Lentils)   page 153
A CHUTNEY/KACHOOMAR OF YOUR CHOICE
pages 242–248

LAMB AND BEEF
DISHES

· Lamb and Beef Dishes ·

I have no memory of ever having been squeamish about eating meat, only a growing awareness that my appetite for it was in no way marred by guilty concern about carnivorous living or diminished by religious taboos.

We were Muslims in India; at least in name. I was a post-partition child of parents who hadn't yet crossed the border. We lived in cosmopolitan Bombay and had no orthodox religious training or identity, but to be a Muslim who had not defected to the promise of safety and prosperity was a complex and confusing thing. When we sat down at the long scrubbed wooden benches at our tables in the basement dining hall at school, to eat our *tiffin*, I was conscious every time I unpacked my containers that I was asserting my right to be Indian despite being a strict carnivore, a minority in a world of vegetarians. It is certainly a possibility that this private rebellion, the only political expression I was capable of at that young age, nurtured in me a strong relish for meat.

When we moved to Pakistan, more than a decade and a half later, I found myself in a society of committed meat lovers, where everyone eats meat as often as they can afford it and vegetables are only seen as something possibly to be added to a meat dish to change its flavour, or to turn to as a last resort on economic grounds. To assert my Indian identity in this changed context, it became necessary to learn to eat vegetables. People eat so much meat in Pakistan that the one thing successive governments have agreed about is the declaration of two days a week as 'meatless days', to ration the slaughter of animals. On these days no meat can be sold in shops, and no lamb or beef dishes will be served at restaurants or indeed at any public place. Theoretically poultry and fish are finally given a chance. In reality people stock up in advance. On each Monday before the statutory fast, almost as much meat is sold as would have been if the shops had remained open through the week. *Tikka* and *kabab* sellers, bowing to public demand and taste for red meat, camouflage their *seekh* and *boti kababs* so well that I, for one, have never been convinced that they were really made with chicken or fish.

In the subcontinent we don't like to cook our meat so rare that it's almost dripping blood. Westerners often complain that we cook our food to death. We have a happier, more complimentary expression for it. To describe meat as being so tender that it melts like butter in the mouth, or as having the texture of *halwa*, is high praise. My test to see whether a piece of cooked meat can be broken into easily is by pressing it gently using only the tips of my thumb and forefinger. Depending on the recipe, the meat may be brought to this tender state through a slow process of *dum* cooking, in which the saucepan is sealed tightly shut, perhaps with a heavy weight placed on the lid to hold in the steam; or it might well be *bhunna* or stir-fried; or else grilled, boiled, steamed or braised; or it might even be marinated with the help of natural tenderizers beforehand, which makes the meat soft and edible and saves having to cook it for ages, by whatever method. Papaya and *kachri* are both natural tenderizers and have been used for this purpose for generations. Salt and lemon juice, salt and grated ginger, olive oil and vinegar, mustard oil and ginger, yoghurt with garlic and ginger, are all different prescriptions for marinating the meat to tenderize it before cooking.

It's important to be skilled at recognizing how far or close your meat is to being ready. This eliminates the danger both of overcooking the meat so much that it falls off the bone or disintegrates, as well as it being left too rare or undercooked by Indian standards, when it risks drawing comparisons with a rhino's hide! This skill or judgement will also enable you to know just when to add water or how much, at what stage to add different vegetables or yoghurt, or when to *dum* and when to speed up the process and dry up any excess moisture that there may be. Recipes can guide you, but it is hard to give exact timings because there is no uniform way of predicting what quality of meat you will bring home from the butcher.

In subcontinental English, 'mutton' is the name for the meat of both goat and kid. Sheep and lamb are eaten much less. While it is generally true that some mountain people in the North-West Frontier Province, Baluchistan, Gilgit, Kashmir and Ladakh may relish sheep's meat, most flat-land dwellers would immediately wrinkle up their noses in various expressions of distaste at the very thought. It is notorious for being smelly. According to popular belief, this is because it is a fatty meat, from an animal clad in a blanket of thick wool – entirely inappropriate for life in a hot country. I am not sure whether the explanation is fact or folklore, but I am witness to the truth of it being a more strongly flavoured meat in that part of the world. Our mutton, or goat's meat, is leaner, more tender and delicately flavoured than lamb. Popularly known as *chotey ka gosht* – meat from the small one, as opposed to beef which is *barey ka gosht*, meat from the big one – it ranks at number one in the hierarchy of meats and is second only to chicken, if we allow poultry to compete. Of the two, beef is without question the one looked down upon and regarded as of poorer quality. It costs less and is mainly used as mince for *qeema*, *seekh* and *shami kababs*. There are some joints of beef, such as the prime undercut, which are highly valued and expensive, and are used in making elaborate and highly regarded dishes like *passandas*.

It is true that animals in India, Pakistan and Bangladesh are much less well fed than in the affluent countries of the West. It does not follow, as is so often assumed, that the meat is of inferior quality. If we judge quality in relation to correct food value and nutritional balance, then it is clear why health experts and nutritionists are beginning to express such concern about the dangerous effects of eating too much inorganically fattened meat on people living in Europe and America. In many countries of the developed world, animals are specially bred and fattened on rich synthetic diets to make their flesh more tasty for human consumption. I was shocked to read a recent newspaper report which revealed that in Sweden the specially prepared meals for animals bred for slaughter on a large cattle farm were discovered to be frequently non-vegetarian and cannibalistic. Carcasses of dead animals were recycled into scientifically balanced diets for other animals. Personally I would feel a lot safer eating an under-developed, traditionally grass-eating, bush-chewing, vegetarian goat or cow.

What we lose in richness we more than make up for in freshness. The meat we buy in our markets has probably been slaughtered that same day. It is not an uncommon sight to see live animals harnessed behind the butcher's shop or market stall waiting to be selected by the customer prior to slaughter. Fresh meat has a wonderful glow and delicate flavour which is completely lost in freezing. That moist, plum-red colour of fresh meat is totally absent in frozen meat. My husband, though he frequently tries to delude himself that he is vegetarian, is so tempted by the taste of really fresh meat and feels so deprived of this simple pleasure living in England, that on a recent holiday in Kashmir he would describe every baby goat we saw grazing on the hillside only in terms of a possible *qorma* for our evening meal!

If you can afford it, use choice cuts and tender meat. There is no truth, only bigotry and prejudice, in the belief that 'tough old meat is best for curries as the longer it cooks the better it absorbs spices'. I am myself a believer in the virtues of slow cooking but there can be no substitute for good quality. However, none of us can afford the most expensive meat all the time. While it is necessary to recognize that there is a qualitative difference between fresh and frozen, cheap and expensive cuts, it's just as important to know that we can prepare delicious meals and delight the most discriminating palates even when breaking some of these sacred gourmet commandments. While tough meat will take longer to cook, cheap cuts are just as nutritious as expensive ones. If you have the time, let it cook slowly. Slow cooking really does bring out the best in meat. The meat retains its moisture, does not shrink, and the goodness is not burnt away as with more rapid cooking techniques. I know many cooks are snooty about using a pressure cooker and rule it out altogether. I confess that I do use one but only when I am stuck for time or when cooking with mutton rather than lamb.

When preparing meat for cooking trim away all excess fat, skin and muscle. Because we eat with our hands, meat eaters in the Indian subcontinent know well that half the pleasure of eating meat is to pick it up and chew it right off the bone. Traditionally some pieces will always be cut with the bone and some cubes of meat will be boneless. It is not unusual to put a mixture of cuts from the shoulder, leg or other parts of the animal into the same cooking pot. I often buy a whole lamb or half a lamb and divide it up into a mixture of pieces from different parts and freeze it in small portions for use at a future time. It really is a question of personal preference. If you prefer to use cubed meat off the bone, which I grant you is easier to tackle when eating with knives and forks, there is no reason why you should not do so.

There are several recipes in this section in which I have avoided giving specific, overall cooking times for the meat. The reason I chose to do this was so that the recipes would work equally well whatever the cut or quality of your meat. Most of the dishes concerned are made with cubed lamb/mutton, on or off the bone, which in general should take between an hour to an hour and a half to cook.

Achar Gosht
(Lamb in a Pickle Sauce)

You must not let the name of this recipe misguide or frighten you. The meat is *not* pickled, but is given this name as a compliment and in recognition of the fact that the combination of flavours produced by the green chillies and the selection of certain whole spices, notably *kalonji*, used in the dish, are characteristic of a wide variety of pickles and closely associated with them. It is also probably worth knowing that this dish is not as chilli hot as you might at first imagine, as the seeds which contain most of the heat in a chilli are entirely removed before use.

For this recipe you need a variety of green chilli sometimes called the 'Spanish chilli' by English greengrocers. It is a Mediterranean variety and is larger, fatter and less hot than the typically small, slender, Indian green chilli, but very similar in flavour. Do not use green peppers as a substitute as their taste is identifiably different and will dramatically alter the classical nature of this dish.

2 lb/900 g lean lamb, on or off the bone, cut into 1–1½ in/2·5–3·8 cm cubes, fat trimmed off (*gosht*)

1 lb/450 g onions, peeled and roughly chopped (*pyaz*)

4 fl. oz/120 ml cooking oil (*tail*) or 2 oz/50 g clarified butter (*asli ghee*)

1 tsp turmeric (*haldi*)

3 tsp ground coriander (*dhania*)

1 tsp red chilli powder (*lal mirch*)

8 oz/225 g natural yoghurt (*dahi*)

salt to taste (*namak*)

12 large Spanish green chillies (*bari hari mirch*)

2½–3 tsp nigella seeds (*kalonji*)

2½–3 tsp white cumin seeds (*sabut safeid zeera*)

2½–3 tsp fenugreek seeds (*methi dana*)

Fry the onions in plenty of cooking oil or *asli ghee*. When golden brown, add the meat and fry well to brown it and seal in the juices. Add the turmeric, coriander, red chilli powder, yoghurt, and salt. Stir-fry the meat and spices together for a few minutes until they are well mixed and have turned just a shade darker.

Add 8 fl. oz/250 ml water, bring to a boil, then immediately turn the heat down, covering the saucepan with a well-fitting lid, and simmer over low heat until the meat is tender. Check a few times during this period to ensure that there is sufficient moisture in the pan and that the meat and spices are not sticking to the bottom. Add more water if you need to.

While the meat is cooking, slit the chillies down one side, remove the seeds and wash them thoroughly in cold running water. I would recommend that you wear gloves for this as the chilli can get under the fingernails and burn painfully. Mix together the three sets of seeds and, keeping a teaspoonful aside, stuff the rest into the seeded chillies.

When the meat is about two-thirds cooked (which can take between 45 minutes and $1\frac{1}{2}$ hours, depending on its quality), carefully arrange the stuffed chillies in the saucepan and add the teaspoon of whole spices kept in reserve. Do not worry if some of the seeds fall out into the gravy while you stir or as the food cooks – it is inevitable. In fact if you are feeling lazy, you can just throw in the whole spices separately and not bother to fill the chillies at all – I have sometimes done just this and the dish tasted every bit as good. You can add more water at any stage if you think you need to, but take care that the gravy does not become too watery. When the chillies change colour and the lamb is tender your dish is ready.

Steak à la Passandé
(*Beef Passanda*)

My mother was so proud of her *Passanda* recipe and, wishing to emphasize the fact that it was made only from the finest quality beef undercut available in Pakistan, felt it was something of a betrayal to simply call it by a name as commonplace as *passanda*. . . . So to indulge her, in our home, we teasingly referred to it by a French name.

With this background of intense family indoctrination I was extremely disconcerted on coming to England to find lamb *passandas* on restaurant menus everywhere and not a hint of the existence of the fine beef *passandas* I had always known. My initial reaction was quite strongly to reject the possibility that there was any such thing. I have since been forced to accept the *de facto* position that lamb *passandas* exist. I remain, however, privately convinced to the contrary, trusting more the knowledge passed down to me by generations of quality beef *passanda* eaters, perched on our family tree. This recipe that I am now sharing with you is the authentic dish, which fact is surely borne out by its taste which is infinitely superior and bears little or no resemblance to that mild, almost bland invention that has usurped its name.

2 lb/900 g good quality beef, cut into slices approx. 2 × 3 in/5 × 7·5 cm and ½ in./1·2 cm thick (*gai ka gosht*)

8 oz/225 g natural yoghurt (*dahi*)

3 medium onions, peeled and coarsely chopped (*pyaz*)

clarified butter *or* cooking oil (*asli ghee/tail*)

1 in./2·5 cm cube fresh ginger, peeled and finely grated or chopped (*adrak*)

1½ tbsp crushed garlic cloves (*lehsun*)

1 tbsp ground coriander (*dhania*)

4–5 large cardamoms (*bari elaichee*)

1 tsp red chilli powder (*lal mirch*)

salt to taste (*namak*)

10–12 small cardamoms (*choti elaichee*)

For the garnish

2 tbsp fresh coriander leaves, finely chopped (*hara dhania*)

Flatten and tenderize the slices of beef by pounding them with a blunt-edged knife or kitchen mallet. Spread the yoghurt over the meat and leave it to marinate for 2–4 hours.

Fry the onions in *asli ghee* or cooking oil until golden brown. When ready, remove them from the saucepan with a slotted spoon and blend them to a paste.

Put the meat, onion paste and all the remaining ingredients, except for the small cardamoms and fresh coriander, in the same oil in which you browned the onions and mix them well together over a medium flame. After a few minutes, turn the flame down to its lowest point, cover the saucepan and simmer until tender. Coarsely grind the small cardamoms and add them to the saucepan just before the meat is done.

You may find that you need to add some water from time to time to prevent the spices from sticking to the bottom of the saucepan and burning. Be careful that you don't add too much, as the gravy in this dish should be thick and vibrant, not watery. Garnish with fresh coriander when serving.

Shaljum Gosht
(Lamb with Turnips)

Originally a Kashmiri recipe, this dish was introduced to the Punjab by migrant and settler families. There it gained immense popularity and became such a household favourite that it earned itself an equally important place in Punjabi cuisine.

Shaljum gosht, with its ample gravy and distinctive aroma, is normally eaten with *khushka*, plain boiled rice, by Kashmiris and Punjabis alike. If you prefer to do something more special with your rice, then a simple *pullao* would be the most appropriate choice, as a heavily seasoned rice would only detract from the taste of the lamb delicately flavoured with turnips.

2 lb/900 g lean cubed lamb, on or off the bone according to personal preference (*gosht*)

1–1½ lb/450–700 g white turnips (*shaljum*)

salt to taste (*namak*)

1 medium onion, peeled and chopped (*pyaz*)

cooking oil (*tail*)

1½ in./3·75 cm cube fresh ginger, peeled and finely grated (*adrak*)

8 medium garlic cloves, crushed (*lehsun*)

2 dsp ground coriander (*dhania*)

½ tsp turmeric (*haldi*)

1 tsp red chilli powder (*lal mirch*)

6 oz/175 g natural yoghurt (*dahi*)

8 oz/225 g tomatoes, chopped (*timatar*)

1 tsp sugar (*shakar*)

whole garam masala spices

6 black peppercorns (*sabut kali mirch*)

4 cloves (*laung*)

1 large cardamom (*bari elaichee*)

2 small cardamoms (*choti elaichee*)

½ in./1·2 cm cinnamon stick (*dalchini*)

1 bay leaf (*tejpatta*)

1 tsp white cumin seeds (*sabut safeid zeera*)

For the garnish

2 tbsp fresh coriander leaves, finely chopped (*hara dhania*)

Peel the turnips and, depending on their sizes, halve or quarter them into fairly large pieces. Prick holes in them with a fork, liberally rub with salt and put to one side. After 15–20 minutes wash them well in cold running water, and pat them dry with a paper towel.

Fry the chopped onions in cooking oil and, once they are soft and translucent, sprinkle in the whole *garam masala* spices. Add the turnip pieces when the onions are a pale golden brown and continue to fry gently over a low flame. When the turnips are lightly sautéed, lift them out of the pan, leaving behind as much of the onion as possible. Put the turnips aside.

To the browned onions and whole spices add the fresh ginger, garlic, ground coriander, turmeric, red chilli powder and some salt, and stir-fry for 1–2 minutes. Add the meat, and continue to brown the meat and spices, stirring them well together for a few minutes. Add a little water to the yoghurt, whisk it with a fork and pour it in with the meat. Stir some more to mix all the ingredients well and cover the saucepan with a tightly fitting lid. Gently cook the meat until it is about half done – about 30–45 minutes – at which stage you should add the chopped tomatoes and 8 fl. oz/250 ml hot water to make a gravy. Cover and continue to simmer until the meat is three-quarters cooked, then add the fried pieces of turnip and the sugar. Decide at this stage whether you think you need to add any more water.

The finished dish should have a gravy of medium weight, neither too thick nor too watery. Garnish with chopped fresh coriander and serve.

Kharey Masalay ka Gosht
(*Lamb in Whole Spices*)

This is one of the first recipes I learned when I started to cook and has always been a great family favourite. It demonstrates, with amazing clarity, how completely the flavour of spices is transformed when used whole rather than ground. You may already be familiar with the flavours of those whole spices which belong to the *garam masala* family, as they are frequently used whole. Here you will experience brand new tastes even from those commoner spices such as coriander seeds, more often seen in their ground form. The combination of whole spices used to cook this dish is just sensational. Another pleasure of cooking entirely with whole spices is the comparative simplicity of cooking a dish that minimizes the need to peel, crush, grind, grate or chop!

2 lb/900 g leg of lamb, cubed on or off the bone, with all fat removed (*gosht*)

6–7 tbsp clarified butter or 3 fl. oz/75 ml cooking oil (*asli ghee/tail*)

8–10 oz/225–275 g onions, peeled and sliced into rings or half rings (*pyaz*)

8 small or 4 large garlic cloves, peeled (cut large cloves in half) (*lehsun*)

1½ in./3.8 cm cube fresh ginger, peeled and finely diced (*adrak*)

10–12 whole, large, dried red chillies, or to taste (*sabut lal mirch*)

1 tsp white cumin seeds (*sabut safeid zeera*)

1 tsp coriander seeds (*sabut dhania*)

4 large cardamoms (*bari elaichee*)

½ tsp black peppercorns (*sabut kali mirch*)

½ tsp nigella seeds (*kalonji*)

8 oz/225 g tomatoes, roughly chopped (*timatar*)

5 oz/150 g natural yoghurt, lightly whisked (*dahi*)

salt to taste (*namak*)

For the garnish

2 tbsp fresh coriander leaves, finely chopped (*hara dhania*)

Using a wok or other wide, heavy-bottomed cooking utensil, heat the clarified butter or oil and fry the pieces of meat over a medium flame to seal in the juices. After stirring the meat around for about 5 minutes so that it browns evenly, add the onions, along with the garlic, ginger, red chillies and other whole spices. Stir well to mix together and cook over medium heat for about 5 minutes before adding the tomatoes. Cover the pan and cook for a further 10 minutes, then add the yoghurt and salt, mixing them with the meat and spices. After bringing to a boil, turn the heat down and simmer in a covered pan until the meat is tender.

Once the meat is cooked, if you find the gravy still too watery, take off the lid and cook over medium to high heat to allow the excess liquid to evaporate quickly. When ready, the meat should have a rich colour and a thickish gravy. This dish ought to cook in its own juices and the water released from the yoghurt, onions and tomatoes; but if the meat you are using is tough and the moisture evaporates before it is tender you may need to add a little water. Garnish with chopped fresh coriander.

NB. When eating this dish do not eat the whole spices, but put them to the side of your plate.

Hari Chutney Main Gosht
(Lamb in a Fresh Coriander Chutney)

This is an unusual recipe in which delicately spiced lamb is cooked in natural yoghurt and flavoured, at the end, with a chutney of fresh coriander leaves, mint leaves, and green chillies. The use of blended green chutney produces a burst of fresh flavour which is instantly absorbed by the meat.

2 lb/900 g leg of lamb, cut into lean small 1–1½ in./2·5–3·8 cm cubes on or off the bone according to preference (*gosht*)

10 oz/275 g onions, peeled and finely chopped (*pyaz*)

4 fl. oz/120 ml cooking oil (*tail*)

10 garlic cloves, crushed (*lehsun*)

2 tbsp peeled and finely grated fresh ginger (*adrak*)

½ tsp turmeric (*haldi*)

¼ tsp red chilli powder (*lal mirch*)

1 tsp ground coriander (*dhania*)

1 tsp salt, or to taste (*namak*)

10 oz/275 g natural yoghurt (*dahi*)

1 tsp freshly ground *garam masala* (see page 17)

1 cup fresh coriander leaves, finely chopped (*hara dhania*)

½ cup fresh mint leaves, finely chopped (*pudeena*)

4 green chillies (*hari mirch*)

2 tbsp lemon juice (*neebo ka ras*)

Brown the chopped onions in the cooking oil. When they change colour, add the garlic and ginger, and stir for a minute before adding the turmeric, red chilli powder, ground coriander and salt. Stir the spices around to brown them a little, being careful not to burn them.

Add the meat and mix well with the spices. Once the colour of the meat changes and it loses its raw appearance, add the yoghurt, lightly whisked with a fork, and stir it in. Put in the freshly ground *garam masala*, cover the saucepan with a well fitting lid, turn the heat down very low, and simmer. If your meat is truly tender it should cook in its own juices within an hour. If not, you may add a little water should you need to, and cook for longer until the meat is done.

While the meat is slowly simmering, blend the fresh coriander, mint, green chillies and lemon juice in an electric blender or processor to a smooth chutney paste. Once the meat is cooked, pour in this green chutney, cover and cook it only for another 10–15 minutes, over low heat. This dish does not have a gravy but a thick sauce which clings, with the chutney, to the meat.

Daal Gosht
(Lamb or Mutton with Split Chickpeas)

A great favourite for family meals in the Punjab. The traditional way to cook *daal gosht* is with *channay ki daal* (split chickpeas). This *daal* is known for being hard to digest and, if you find it makes you fart too much, you would be forgiven if you used split *moong* lentils instead. I love the *channa*, farts and all, so I usually swallow some carminative mixture and pray that it silences the problem sufficiently to escape any embarrassment!

I like to use leg of lamb or mutton for this recipe. My butcher removes all the excess fat and then cuts the joint into medium sized pieces, some of which are on the bone and others just lean cubes of meat. I would make a special plea in favour of including some pieces on the bone as the bone and marrow add a noticeable richness to the flavour of the dish.

I often use my slow cooker to make this recipe. This is not essential but *daal gosht* is exceptionally good when allowed to cook gently for a long time. One distinct advantage of the slow cooker is that it dispenses with any need to watch over the dish or to stir it while it is cooking. Here we are aiming for a dish in which the meat is extremely well done and the yellow grains of *daal*, although completely soft, remain distinct. The *bhagar* of hot oil and crisply browned onions at the end adds the final touch that makes it irresistible over-riding lurking concerns about social inconvenience.

1–1½ lb/450 g lamb or mutton, cut into medium-sized pieces (*gosht*)

1 lb/450 g split chick peas (*channa daal*)

2 medium onions, peeled and chopped (*pyaz*)

cooking oil (*tail*)

6 medium garlic cloves, crushed (*lehsun*)

1 tbsp finely grated fresh ginger (*adrak*) and a few thinly cut strips

1 tsp turmeric (*haldi*)

2 tsp ground coriander (*dhania*)

1 tsp red chilli powder (*lal mirch*)

3 small tomatoes, chopped (*timatar*)

2–3 fresh green chillies (*hari mirch*)

1–2 tbsp fresh mint leaves, finely chopped (*pudeena*) (optional)

1½ tsp freshly ground *garam masala* (see page 17)

salt to taste (*namak*)

For the bhagar

1 small onion, peeled (*pyaz*)

4 tbsp cooking oil (*tail*)

5–8 *karri* leaves (*karri patta*) (optional)

3–4 whole dried red chillies (*sabut lal mirch*) (optional)

For the garnish

2–3 tbsp fresh coriander leaves, finely chopped (*hara dhania*)

Fry the onions in some oil in a heavy-bottomed saucepan. When they are a rich golden colour, turn the heat right down and add the garlic, ginger, turmeric, ground coriander and red chilli powder. Stir in the spices to mix them well with the fried onions, and fry for a few minutes until they release their aroma and darken just a little. Then add the meat to the spice mixture and stir well until the pieces are fully covered with the spices and evenly browned. Stir the chopped tomatoes in with the meat.

If you are using a slow cooker this is the stage at which you should transfer the meat to it, and, if using lamb, also add at the same time the washed chickpeas with enough water to cover them. Leave it to cook on a low setting for 8–10 hours. If you are cooking with mutton, add the chickpeas 2 hours after the meat.

If you are cooking on a conventional cooker and you have tender lamb, add the washed chickpeas once the meat has been browned; cover with water and simmer gently. If you are using mutton, let the meat cook for about 45 minutes before you add the chickpeas. The reason for the different timings is that, when the meat is quite tender and the dish is ready to be served, the grains of *daal* must be plump and clearly visible rather than overcooked to the point where they dissolve into a thick soupy consistency.

At the end stir in some thinly cut strips of fresh ginger root, chopped green chillies, fresh mint leaves and salt to taste, and simmer for a further couple of minutes. Transfer the *daal gosht* to your serving dish and sprinkle the ground *garam masala* over the surface.

To prepare the *bhagar*, cut the onion into fine rings or half rings. Heat the oil and fry the onion rings to a crisp golden brown. Just before the onions are ready you may add the *karri* leaves and whole red chillies if you have chosen to use either or both. Pour the sizzling mixture on to the serving dish just before eating. Do not stir it in. Garnish with fresh coriander.

Lamb Qorma

The mere mention of a *qorma* inevitably conjures up in my mind fragrant images of the luxuriant foods typically associated with weddings, festivals and special family gatherings. Yet, a *qorma* need not be lavish and is by no means reserved for eating only at such select occasions. Nor is it the case that it is only ever seen keeping company with those traditionally accepted old friends like *biryanis*, *sheermaals*, *zardas* and *firnis*.

By some standards this recipe would qualify as fairly lightweight. It uses no fresh cream, pistachios or almonds, and is spiced with comparative restraint. But it keeps the essential rich quality of an authentic *qorma*, instantly recognizable by its thick, vibrant gravy, the unmistakable aroma and flavour of *kewra* and cardamom, and you are encouraged to use saffron if you can possibly afford it. I actually prefer it to the heavier version which can give you a hangover the next day, although there are several gluttons I know who would swear that the experience of sheer indulgence had been well worth any excess.

You will discover that the process for cooking a *qorma* is a little more elaborate than for some other dishes you may have tried but, as *qorma* recipes go, this one is revolutionary in its simplicity.

2 lb/900 g lean leg of lamb (*gosht*)
8 oz/225 g onions, peeled and coarsely chopped (*pyaz*)
8 oz/225 g clarified butter *or* 10 tbsp cooking oil (*asli ghee/tail*)
4–5 large cardamoms (*bari elaichee*)
10–12 small cardamoms (*choti elaichee*)
6–8 garlic cloves, crushed (*lehsun*)
1½ in./3·8 cm cube fresh ginger, peeled and finely grated (*adrak*)

1½ tbsp ground coriander (*dhania*)
1 tsp red chilli powder (*lal mirch*)
1½ tsp salt (*namak*)
8 oz/225 g natural yoghurt, lightly whisked (*dahi*)
1½ tsp *kewra* (optional)
a pinch of saffron as generous as you can afford (*zafran*)

Ask your butcher to trim away all the excess fat from the meat, to cut the joint of lamb into medium-sized cubes and to give you a selection of meat pieces both on and off the bone.

Brown the onions in *asli ghee* or cooking oil. When they turn a deep honey golden, lift them out of the saucepan with a perforated spoon, leaving a few strands behind in the oil. Now place these fried onions in the container of an electric blender and give them a few short whizzes so that they are considerably broken down into a rough paste. Grind both the large and small cardamoms just enough to reduce them to a crude powder. Mix these crushed cardamoms with the onion paste and reserve for use later.

Add the meat to the *asli ghee* or oil in which you fried the onions, and stir over a medium high heat. After a few minutes, when the meat has lost its raw colour and the juices are safely sealed in, add the garlic, ginger, ground coriander, red chilli powder and salt. Keep stirring briskly to prevent the spices from sticking to the bottom of the pan. As soon as the spices are evenly distributed and begin to turn a shade darker, losing their raw quality (a couple of minutes only), pour in the yoghurt and stir once again to mix the ingredients well. Cover and cook over extremely low heat. If you have good quality meat, then in about $1-1\frac{1}{2}$ hours it will be absolutely tender. About halfway through the cooking you may need to add some water. If you have tougher meat then continue to add a little water from time to time until the meat is quite cooked.

When the meat is close to being ready, add the onion and cardamom paste prepared earlier, and cook gently until the lamb is very well done and ready to eat. If your dish has too watery a gravy at this stage then you must have added too much water. Turn the heat up and evaporate some of the excess moisture. A *qorma* should have a thick sauce.

About 5 minutes before the *qorma* is completely ready, add the *kewra* and saffron and cover the saucepan with a well-fitting lid so that their aroma can be absorbed by the meat and the gravy through the trapped steam as the *qorma* simmers gently.

Gobi Gosht
(Lamb with Cauliflower)

Follow the recipe for Lamb *Qorma*, omitting the last paragraph that asks you to add the saffron and *kewra*.

A medium cauliflower is added only after the meat is fully cooked. However, it should first be chopped up into small florets and stir-fried separately in a wok. After adding these fried florets to the cooked meat, sprinkle in some finely chopped fresh ginger, chopped green chillies and about 4 tbsp finely chopped fresh coriander. Stir them in well and simmer gently for a few minutes before transferring the food to a serving dish.

Bund Gobi Gosht
(Beef with Cabbage)

This is cooked in exactly the same way as the Lamb with Cauliflower. Finely chopped or shredded cabbage is first stir-fried separately before being added to the meat. It could be made with either lamb or beef but is distinctly tastier with beef.

Turai Gosht
(Lamb with Courgettes)

Again follow the recipe for *qorma* to cook the meat omitting the saffron and *kewra*. If you want a less rich meat base then follow the recipe for *Aloo Gosht* on page 73. Cook the courgettes first and, if following the recipe for Aloo Gosht, add them to the meat together with some browned onions (1 small onion chopped and separately fried), when the meat is about 15 minutes away from being ready. In either case just before serving, squeeze some lemon juice into the dish to add a refreshingly sour tang to its flavour.

Aam Qaliya
(Lamb with Green Mangoes)

Credit for this recipe must be given to my sister's mother-in-law at whose house in Karachi last year I encountered it for the first time. Although Mrs Shah is known to be a brilliant cook, in a family of stunning cooks, here she has surpassed even herself. A *qaliya*, by the way, is simply a more elaborate sort of *qorma*. What makes this dish such a discovery is the wonderfully exotic combination of lavish *qorma* ingredients such as saffron, cardamoms and rosewater together with halved, unripe mangoes that have been stewed in turmeric water and garnished with slivers of blanched almonds.

1 × Lamb *Qorma* recipe (see
  page 62)
1 lb/450 g unripe small green
  mangoes (*katchay aam*)
1 dsp turmeric (*haldi*)
1 tsp granulated sugar (*shakar*)

For the garnish
15 almonds, blanched and slivered
  (*badam*)

Make a Lamb *Qorma* as on page 62, omitting only the *kewra*.

While that is cooking, peel and halve the mangoes, removing the soft white seed inside them. Add the turmeric to a saucepan full of water and boil the mangoes. Once the mangoes are tender, strain them in a colander and discard the turmeric water. Arrange the mango halves in the saucepan with the lamb, add the sugar, cover with a tightly fitting lid and simmer for a short time on low heat.

Serve garnished with slivers of blanched almonds sprinkled over the surface of the dish.

SABUT RAAN
(Whole Roast Leg of Lamb)

In an Indian home, to cook and serve meat in this style is a true sign of affluence, unstinting hospitality or a generous and extravagant host. Eating habits in all cultures express volumes about their people. I have often heard westerners express amazement at the amount of rice or bread we consume with our meals and comment on the relatively small quantity of 'food' that accompanies them; which also leads the western mind to wonder about whether our bodies are receiving sufficient nutrition. In just the same way, I admit that we frequently remark on the sheer weight of meat per head that is eaten at meals in the West and marvel at the resilience of the human digestive system which survives such regular onslaughts.

Here I am giving you two recipes to choose from. In the first, the lamb is highly seasoned, with a freshly prepared spicy yoghurt, and uses onions as the base for a more than generous gravy. The second recipe is comparatively mildly spiced, and uses lemon juice in place of the yoghurt and onions, to produce a moist, delicately flavoured roast leg of lamb.

You may want to ask your butcher to chop off the end bone to make it easier to fit the leg into a roasting pan. Remember that in Indian cookery it is a must to trim away as much fat as possible before preparing the meat. This makes it crucially important to baste the joint frequently in the pan juices to prevent the meat from drying out. Since the fat has been removed, it will be impossible for the meat to be basted naturally. Allow the leg of lamb to roast slowly to avoid shrinkage.

Apart from being differently prepared and spiced, there is one other feature which distinguishes an Indian *raan* from a roast leg of lamb. This is the special soft texture of the cooked meat which we like to be extremely tender, almost *halwa*-like, melting away in our mouths.

Sabut Raan I

This first recipe can be made either in the oven, as described here, or as a sort of pot roast on the cooker. Once you have drenched the whole leg of lamb in its marinade for the prescribed length of time, cook it by whichever method you find more convenient.

1 leg of lamb, approx. 4 lb/1·8 kg in weight, fat removed (*raan*)
1 tbsp poppy seeds (*khas khas*)
1 dsp coriander seeds (*sabut dhania*)
10 cloves (*laung*)
15 black peppercorns (*sabut kali mirch*)
2 in./5 cm cinnamon stick (*dalchini*)
2 large cardamoms (*bari elaichee*)
1 bay leaf (*tejpatta*)
2 tbsp crushed garlic (*lehsun*)
2 tbsp finely grated fresh ginger (*adrak*)

2 tbsp finely grated unripe green papaya (*hara papita*) (optional)
salt to taste (*namak*)
8 oz/225 g natural yoghurt (*dahi*)
8 oz/225 g onions, peeled and coarsely chopped (*pyaz*)
clarified butter or cooking oil (*asli ghee/tail*)

For the garnish
crisply fried onions (*pyaz*)
fresh sliced tomatoes (*timatar*)
wedges of lemon (*neeboo*)

In a non-stick or cast-iron frying pan or *tava*, dry roast the poppy seeds, coriander seeds, cloves, peppercorns, cinnamon, cardamoms and bay leaf until they take on a slightly darker colour and release their aromas. Grind them to a fine powder. Mix these freshly roasted and ground spices, the garlic, ginger, papaya and salt with the yoghurt and whisk lightly with a fork.

Prick deep holes into the meat or else make knife gashes all over the leg. Rub the marinade well into the meat, pouring any excess there may be over it and set it aside for at least 1–2 hours, or even longer, depending on how strongly you want the flavour of the spices to be absorbed by the meat.

Fry the onions to a pale golden colour in the *asli ghee* or oil. Place the joint in all its marinades in a greased roasting pan and pour the clarified butter or oil with the fried onions over it. Add about ½–1¼ pints/450–750 ml water and put it in an oven pre-heated to 350°F/180°C/Gas 4. Turn the joint over every 15 minutes for about 2–2½ hours, until the meat is completely tender. I often add an additional cup or more of water while the joint is cooking to allow for evaporation. This keeps the joint succulent and moist and, combined with the yoghurt and onions, also serves to make a generous, rich and wonderful gravy.

Lift out the meat and place it in a serving dish with some of the gravy poured over it. You should have plenty of gravy, so serve the rest in a sauce boat. Garnish with crisply fried onions, fresh tomatoes and wedges of lemon.

Sabut Raan II

1 leg of lamb, approx.
  3½–4 lb/1·6–1·8 kg, fat removed
  (*raan*)
salt to taste (*namak*)
1½ tbsp crushed garlic (*lehsun*)
1½ tbsp finely grated fresh ginger
  (*adrak*)

1 tsp black peppercorns, freshly
  ground (*sabut kali mirch*)
½ tsp red chilli powder (*lal mirch*)
5–6 tbsp lemon juice (*neeboo ka ras*)
clarified butter (*asli ghee*)

Mix the salt and other spices well with the lemon juice. Prick deep holes in
the meat with a fork or, better still, make deep knife gashes all over it. Place
the meat in a dish and pour the marinade over it, rubbing it thoroughly into
the holes or gashes. Set it aside for an hour or two.

When you are ready to cook, smear the joint generously with clarified
butter. This is especially important because in Indian cookery all the fat on
the joint is removed. Place it in a clear roasting bag, seal it and put it in an
oven preheated to 350°F/180°C/Gas 4 for about 2 hours. This is the ideal
way to roast the joint because it bastes and browns and is kept perfectly
moist in the bag. When tender, transfer to a serving dish and pour the
gravy from the bag on to the joint.

Spicy Beef Pot Roast

3 lb/1·4 kg topside of beef, all fat
  trimmed off (*gai ka gosht*)
5–6 tbsp clarified butter (*asli ghee*)
8 oz/225 g onions, peeled and
  chopped (*pyaz*)
1 tbsp desiccated coconut (*naryal*)
1 dsp white poppy seeds (*khas khas*)
1 dsp fennel seeds (*sonf*)
1 tsp white cumin seeds (*sabut safeid
  zeera*)

½ tsp coriander seeds (*dhania*)
6 oz/175 g natural yoghurt (*dahi*)
2 tbsp crushed garlic cloves (*lehsun*)
2 tbsp finely grated fresh ginger
  (*adrak*)
1 tsp red chilli powder, or to taste
  (*lal mirch*)
1 tsp turmeric (*haldi*)
salt to taste (*namak*)

Using a heavy-bottomed pan, heat the clarified butter and fry the chopped onions until they are a golden brown. Lift them out of the pan with a perforated spoon and blend them to a smooth paste. Grind the coconut, poppy, fennel, cumin and coriander seeds to a fine powder. Mix together with the yoghurt, onion paste, garlic, ginger, red chilli powder, turmeric and salt. Cut deep knife gashes in the meat to enable it to absorb the spices well. Rub the spicy marinade all over it and set aside for at least 2 hours.

Now place the meat the marinade in the same saucepan containing the clarified butter in which you earlier browned the onions. Add 16 fl. oz/475 ml water and after bringing it to a quick boil, turn the heat down low and cook gently in a covered pan. Turn the meat over every now and again to prevent the spices from sticking to the bottom and to ensure it cooks evenly. You may or may not need to add more water during the cooking process depending on how quickly or slowly the joint cooks. At the end, when the joint is completely tender, if there appears to be too much gravy, simply turn the heat up and evaporate some of the excess moisture.

SPICY LAMB CHOPS AND CUTLETS

Indian lamb chops and cutlets are seasoned with spices, then gently cooked over a low heat until the spices are completely absorbed and the meat is perfectly tender. There are, however, variations to this method and as shown in my second recipe they are also sometimes, as a final touch, dipped in egg and coated with breadcrumbs which adds a delicious outer crispness.

For as long as I can remember, lamb chops and cutlets have always been for me a special treat at meal times. Mutton *champ* as they are collectively called in the vernacular, are a popular item on the menus of every *Irani* hotel and restaurant. These eating places are unique roadside cafés at the hub of subcontinental inner-city culture where the flow of human traffic is constant..It is seldom quiet in an *Irani* restaurant, most of which run a full house from dawn, when they open, to the early hours of the next morning when business from hungry truckers, taxi-drivers, builders, labourers, shoppers, passers-by, hangers-on and dope peddlers quietens down for a few hours – just long enough to put out the rubbish and feed the leftovers to stray cats and dogs.

In Karachi, some years ago, these one-star eating houses were discovered by the rich trend-setters of the city. Cushioned in their de luxe Toyotas and air-conditioned Mercedes against all risk of contamination from humans and bacteria alike, they would drive on to the kerb just outside one of the popular *Irani* restaurants and blow their horns impatiently to demand 'car service', clearly delighted to have found the best deal in town. In these circles such fun-filled evenings were fashionably known as 'going slumming'.

Lamb chops are also a very popular item on the menus of many Indian restaurants in London. For some inexplicable reason, they feature as Starters, a concept totally foreign to classical Indian cuisine, but one which I once found was fiercely defended by the management when I attempted to order some chops to accompany my main meal.

Spicy Lamb Chops or Cutlets in a Sauce

Use either loin chops, or rib chops and cutlets taken from the best end of neck as individual cuts, with all excess fat trimmed off.

1½ lb/700 g lamb chops or cutlets, weighed without fat (*champ*)
6–8 garlic cloves, crushed (*lehsun*)
1 fat 1 in./2·5 cm cube fresh ginger, peeled and finely grated (*adrak*)
1 tsp red chilli powder, or to taste (*lal mirch*)

½ tsp freshly ground *garam masala* (see page 17)
salt to taste (*namak*)
4 oz/100 g natural yoghurt (*dahi*)
cooking oil (*tail*)
8 oz/225 g onions, peeled and finely chopped (*pyaz*)

Mix the garlic, ginger, red chilli powder, *garam masala* and salt with the yoghurt, and coat the chops with this paste. Heat a little oil in a heavy-bottomed pan and place the chops in it with all the spicy yoghurt sauce. After briefly frying them over a high heat, cover with a tightly fitting lid and cook slowly over a low flame until the meat is tender (about 45 minutes). It should not be necessary to add any water as the meat cooks in its own juices and moisture released by the yoghurt. If, however, the meat is tough and all the moisture evaporates before it is fully cooked, you may add a little water at a time, to prevent the spices from sticking to the bottom of the pan, and continue to simmer until all the chops are well done.

Lift the chops out of the pan on to a plate and put them to one side for the moment. If there is only very little moisture left in the saucepan add a small quantity of water and make a thick gravy, scraping off the spices from the sides and bottom of the pan; spoon off any excess oil that may be floating on the surface of this gravy and reserve.

Take a fresh saucepan or large frying pan and, heating the minimum oil necessary, fry the onions, stirring more or less continuously until they are a deep golden brown. When they reach the desired colour, put the cooked chops back in, and fry them over a medium flame for a few minutes. Then pour in the gravy and continue to fry for a few minutes more. You will know your dish is ready when the oil separates from the gravy.

Spicy Lamb Chops or Cutlets in Breadcrumbs

1½ lb/700 g lean double loin chops, or rib chops and cutlets taken from the best end of neck with all excess fat trimmed off, weighed without fat
2 oz/50 g onion, peeled and roughly chopped (*pyaz*)
1 in./2·5 cm cube fresh ginger, peeled and finely grated (*adrak*)
6–8 garlic cloves, crushed (*lehsun*)
¼ tsp freshly ground *garam masala* (see page 17)

1 tsp red chilli powder, or to taste (*lal mirch*)
1 tsp ground coriander (*dhania*)
½ tsp turmeric (*haldi*)
½ tbsp pomegranate seeds, finely ground (*anardana*)
salt to taste (*namak*)
2 tbsp natural yoghurt (*dahi*)
cooking oil (*tail*)
1 egg, beaten (*unda*)
breadcrumbs (*double roti kay crumm*)

Blend the onion to a smooth paste. Mix all the spices and salt with the yoghurt and onion paste. Rub this spicy paste over the chops and set aside for 15–30 minutes. Heat a little oil and fry the chops on both sides, then turn the heat down and cook slowly until they are tender (about 45 minutes). Add a small quantity of water if necessary. When the meat is completely cooked and all the moisture has evaporated, lift the chops on to a plate with as much of the thick sauce clinging to them as possible. Dip each one in beaten egg and coat with breadcrumbs. Fry them to a golden brown colour shortly before serving. This is absolutely delicious as what you get is a crisp outer coating with soft well-seasoned meat on the inside.

Palak Gosht
(Spring Lamb with Spinach)

Fresh spinach is available in season from most greengrocers. Imported Cyprus spinach can be found almost all the year round at Indian and Cypriot shops. The Cyprus spinach is closer to the sort grown in the subcontinent and has a much more highly developed flavour, so try and spot it if you can. For the sake of convenience you could opt for frozen leaf spinach which works perfectly adequately with the recipe, but your dish will lose a great deal of the pleasure that comes from the unrivalled taste of fresh spinach.

2 lb/900 g leg of lamb, cut into lean small 1½ in/3·8 cm cubes, on or off the bone (*gosht*)

1 lb/450 g fresh spinach (*tazi palak ka saag*), *or* frozen spinach

6 oz/175 g onions, peeled and finely chopped (*pyaz*)

6 tbsp cooking oil (*tail*)

1 tbsp crushed garlic (*lehsun*)

1 tbsp finely grated fresh ginger (*adrak*)

½ tsp turmeric (*haldi*)

1 tsp red chilli powder (*lal mirch*)

2 tsp ground coriander (*dhania*)

½ lb/225 g tomatoes, finely chopped (*timatar*)

salt to taste (*namak*)

2 green chillies, finely sliced (*hari mirch*)

Wash the spinach carefully. Cut off and discard the thick stems. Hold the spinach leaves together in a bunch and cut across at ½ in./1·2 cm intervals. Cut these strips also at ½ in./1·2 cm intervals but in the opposite direction. Put aside for use later.

Fry the onions in the oil until they turn golden brown. Then add the garlic and ginger and fry for 1 minute before adding the remaining spices. Stir-fry the onion and spice mixture for a few minutes before adding the meat. Stir to mix the ingredients well and brown the meat to seal in its juices. Add the tomatoes, salt and 4 fl. oz/120 ml water, and simmer over very low heat for 20–25 minutes in a covered saucepan. During this time check a few times to see that it is not sticking to the bottom. At the end of this time you could add another 4 fl. oz/120 ml water. By this stage the meat should be half cooked. If your meat is not of the best quality you may need to add some more water and extend the cooking time.

Once the meat is about half cooked or even a little more, add the fresh spinach and mix it in well. Continue cooking slowly over low heat until the meat is absolutely tender. Finally, turn the heat up, add the finely sliced green chillies and stir-fry until most of the extra moisture evaporates and you are left with a rich, thick sauce, the spinach clinging to the meat.

Aloo Gosht
(Lamb and Potatoes in Gravy)

This is a wholesome dish, very popular in the Punjab, and is associated with homely unpretentious cooking of the finest sort. It tends to be taken a little for granted, yet I know how after a period of eating more adventurously a craving sets in that will be satisfied by nothing else.

2 lb/900 g lamb rib chops with all fat removed, or leg of lamb cut into medium sized pieces, on or off the bone (*gosht*)

1½ lb/700 g medium potatoes, peeled and quartered (*aloo*)

12 oz/350 g onions, peeled (*pyaz*)

4 fl. oz/120 ml cooking oil or clarified butter (*tail/asli ghee*)

1 dsp crushed garlic (*lehsun*)

1 dsp finely grated fresh ginger (*adrak*)

½ tsp turmeric (*haldi*)

1 tsp red chilli powder (*lal mirch*)

2 tsp ground coriander (*dhania*)

½ tsp ground white cumin (*safeid zeera*)

8 oz/225 g tomatoes, chopped (*timatar*)

salt to taste (*namak*)

3 tbsp coriander leaves, finely chopped (*hara dhania*)

Chop half the onions and grind the remainder to a smooth paste. Fry the chopped onions a golden brown in the oil or *asli ghee*. Add the garlic, ginger and other ground spices and fry for a few moments before putting in the onion paste. Continue stir-frying over low heat for another minute or two, taking care not to let the mixture stick to the bottom of the pan.

Add the meat and mix it well with the spices. When the meat has browned mix in the chopped tomatoes, 16 fl. oz/475 ml water and some salt. Cover the pan and simmer over low heat until the meat is almost tender (about 40 minutes). Add the potatoes, 2 tablespoons of the chopped coriander leaves and some more water if necessary. (This dish should have a fairly generous gravy.) When both the meat and potatoes are cooked your dish is ready. If you add the potatoes too soon and they cook first, take them out of the pan and keep them to one side until the meat is ready. Garnish with the remaining fresh coriander and serve with a dish of rice.

Timatar Gosht
(Lamb in a Rich Tomato Gravy)

A few tomatoes are often used to add flavour or colour to the gravy in any number of dishes. Here more than double that usual quantity is used to produce a distinctively rich, sweet and sour flavour.

2 lb/900 g lean lamb, cubed, on or off the bone (*gosht*)

2 lb/900 g tomatoes (*timatar*)

8–10 oz/225–275 g onions, peeled and finely chopped (*pyaz*)

cooking oil or clarified butter (*tail/asli ghee*)

8 garlic cloves, crushed (*lehsun*)

2 in./5 cm piece fresh ginger, peeled and finely grated (*adrak*)

1 tsp turmeric (*haldi*)

3 tsp ground coriander (*dhania*)

1 tsp ground white cumin (*safeid zeera*)

1½ tsp red chilli powder, or to taste (*lal mirch*)

salt to taste (*namak*)

3–4 tsp fresh green chillies (*hari mirch*)

For the garnish

3 tbsp fresh coriander leaves, finely chopped (*hara dhania*)

Fry the onions in some oil or *ghee* until they take on the colour of almonds. Add the garlic and ginger and stir for a minute before adding the other ground spices and some salt. Stir-fry the onions and spices together for a few minutes until they darken a shade and release their aroma. Put in the meat and fry over low heat with the spices. When the meat has browned, chop and add half the tomatoes and a little water and simmer gently until it is almost cooked (about 45 minutes–1 hour).

In the meantime take the remaining tomatoes and put them whole either in the oven or cook them on the stove over a very low flame adding only a few drops of water to prevent the saucepan from burning. When the tomatoes soften, peel and then chop them. Once the meat is nearly done add these tomatoes with a few whole green chillies and continue to cook slowly until the lamb is perfectly tender. Garnish with fresh coriander.

Loki Gosht
(Lamb with Marrow)

This dish has a light, generous gravy which needs to be served with rice to be fully appreciated and enjoyed. Those of us who are wheat eaters and insist on having some kind of *roti* with our meals, relish eating a dish of this kind in a small bowl so we can dunk our bread in its delicious gravy.

2 lb/900 g lamb, cut into lean medium pieces, on or off the bone (*gosht*)

1½ lb/700 g marrow, peeled and cut into largish pieces (*loki*)

8 oz/225 g onions, peeled and finely chopped (*pyaz*)

4 fl. oz/120 ml cooking oil, or clarified butter (*tail/asli ghee*)

1 in./2·5 cm cinnamon stick (*dalchini*)

3 large cardamoms (*bari elaichee*)

4 cloves (*laung*)

1 bay leaf (*tejpatta*)

10 black peppercorns (*sabut kali mirch*)

8 garlic cloves (*lehsun*)

2 in./5 cm cube fresh ginger, peeled and grated (*adrak*)

1 tsp turmeric (*haldi*)

3 tsp ground coriander (*dhania*)

1 tsp ground white cumin (*safeid zeera*)

1½ tsp red chilli powder (*lal mirch*)

salt to taste (*namak*)

12 oz/350 g tomatoes, chopped (*timatar*)

5 tbsp fresh coriander leaves, finely chopped (*hara dhania*)

Fry the onions a pale golden brown in the oil or *asli ghee*. Add the cinnamon, cardamoms, cloves, bay leaf and peppercorns and fry these with the onions over low heat for just a minute. Then put in the pieces of marrow and fry them together, still over low heat, for 15–20 minutes so they are lightly browned. The onions will turn a darker brown during this time, but take care that they do not burn. Lift the marrow pieces out of the pan using a fork so you leave behind most of the onions. Add some more oil if you need to and add the garlic, ginger, ground spices and some salt.

Keeping the heat low, almost immediately add the meat and stir well to mix with the spices. When the meat has browned put in the tomatoes, 16 fl. oz/475 ml water and bring to a boil. Then cover the pan, turn the heat right down and simmer. When the lamb is almost tender (about 45 minutes–1 hour), put back the fried marrow pieces, stir in 3 tablespoons of the chopped fresh coriander, add some more water if you need to for the gravy and simmer slowly until the meat and vegetables are cooked. Garnish with the remaining fresh coriander.

Karela Gosht
(Lamb with Bitter Gourds)

If you are looking for something unusual with a completely new taste to cook for friends or family this is an excellent choice. Refer to the recipe for Bitter Gourds with Onions, in the section on vegetable dishes, for information on where to buy *karelay* and tips on what to look out for when selecting them (page 128).

2 lb/900 g lean lamb, cubed, on or off the bone (*gosht*)

2 lb/900 g young bitter gourds (*karelay*)

salt to taste (*namak*)

clarified butter or cooking oil (*asli ghee/tail*)

½ lb/225 g onions, peeled and cut into rings or half rings (*pyaz*)

1½ in./3·8 cm cube fresh ginger, peeled and finely grated (*adrak*)

6–8 garlic cloves, crushed (*lehsun*)

½ tsp turmeric (*haldi*)

2 tsp ground coriander (*dhania*)

1 tsp red chilli powder (*lal mirch*)

½ lb/225 g ripe tomatoes, chopped (*timatar*)

½ unripe green mango, peeled and grated (*katcha aam*), or

4 fl. oz/120 ml lemon juice (*neeboo ka ras*)

Scrape the *karelay* well and slit them open lengthwise to scoop out the seeds. (If you are a connoisseur of their bitter flavour, you may want to keep the very young seeds, which are still soft and marrow like, to use a little later in the cooking.) Cut the gourds across into fine rings and rub them with salt. After half an hour wash them thoroughly in cold water and squeeze gently to remove the excess moisture. Heat some oil and fry these rings until they are a pale golden colour and lift them out with a slotted spoon. In this same oil, now fry the onions until golden brown. Lift these out as well, and set them aside with the *karelay* for later use.

Still using the same oil, fry the ginger, garlic, turmeric, coriander and red chilli powder for a few minutes before adding the meat. Brown the meat for a further few minutes then add the chopped tomatoes with a little water. Cover and simmer over low heat until the meat is just about done (about 45 minutes–1 hour). At that stage, put back the fried bitter gourds and onions and continue to simmer over low heat with a tightly filling lid. After 5 minutes add the grated raw mango or lemon juice and cook gently for a few more minutes until the meat is completely tender.

Mary Manezes' Lamb in Coconut Milk

This recipe was given to me as a present by a woman who is without doubt the finest cook in Mangalore. It is my pleasure to share with you her gift which carries the rich coconut flavour that is the hallmark of so many South Indian dishes. It is deliciously uncomplicated and proves my point that many of our finest creations can be painless.

2 lb/900 g lamb, cut into lean medium pieces, on or off the bone (*gosht*)

16 fl. oz/475 ml coconut milk (*naryal*) (see below)

1 large and 1 small onion, peeled (*pyaz*)

1 in./2·5 cm cube fresh ginger, peeled and finely grated (*adrak*)

2 tomatoes, chopped (*timatar*)

3 green chillies, or to taste (*hari mirch*)

salt to taste (*namak*)

5 whole dried red chillies, or to taste (*sabut lal mirch*)

6 cloves (*laung*)

2½ in./6·3 cm cinnamon stick (*dalchini*)

1 tsp ground white cumin (*safeid zeera*)

3–4 medium garlic cloves (*lehsun*)

2–3 tbsp tamarind juice (*imli*), or few drops lemon juice (*neeboo ka ras*)

1 tsp white poppy seeds (*khas khas*)

1 tsp turmeric (*haldi*)

a few mint leaves (*pudeena*)

a few coriander leaves (*hara dhania*)

4 fl. oz/120 ml cooking oil (*tail*)

1 lb/450 g potatoes, peeled (*aloo*)

Cook the lamb in half the coconut milk. (This is available canned or may be prepared by watering down canned cream of coconut. Alternatively, slab creamed coconut may be used. Dilute 2½ oz/65 g with 16 fl. oz/475 ml warm water.) When the meat is simmering add to it the small onion, coarsely chopped, the grated ginger, chopped tomatoes and green chillies. Allow the meat to continue simmering gently, covered, until it is three-quarters cooked (about 45 minutes).

Meanwhile, put the large onion, some salt, and all the remaining ingredients, except the oil, potatoes and remaining coconut milk, in a blender and reduce them to a paste. Then heat the oil and fry this paste, stirring continuously for about 5–6 minutes. Cut the potatoes into large cubes. Add the blended spice and onion paste and the potatoes to the meat, pour in the remaining coconut milk, and simmer until the meat is completely tender and the potatoes are cooked. If you prefer to have a milder coconut flavour, then omit the final addition of coconut milk.

Lamb/Beef DoPyaza
(Lamb/Beef with Onions)

In this dish onions are used, as in so many other dishes, with the spices as a base for the gravy, but they also feature more prominently as vegetables in their own right. Consequently they are used not only in double the normal quantity but at two separate stages of the cooking process. Whole *garam masala* spices are used in this recipe which counteract the sweetness of the onions and are, in turn, made more mellow by their flavour. It really is a superb dish and an old North Indian classic. Remember not to eat the whole spices that find their way on to your plate but to put them to one side.

2 lb/900 g lean lamb or beef, cubed, on or off the bone (*gosht*)
1½ lb/700 g onions, peeled (*pyaz*)
cooking oil or clarified butter (*tail/asli ghee*)
8 medium garlic cloves, crushed (*lehsun*)
1½ in./3·8 cm cube fresh ginger, peeled and finely grated (*adrak*)
6 whole red chillies (*sabut lal mirch*)
salt to taste (*namak*)
½ lb/225 g tomatoes, chopped (*timatar*)

6 green chillies, or to taste, chopped (*hari mirch*)
fresh coriander leaves finely chopped (*hara dhania*)

whole garam masala spices
3 small cardamoms (*choti elaichee*)
1 large cardamom (*bari elaichee*)
4 cloves (*loung*)
½ tsp black cumin seeds, (*sabut kala zeera*)
8 black peppercorns (*sabu kali mirch*)
1 in./2·5 cm cinnamon stick (*dalchini*)

Coarsely chop half the onions. Heat some oil or *ghee* and fry the meat until it changes colour. Add half the quantity of garlic and half the ginger and fry for another minute. Then put in the chopped onions, the whole *garam masala* spices, red chillies and salt with 8 fl. oz/250 ml water and, after bringing to a quick boil, simmer gently.

When the meat is half cooked, add the tomatoes, and the remaining garlic and ginger. Cut the rest of the onions into rings or half rings. Add these onions to the meat when it is approximately three-quarters cooked, so that when the dish is ready these onions will still be visible. When the meat is quite tender stir in the chopped green chillies and fresh coriander and serve.

KOFTAY
(Meatballs)

It is entirely in keeping with the spirit of this book to declare openly, right at the beginning, that even the simplest *kofta* dishes require a fair amount of preparatory work. You would be perfectly justified in wondering why a cook as self-confessedly lazy as me ever seriously contemplates cooking *koftay*! If you cannot take it on trust that it is a superior, distinctive and wonderfully delicious invention, then I hope this glowing testimonial encourages you to give the *koftay* a chance to win you over themselves.

Here you have a recipe as close to being infallible as is possible – a godsend for those times when we want to minimize all risks and feel confident that the meal we are planning is certain to succeed. A sense of achievement is particularly gratifying with this dish because *koftay* are renowned for being difficult to make well, and quality *koftay* are taken to be the mark of a truly gifted cook. There are two basic secrets behind the success of this recipe. The first is in the use of *khas khas* or white poppy seeds which contain the magic that keeps your meatballs soft; the other is *gram* flour, used to bind the meat so that the meatballs hold together. Dry-roasting the *gram* flour is a real inspiration, as otherwise its uncooked taste and smell would remain distinctly identifiable and permeate the meat, detracting from the delicate flavour of the cardamoms and other spices.

A final word about the practical advantages of *koftay* which, I find, frequently tip the scales in favour of this dish: they freeze extremely well and because they are cooked in plenty of gravy it is possible, even for those of us who do not own a microwave, to thaw them out quickly by placing the whole frozen block with some added water in a covered saucepan on a conventional stove. *Koftay* are also a dinner-party favourite with us because they can be cooked completely ahead of time and require no last-minute attention. It is not an insignificant bonus for me that they offer an economical way of serving a large number of people with a special meal.

Koftay

(Meatballs in Gravy)

For the gravy
8 oz/225 g onions, peeled and
  chopped (*pyaz*)
5 tbsp cooking oil (*tail*)
1 tbsp grated fresh ginger (*adrak*)
1 tbsp crushed garlic (*lehsun*)
2 tsp ground coriander (*dhania*)
1 tsp red chilli powder, or to taste
  (*lal mirch*)
½ tsp turmeric (*haldi*)
4 oz/100 g natural yoghurt, lightly
  whisked (*dahi*)
2 medium ripe tomatoes, or tinned
  plum tomatoes, chopped (*timatar*)
salt to taste (*namak*)

For the koftay
1 lb/450 g lean beef, finely minced
  (*qeema*)
4 oz/100 g onion, peeled and ground
  into a smooth paste (*pyaz*)
1 tbsp grated fresh ginger (*adrak*)

½ tbsp crushed garlic (*lehsun*)
1 dsp ground white cumin (*safeid
  zeera*)
½ tsp red chilli powder (*lal mirch*),
  or to taste
1 tbsp *gram* flour (*besan ka ata*),
  dry-roasted in a non-stick frying
  pan, *tava* or cast-iron pan until it
  turns a shade darker and releases
  its aroma
a pinch of ground nutmeg (*jaiphal*)
a pinch of ground mace (*jaivitri*)

freshly ground in coffee grinder
12 black peppercorns (*kali mirch*)
3 large cardamoms (*bari elaichee*)
6 small cardamoms (*choti elaichee*)
1½ tsp white poppy seeds (*khas khas*)

For the garnish:
2–3 tbsp fresh coriander leaves,
  finely chopped (*hara dhania*)

First prepare the gravy. Fry the onions in the oil until they turn a rich shade of honey. Lift them out with a perforated spoon and blend to a smooth paste. Return this paste to the same oil and, working over medium heat, add the grated ginger and crushed garlic. Stir for about a minute or two. Turn down the heat and put in the other spices and stir for a few more moments until the spices lose their raw smell. Slowly pour in the yoghurt and blend it in. Next add the tomatoes and stir them into the mixture, squashing them with the back of a cooking spoon. Once this mixture has been gently simmering for 5 minutes, add 16 fl. oz/475 ml water to make the gravy. After bringing it rapidly to a boil, let it cook slowly for about half an hour while you prepare the meat.

Measure out all the *kofta* ingredients and mix them all together. Knead well to ensure that the spices are spread evenly, and that the mince becomes smooth in texture. Once this is done pull off a sufficient quantity at a time to roll into the size and shape of a golf ball. I find it easiest to get a nice round shape by rolling the meat between the palms of my hands.

When all your meatballs are ready, turn the heat up under the saucepan in which the gravy has been cooking and bring it once again to the boil. Immediately turn down the heat to the lowest point on your cooker and carefully put the meatballs in one at a time.

Leave to cook for 40–50 minutes. After every 15 minutes, stir gently so the meatballs roll over and shift their positions. If you find it easier, just rock the saucepan slightly so the meatballs cook evenly all round. If you are serving the *koftay* with rice, you will probably want a little more gravy than if you were planning to eat them with *chapattis*. The gravy should be fairly generous and neither too thick nor too watery. Add some water if you think it is needed. Garnish with fresh coriander.

Nargissi Kofta

In the kingdom of meatballs these have always reigned supreme. The name, which is perhaps more of a title, is derived from *nargis*, the Urdu word for the narcissus flower, and was probably chosen as a way of paying tribute to the beauty of a dish in which the yellow and white centres are reminiscent of narcissi in a field. To the cook, a *nargissi kofta* is an oval shaped meatball with a hard-boiled egg in the centre, with a wrapping of finely ground, highly seasoned, minced lamb or beef.

The main difference between this and the previous recipe for plain *koftay* is that here the mince is first cooked with spices, then ground like a fine pâté, before being firmly folded around the eggs. After this these meatballs are lightly fried before being deftly cut open into two. They may now be served, face up, just as they are, as *nargissi kababs* or else accompanied by a rich gravy which could be on the side or poured over the *kofta* halves, decoratively arranged in a shallow dish.

For the meatballs
1 lb/450 g extra lean lamb or beef,
  minced (*qeema*)
2 small to medium onions, peeled
  (*pyaz*)
5 medium garlic cloves (*lehsun*)
1 in./2·5 cm cube fresh ginger,
  peeled and cut in half (*adrak*)
4–5 whole dried red chillies, or to
  taste (*sabut lal mirch*)
1½ tsp white cumin seeds (*sabut
  safeid zeera*)
1 dsp yellow split chickpeas (*channa
  daal*)
1 tsp salt (*namak*), or to taste
cooking oil (*tail*)
1 tsp freshly ground *garam masala*
  (see page 17)
1 tbsp dry roasted *gram* flour (*besan*)
3–4 tbsp fresh mint leaves finely
  chopped (*pudeena*), *or* fresh
  coriander leaves (*hara dhania*)

3 fresh green chillies (to taste, or
  remove seeds to reduce heat),
  chopped (*hari mirch*)
6 eggs (*unday*)

For the gravy
8 oz/225 g onions, peeled and
  chopped (*pyaz*)
5 tbsp cooking oil (*tail*)
1 tbsp grated fresh ginger (*adrak*)
1 tbsp crushed garlic (*lehsun*)
2 tsp ground coriander (*dhania*)
1 tsp red chilli powder (*lal mirch*)
½ tsp turmeric (*haldi*)
2 oz/50 g yoghurt (*dahi*)
2 medium, ripe tomatoes or tinned
  plum tomatoes, chopped (*timatar*)
3–4 tbsp fresh coriander leaves,
  finely chopped (*hara dhania*)

Place the minced meat in a heavy-bottomed saucepan and pour in enough water to just cover it. Add one of the onions, coarsely chopped, the peeled whole garlic cloves, the peeled halved ginger, whole red chillies, cumin seeds, yellow split chickpeas and salt. Bring rapidly to a boil and then turn the heat down to just below medium and allow to simmer briskly until almost all the moisture has evaporated. Then turn the heat down very low and, stirring constantly, continue to cook the meat until the last traces of moisture evaporate. Remove from the heat.

Finely chop the remaining onion and fry it in some oil until it is a golden brown colour. Lift out of the oil with a perforated spoon and add to the cooked minced meat, along with the ground *garam masala*, dry-roasted *gram* flour, mint and chopped green chillies. Put this whole mixture into a food processor and reduce to a smooth paste.

Hard-boil five of the eggs and let them cool. Divide the mince into five equal parts and firmly wrap round the hard-boiled eggs. When they are all prepared, beat the remaining egg and dip each meatball in it. Shallow-fry them carefully, one at a time, so that they are evenly brown on all sides. Put them to one side to cool while you make the gravy.

Cook the gravy in exactly the same way as described in the recipe for plain *koftas* (page 80).

Present the *koftas* cut open into halves and garnished with a few leaves of fresh coriander. Heat the gravy and serve it either separately or poured over the *koftas* in a shallow dish. Remember to pour the gravy over the meatballs only moments before they are eaten as they might fall apart if left soggy for too long.

QEEMA
(Minced Meat)

We spend so much time and effort learning how to cook new things and experimenting with unusual ingredients and recipes that we can easily ignore the simplest, most obvious possibilities that are right under our noses. I also believe that in the case of minced meat a kind of gastronomic snobbery has led us to think of it as an unimaginative way of eating meat. It is impossible to believe this once you have experienced even a few of the many delicious *qeema* recipes in Indian cookery. Indian minced meat dishes rise effortlessly above this mundane image and can hold their own at any table. There are numerous recipes you can create by making tiny variations to the basic ingredients. *Qeema* could only be called boring in that it is simple and quick to make, with very little room for error.

It is probably true that it is cheaper to cook with minced meat than some other joints or cuts of meat. But surely that is no bad thing? It is probably one of the reasons why so many different ways of eating it exist. However, in Britain, ready-minced meat is usually of an inferior quality, made from meat scraps, and is often fatty. Buy lean minced meat from a butcher you can trust, or mince it at home if you have a mincer or food processor.

The selection of vegetables cooked with minced beef in the recipes that follow are those which traditionally go together. Although I'm not a strict traditionalist cook, I have found that it does not pay to innovate too liberally, disregarding the traditional roots of a cuisine. If, for example, you cooked *qeema* with Brussels sprouts, I'm sure it would be awful.

Bhunna hua Qeema Masalaydar
(Spicy Minced Beef Braised with Tomatoes)

1 lb/450 g lean beef, minced (*qeema*)

8 oz/225 g onions, peeled and coarsely chopped (*pyaz*)

4 fl. oz/120 ml vegetable cooking oil (*tail*), or clarified butter (*asli ghee*)

4 large garlic cloves, crushed (*lehsun*)

1 in./2·5 cm cube fresh ginger, peeled and finely grated (*adrak*)

1 tsp red chilli powder (*lal mirch*)

½ tsp turmeric (*haldi*)

2 tsp ground coriander (*dhania*)

1 tsp ground white cumin (*safeid zeera*)

1 × 14 oz/400 g can peeled plum tomatoes in juice (*timatar*)

1 tsp salt, or to taste (*namak*)

For the garnish

1 small onion, peeled (*pyaz*)

2–3 tbsp fresh coriander leaves, finely chopped (*hara dhania*)

finely sliced green chillies to taste (*hari mirch*)

or

sliced hard-boiled eggs (*unday*)

fresh coriander as above (*hara dhania*) and/or mint (*pudeena*)

Using a heavy-bottomed cooking utensil, fry the coarsely chopped onions in oil until they are deep golden brown. Turn down the heat as low as possible and put in the crushed garlic and grated ginger. Stir for about a minute then add the remaining spices while continuing to stir for approximately another minute until the mixture darkens a little and the spices release their aroma. Take care not to let the spices burn. If you find them sticking to the bottom of the pan, remove it at once from the heat and add a few drops of water.

Now add the minced beef and turn the heat up. Mix the meat and spices well together, stirring vigorously to break up any lumps that may form in the meat. When the meat is well fried, stir in the tomatoes, squashing them up with your spoon, add the salt and cover the saucepan, leaving it to simmer briskly over medium heat. Cook for about 30 minutes, stirring occasionally. At the end of this time take the lid off the pan and allow any liquid that may be left to evaporate. When the oil separates and is visible on the surface your dish is almost ready. As a final touch fry the *qeema* over high heat, stirring constantly so it is well browned or *bhunnoed*.

Garnish the dish either with finely chopped raw onion, fresh coriander and green chillies (optional) or with hard-boiled eggs cut lengthwise in half, which look decorative sprinkled with fresh coriander and/or mint.

Aloo Qeema
(Minced Beef with Diced Potatoes)

1 × *qeema* recipe (see page 84)
1 lb/450 g potatoes, peeled (*aloo*)

Prepare the *qeema* as above.

Dice the potatoes into equal sized cubes and add them to the minced meat about 15 minutes before it is ready. Precisely when you add the potatoes will depend on how large or small you prefer to keep them.

If you are serving the dish as soon as it is ready, then the potatoes should be almost completely cooked by the time you fry the minced meat over high heat at the end. Stir gently and only occasionally to prevent the meat from sticking to the bottom of the pan, taking care not to break up the potatoes. If you are cooking ahead of time and will not be serving the food until some later time, then turn off the heat before the potatoes are fully cooked. Perhaps you should also take the lid off the pan to allow it to cool as the potatoes will continue to soften while the meat retains its heat. Finish cooking just prior to serving. It is important to ensure that the potatoes do not *over*cook as they will disintegrate.

Palak ka Saag Qeema
(Spinach and Minced Beef)

1 × *qeema* recipe (see page 84)
1½ lb/700 g fresh spinach, weighed
   with stalks *or* frozen spinach
   (*palak ka saag*)

Wash and chop up the spinach discarding the thick stalks. Add to the minced beef about 15 minutes after it has been left on a brisk simmer. If you are using frozen spinach then you can add it, still frozen, to the meat. The frozen block of spinach will release some additional moisture as it dissolves which should be evaporated over high heat at the same time as any excess liquid in the pot is dried off during the final stir-frying over high heat.

Methi ka Saag aur Qeema
(Fenugreek Leaves with Minced Beef)

1 × *qeema* recipe (see page 84)
1 bunch fresh fenugreek leaves, *or*
  2–3 tbsp dried fenugreek leaves
  (*methi ka saag*)

chopped green chillies to taste (*hari mirch*)

Prepare the *qeema* as above.

If you find fresh fenugreek leaves then add them to the mince about 20 minutes after it has been left to simmer. Break the leaves, do not cut them with a knife, and throw them in. You must not add any water at this stage.

If using dried leaves, place them in a fine sieve and soak them in cold water for about 15 minutes. You need a smaller quantity of the dehydrated leaves as their flavour and aroma is much stronger. Tastes vary about how strong the flavour should be and you must feel free to alter the quantity of fresh or dried fenugreek to suit your own preference.

When the dish is ready you can add some chopped green chillies and let it cook for another 2–3 minutes. If you want the flavour of the chilli without its heat, remove all the seeds and wash well before use.

Gobi Qeema
(Cauliflower in Minced Beef)

1 × *qeema* recipe (see page 84)
1 small cauliflower (*phool gobi*)
fresh peeled ginger cut into 12 fine
  2 in. strips (*adrak*)
green chillies to taste, finely sliced
  (*hari mirch*)

For the garnish
fresh coriander leaves, finely
chopped (*hara dhania*)

Wash and cut the cauliflower into small florets. Fry these florets separately and add them to the *qeema* about 10–15 minutes after it has been left to simmer. When the dish is almost ready and just before you finally stir-fry over high heat, add the fine strips of fresh ginger and green chillies. Garnish with lots of finely chopped fresh coriander.

Baingan Qeema
(Aubergines and Minced Beef)

1 × *qeema* recipe (see page 84)
1 medium aubergine (*baingan*)
4 oz/100 g onions, peeled and finely
   chopped (*pyaz*)
cooking oil (*tail*)
2 garlic cloves, crushed (*lehsun*)
1 tsp freshly ground *garam masala*
   (see page 17)

4 oz/100 g natural yoghurt (*dahi*)
salt to taste

For the garnish
2 tbsp fresh coriander leaves, finely
   chopped (*hara dhania*) and/or
   mint (*pudeena*)

Cook the aubergine whole in its skin until it is soft all the way through. It is best to do this in the oven, wrapped in foil, at 400°/200°/Gas 6 for 30–40 minutes. If this is not possible then cook it in a little water in a pan on top of the stove. Once the aubergine is cooked, peel and mash it with a fork.

Fry the onions in oil until deep brown and then lift them out with a slotted spoon. Mix the browned onions with the mashed aubergine, crushed garlic, *garam masala*, yoghurt and a little salt. Fry over medium heat for 5 minutes, stirring all the time. Add the aubergine to the *qeema* some 10 minutes before it is fully cooked. Garnish with finely chopped fresh coriander and/or mint.

Matar Qeema
(Green Peas in Minced Beef)

1 × *qeema* recipe (see page 84)
8 oz/225 g shelled peas (fresh or
   frozen) (*matar*)

For the garnish
spring onions, finely chopped (*hari
   pyaz*)
fresh coriander or mint leaves, finely
   chopped (*hara dhania/pudeena*)

Add the peas to the mince about 10 minutes before it is fully cooked. Carry on with the recipe as usual. Garnish with finely chopped spring onions and fresh coriander or mint leaves.

Hari Mirchon ka Qeema
(Minced Beef with Green Chillies)

As in the recipe for *Achar Gosht* (see page 53) this dish works best if you cook it with the large 'Spanish' green chilli after removing its seeds. The minced beef is first cooked with onions, ground spices and yoghurt, after which these mild chillies, carefully filled with fennel, nigella, fenugreek and cumin seeds, are gently placed in the meat and cooked by the steam trapped in the saucepan with a tightly fitting lid. This variety of chilli is much milder than the smaller slim green chilli usually used in Indian food, and since they are seeded as well, you will enjoy their flavour which fills the dish, without being troubled by their heat.

1 lb/450 g lean beef, minced (*qeema*)

8 oz/225 g onions, peeled and finely chopped (*pyaz*)

cooking oil (*tail*)

1 tbsp crushed garlic (*lehsun*)

1 tbsp finely grated fresh ginger (*adrak*)

1 tsp turmeric (*haldi*)

2 tsp ground coriander (*dhania*)

$\frac{1}{4}$ tsp red chilli powder (*lal mirch*) (optional)

8 oz/225 g natural yoghurt (*dahi*)

salt to taste (*namak*)

8 large Spanish green chillies (*bari hari mirch*)

$\frac{1}{2}$ tsp each of fennel, nigella, fenugreek and white cumin seeds (*sonf, kalonji, methi dana, safeid zeera*)

Fry the onions to a golden brown colour in some oil. Turn the heat low and add the garlic and ginger, followed a minute or so later by the ground spices. Stir-fry the spices and onions for a few more minutes then add the minced meat. Continue stirring fairly vigorously so that the meat is well mixed with the spices. Cook over a medium flame for about 5 minutes until the meat is well browned, then add the yoghurt and some salt, and leave it to simmer gently, covered, for approximately 20 minutes.

Wash and slit open the chillies, removing any seeds. Mix together the spice seeds and divide these between the chillies. When the *qeema* has simmered for about 20 minutes, place the stuffed green chillies into the saucepan and fold the minced meat over them. Cover the pan with a tightly fitting lid and leave the chillies to cook in the trapped steam over very low heat. When the chillies change colour and soften, and the oil separates, the dish is ready. It is inevitable that some of the whole spices will fall out of the chillies and be mixed in with the *qeema* as you stir and as the dish cooks, so do not worry.

Karelay Qeema
(Minced Beef with Bitter Gourds)

1 × *qeema* recipe as above
1 lb/450 g bitter gourds (*karelay*)
salt (*namak*)
cooking oil (*tail*)
8 oz/225 g onions, peeled and sliced
  into rings or half rings (*pyaz*)

1 raw green mango, grated (*katcha
  aam*) or other souring agent:
  tamarind water (*imli*) (see page
  29) or lemon juice (*neeboo ka ras*)

Scrape the gourds well. Slit them open lengthwise to remove the seeds. Rub with salt and leave aside for up to an hour. Wash thoroughly in several changes of cold water and squeeze dry. (This process lessens the bitter taste of the vegetable.) Cut the gourds across into fine rings. Shallow-fry in oil over medium heat, stirring all the time until they are an even medium brown. Remove with a slotted spoon.

In this same oil now fry the onion and add both the gourds and fried onions to the mince some 15 minutes before it is fully cooked. Also add the souring agent. Carry on with the recipe as before.

Galavat ka Qeema
(Minced Beef Tenderized with Green Papaya)

This is an extremely delicious and highly unusual *qeema* preparation and is really in a class of its own, being as good as some of the best *kababs* you may serve your guests on a special occasion. The use of the unripe green papaya, a wonderful natural tenderizer, is essential for this recipe, and is the ingredient that gives the dish its special unmistakable texture. Papayas are stocked all the year round by specialist Indian grocers, and it is also becoming more common to find them at high-street supermarkets.

2 lb/900 g lean beef, minced (*qeema*)
2½ oz/65 g unripe green papaya (*katcha papita*)
1½ tsp salt, or to taste (*namak*)
1½ tbsp finely grated fresh ginger (*adrak*)
1 tbsp yellow split chickpeas (*channa*)
1½ tsp freshly ground *garam masala* (see page 17)
1 tsp red chilli powder (*lal mirch*)
1½ lb/700 g onions, peeled and finely chopped (*pyaz*)
4 fl. oz/120 ml cooking oil (*tail*)

For the garnish
finely cut strips of fresh peeled ginger (*adrak*)
½ cup fresh coriander leaves, finely chopped (*hara dhania*)
slices of lemon (*neeboo*)
or
finely sliced hard-boiled eggs (*unday*)
fresh coriander leaves, finely chopped (*hara dhania*)

Peel the papaya and finely grate its flesh. Mix the salt, ginger and papaya with the minced meat and knead it well so that it is evenly mixed. Leave to marinate for about 4 hours. Dry-roast the yellow split chickpeas in a frying pan, stirring them around continuously until they just begin to brown a little. Grind them to a fine power in an electric blender. Once the meat mixture has marinated, add to it the *garam masala*, red chilli powder and the ground dry-roasted chickpeas and mix them all together with your hands. You will notice at this stage how the texture of the meat has been broken down by the papaya and it is almost like a paste.

Brown the onions in the oil until a deep honey colour, then add the meat. At this stage you need to work very quickly and hard. Stir the mixture vigorously, breaking up any lumps that form. You will need to pound away at the mixture with a wooden spoon, breaking it up as you stir. All the while you should be working over fairly high heat so that the meat is being well fried. Suddenly the mince will appear to take on the correct texture, free of lumps. When it has been well fried, turn the heat down low and leave it to cook in a tightly covered saucepan in its own steam, stirring it only now and then. When the meat is cooked and the oil separates, your dish is ready. Stir it a few more times over high heat and serve garnished with finely cut strips of fresh ginger, lots of chopped coriander leaves and slices of lemon or, alternatively, with sliced hard-boiled eggs and fresh coriander.

GOSHT KAY MUKHTALIF KABAB
(Lamb and Beef Kababs)

There must be hundreds of different types of *kababs* that are eaten in the subcontinent. This is the case not only in each region and province, but even every small town, village or district will have its own favourites. *Kababs* are a great class equalizer, identified as much with *bazaar* and street aromas as with banquets or meals in the big houses where rich folk live. I am most familiar with those recipes which originate in the northern areas were people enjoy eating *kababs*, as a matter of course, almost every day of their lives. *Bihari kabab, seekh kabab, shami kabab, katcha kabab, passanda kabab, khatai kay kabab, tikka kabab, chapli kabab, galavat kay kabab, dum kay kabab, nargissi kabab, karhai kabab, gola kabab* and *dhangar kay kabab*, stand out in my mind as some of the more popular ones. These, of course, do not include any of those *kabab* preparations made with chicken, fish or vegetables.

Kababs may be made with ordinary minced lamb or beef; some recipes call for the meat to be so well kneaded that its texture is changed into a soft paste. With some *kababs* it is necessary first to cook the minced meat and then blend it so that it takes on the appearance of pâté. *Kababs* are also made of tender cubed meat, taken off the bone with all excess fat carefully trimmed away. The meat may be seasoned or marinated before cooking or it may first be half cooked by one process and then finished off by another. *Kababs* can be served dry or with a thick clinging sauce. Different traditional chutneys and relishes are served with different *kababs*. A *kabab* dish may be central to the meal or simply take its place beside other dishes on the table. This versatility and wide choice have probably contributed to giving *kababs* the importance they hold in Indian cuisine.

When I think of *kababs*, I am reminded of my college days in Lahore when we practically lived off *naan* and *seekh kababs* from Anarkali market because the food we were given at college was so awful. I think of drive-in *kabab* dinners on cool Karachi evenings where you can park beside an open charcoal fire and order any selection of *tikka* or *boti kababs* and *seekh kababs* that your heart desires. Seconds later they are sizzling and spitting over the coals, while the chef, sitting cross-legged, dangerously close to the fire, fans the flames until they leap up and lick the meat. I do not know which memory is more vivid – the torture of waiting with mounting greed as the smells became stronger and more delicious, or the moment of the dream come true when, as the first morsel melted in the mouth, you knew that every nerve in your nostrils and taste buds unanimously agreed that this was the embodiment of perfection. Perhaps the best after all are my mother's *shami kababs*, ideal for breakfast, lunch, teatime, cocktails, dinner, in-between meals and picnics. I could eat them every day with no trouble at all. For me at least, the others like *chapli kabab* from the North-West Frontier Province or *galavat kay kabab* and *dum kay kabab* are occasional treats. I must put in a special word here too for *katcha kababs* (which I always believed to be a family invention), a sort of Indian hamburger, and a childhood passion of mine which remains delicious to this day.

Shami Kababs

For these *kababs* the minced meat is first cooked in a little water with some *channa daal* and spices. The cooked meat is then blended to a fine pâté-like consistency, stuffed and moulded into beef patty shapes before being fried.

The art of making authentic *shami kababs* lies in being able to prepare the meat in such a way that it needs no egg to hold it in shape. The secret is very simply understood, although admittedly it requires a little practice to execute well. The trick to remember is to use very lean meat, and to cook it until it is very dry, ensuring that every possible drop of moisture has evaporated. If at first you do not succeed, dip each *kabab* into some well beaten egg before it is shallow-fried, and this will hold it safely together.

An Indian meal does not traditionally begin with any starters, but in middle-class circles it is quite common to serve some appetizers with pre-dinner drinks. *Shami kabab* snacks, approximately half the size of those served with meals, are a popular choice.

Makes 6–8 kababs

1 lb/450 g extra lean beef, minced (*qeema*)

1 tsp black peppercorns (*sabut kali mirch*)

4–5 whole dried red chillies, or to taste (*sabut lal mirch*)

1 medium onion, peeled (*pyaz*)

1 dsp split chickpeas (*channa daal*)

salt to taste (*namak*)

oil for frying (*tail*)

1 egg, beaten (optional)

For the stuffing

2–3 green chillies, extremely finely sliced (*hari mirch*)

2 tbsp peeled onions, extremely finely chopped (*pyaz*)

2–3 tbsp fresh coriander leaves, extremely finely chopped (*hara dhania*)

Put all the *kabab* ingredients except for the oil in a saucepan with just enough water to cover, and bring rapidly to a boil. Simmer until most of the moisture has evaporated. At the last stage it will be necessary to stir almost continuously as the mixture cooks, to prevent the food from burning while evaporating as much of the remaining moisture as possible.

When the meat has cooked dry, reduce it to a fine paste in a food processor. (You could, if you wanted, first pick out some or all of the whole red chillies as the meat will already have absorbed much of their flavour and the final product will then be less hot.) Set it aside to cool.

When the ground minced meat reaches room temperature, take enough mixture to roll into the size and shape of a golf ball between the palms of your hands. Make a hollow in the centre of each *kabab* and press in a tiny bit of each of the stuffing ingredients. Carefully working with the palms of your hands, reshape the ball of mince into a flattened round cutlet or patty shape approximately 2–2½ in./5–6·3 cm in diameter, taking care to keep it tightly bonded together to avoid the *kabab* opening up and falling apart.

Using just enough oil to cover the bottom of your frying pan, dipping each *kabab* in the beaten egg if you so choose, fry the *kababs* until they are a crispy brown. Turn only once to minimize the danger of them breaking up.

One great advantage of *shami kababs* is that the main cooking and preparation can be done well in advance, leaving only the quick last-minute frying. I find it useful to make a large batch and to keep them frozen, frying them as and when they are needed.

Chapli Kababs

Chapli kababs are a speciality of the North-West Frontier Province of Pakistan. More recently their popularity and reputation has extended much further afield into the other provinces. Certainly in the large towns and cities of Sindh and Baluchistan, *chapli kababs* can be bought from *Pathan* vendors – people from the Frontier Province – and are eaten in small cafés and pavement stalls, deliciously hot, straight off the stove.

These *kababs* are cooked on large, heavy, cast-iron utensils, gently sloping and concave in shape; a sort of cross between a *karhai*, an Indian wok-like utensil, and a *tava* which is a cast-iron hot-plate. A frying pan serves more than adequately as a substitute. Often, hot *rotis* or unleavened bread may be cooked side by side with these *kababs* on the same *tava*, and spicy beaten eggs are poured on to make delicious scrambled omelettes which are served at the same time and are eaten together. The ingredients which give these *kababs* their distinctive taste are the eggs, tomatoes, pomegranate seeds and cornflour. The other spices may change and are often varied to express the individual pleasure or discretion of the cook.

Makes 6–8 kababs
1 lb/450 g lean beef, minced (*gosht*)
1 tbsp pomegranate seeds (*anardana*)
1 tbsp coriander seeds (*sabut dhania*)
¼ lb/100 g onions, peeled (*pyaz*)
¼ lb/100 g tomatoes (*timatar*)
1 dsp finely grated fresh ginger (*adrak*)
½ cup fresh coriander leaves, finely chopped (*hara dhania*)
¾ tsp ground white cumin (*safeid zeera*)
¼ tsp bishop's weed (*ajwain*) (optional)
½ tsp red chilli powder (*lal mirch*)
1 tsp salt, or to taste (*namak*)
2 oz/50 g or more cornflour (*makkai ka ata*)
2 eggs, beaten (*unday*)
cooking oil (*tail*)

Grind the pomegranate and coriander seeds in a food processor or electric grinder. Finely chop and mix together the onions, tomatoes, ginger and fresh coriander. First add all the ground spices plus some salt to the minced meat, then the cornflour and beaten eggs, and lastly the tomato, onion, ginger and coriander mixture. Mix all these ingredients with the meat, squashing and kneading the mixture with your hands. Divide it into six or eight portions.

Using a frying pan, heat a small quantity of oil. Lightly grease your palms and shape each portion of mince to resemble an oval hamburger. Fry as many at a time as you can manage to fit comfortably in your pan in a single layer. Keep the heat on the medium to low side, cooking the *kababs* for about 10–15 minutes on each side, turning them over no more than once or twice. Serve hot and with the chutney below, if you like.

Chapli Kabab ki Chutney

This is a recipe for a chutney that goes particularly well with the previous *chapli kababs*. It may be served on the side as a relish but is also very effective if poured or spread as a thick sauce over the *kababs* and served hot as a complete dish.

3–4 oz/100 g onions, peeled (*pyaz*)
6 oz/175 g tomatoes (*timatar*)
1 tsp ground white cumin (*safeid zeera*)
2 dsp cooking oil (*tail*)
1 cup fresh coriander leaves (*hara dhania*)

1 cup fresh mint leaves (*pudeena*)
2–3 green chillies, seeded if desired (*hari mirch*)
1 tbsp pomegranate seeds (*anardana*)
salt to taste (*namak*)

Chop the onions and tomatoes very finely. Fry the cumin in the oil for about a minute; add the onions and tomatoes and continue to fry for another 5 minutes or so, stirring continuously. Coarsely grind the remaining ingredients and mix them all together. If using an electric blender take care not to liquidize the ingredients to too smooth a paste; they should retain some texture as they would if ground by hand.

Add some water to blend the ingredients together, perhaps using a little more if making a thick sauce to pour over the *kababs* than you would if serving the chutney as a relish, where it would be preferable to have it in a more concentrated form. Continue to cook for a few more minutes.

Spread hot over the *kababs*, if desired, shortly before serving. The *kababs* can be cooked beforehand and reheated when you need to serve them, either in the oven or under the grill.

Khatai kay kabab
(Kababs in a Sour Sauce)

As a race we seem to have an insatiable appetite for sour tastes. Schoolchildren prefer to suck tamarind or eat unripe green mangoes rather than sweets. One of the most welcome sights at the end of the school day is the man at the gate roasting fresh juicy corn on the cob, liberally doused with the juice of sour limes and sprinkled with salt and chilli powder. Many tea-time snacks have a sour chutney or dip served with them. Here the sauce, not the kabab, is where the hot and sour tastes are concentrated. Serve it on the side as a dip.

For the kababs, makes 12

2 lb/900 g lean beef, finely ground (*qeema*)

1½ tsp freshly ground *garam masala* (see page 17)

8 small green cardamoms, freshly ground (*choti elaichee*)

a pinch of grated nutmeg (*jaiphal*)

a pinch of ground mace (*javitri*)

1 tsp ground white cumin (*safeid zeera*)

1½ tbsp poppy seeds, freshly ground (*khas khas*)

1 tsp red chilli powder (*lal mirch*)

½ small unripe green mango, peeled and finely grated (*katcha aam*)

1½ in./3·8 cm cube fresh ginger, peeled and finely grated (*adrak*)

½ cup fresh coriander leaves, finely chopped (*hara dhania*)

½ cup fresh mint leaves, finely chopped (*pudeena*)

8 oz/225 g onions, peeled (*pyaz*)

2 fresh green chillies, seeded if desired (*hari mirch*)

cooking oil (*tail*)

salt to taste (*namak*)

beaten egg for frying

For the stuffing (optional)

1 egg (*unda*)

1 small onion, peeled (*pyaz*)

1–2 green chillies, or to taste (*hari mirch*)

2 tbsp fresh coriander leaves, finely chopped (*hara dhania*)

1 tbsp lemon juice (*neeboo ka ras*)

salt to taste (*namak*)

For the sauce

2–3 tbsp cooking oil (*tail*)

½ tsp red chilli powder (*lal mirch*)

2 tsp ground white cumin (*safeid zeera*)

1 dsp ground coriander (*dhania*)

½ green mango, peeled and finely grated (*katcha aam*)

6 oz/175 g natural yoghurt (*dahi*)

salt to taste (*namak*)

For the garnish

lemon wedges (*neeboo*)

onion rings (*pyaz*)

sliced tomato (*timatar*)

For the *kababs*, mix together all the ground spices, and add the grated mango and ginger and chopped herbs. Finely chop half the onions and the green chillies, and mix everything with the minced meat. Chop and fry the remaining onions in hot oil, lifting them out once they are golden brown and also add them, still a little oily, to the meat and spices, with a little salt. Knead thoroughly so that the meat acquires a smoother texture and the spices are well distributed and absorbed.

Next prepare the stuffing. Hard-boil the egg and then mash it up well with a fork. Finely chop the onion, green chillies and fresh coriander. Mix all these ingredients together with the lemon juice and some salt to taste.

Divide the meat mixture into twelve equal parts and shape each part to resemble a fat 2½–3 in./6·3–7·5 cm sausage. Indent a narrow trough down the length of the *kababs*, tuck in a little stuffing and re-seal firmly so there are no cracks. Dip each *kabab* into some beaten egg and shallow-fry them over low heat to allow them to cook through. Turn them over during this period so they are evenly browned on all sides.

To make the sauce, first heat some oil in a frying pan, and fry all the spices for a minute or two. Add the finely grated flesh of the green mango and pour in the yoghurt a little at a time, stirring continuously. Add a little water to blend the ingredients and then continue to cook over high heat for a few more minutes. Serve the sauce hot, on the side, in a separate bowl or jug, so that people can serve themselves. Garnish with lemon wedges, onion rings and thin slices of tomato.

Bihari Kabab

These *kababs* are made of lean, cubed lamb cut off the bone, tenderized with green papaya, and well marinated in yoghurt and spices so that the meat acquires the delicious melting quality that is the mark of this recipe.

3 lb/1·4 kg lean lamb, cut into 1½ in./3·8 cm cubes (*gosht*)

1 lb/450 g onions, peeled and chopped (*pyaz*)

mustard oil, preferably (*sarson ka tail*), or other vegetable oil (*tail*)

2 tbsp poppy seeds (*khas khas*)

1 tsp black peppercorns (*sabut kali mirch*)

2 tsp salt, or to taste (*namak*)

1 tbsp crushed garlic (*lehsun*)

2 tbsp finely grated fresh ginger (*adrak*)

1 tsp red chilli powder (*lal mirch*)

1–2 tbsp grated unripe green papaya (*papita*)

2 tbsp natural yoghurt (*dahi*)

Fry the onions in hot oil until they change colour, then lift them out with a slotted spoon and blend to a smooth paste. Grind the poppy seeds and peppercorns to a fine powder, mix with the onions and reserve. Rub the pieces of meat with the salt, garlic and ginger and leave them to marinate for at least 2 hours.

Then mix the red chilli powder, onion paste mix, papaya and yoghurt together with some mustard oil and marinate the meat in this for a minimum of 1 further hour.

When it is time to cook the meat, skewer all the pieces gently through the middle and cook under a grill or in an open barbecue basting regularly, turning all the time to brown the meat evenly.

Seekh Kabab

There are not many foods around today that remain as deeply rooted in a particular community or with a religious group as much as the *seekh kabab* has remained with the Muslims of the subcontinent. In North India, *kabab* shops are a familiar sight to all Delhi-*wallas*, especially visible in areas of Muslim concentration. Although I call them shops they could simply be take-away street kitchens, impromptu cafés or even expensive restaurants. In Old Delhi every second alleyway in Chandni Chowk, behind the Jamia Masjid or the Lal Qila, has several such eating houses, serving amongst other delicacies the ever-popular *seekh kabab*.

In Pakistan *seekh kabab* shops and restaurants seem forever to be mushrooming up with plenty of business for all. In Karachi everyone has their local *kabab* shop within a few minutes' easy walk, and then there are those chefs whose *kababs* have earned them such a reputation that people will venture much further from home to eat them time and again. For some reason most of us living in Pakistan see *seekh kababs* as something you go *out* to eat. It may be, in part, because the taste of the *kababs* barbecued over live coals has the edge over those cooked on gas or electric grills, which is the best most of us can conveniently produce at home. But it has become a state of mind and is more of a tradition than anything else, an excuse for an outing in a place where there are few places to go.

My aunt serves wonderful *seekh kababs* and her guests always express such surprise that they are home-made, and compliment her for being so innovative and enterprising. In fact *seekh kababs* are simpler to make than many other dishes, even in the *kabab* family.

Seekh Kababs I

2 lb/900 g lean beef, minced (*qeema*)

8 oz/225 g onions, peeled and finely chopped (*pyaz*)

4 tbsp cooking oil (*tail*)

6–8 whole dried large red chillies (*sabut lal mirch*)

2 tbsp *gram* flour (*besan*)

1 tbsp coriander seeds (*sabut dhania*)

2 tbsp white poppy seeds (*khas khas*)

1 egg, beaten (*unda*)

2 tbsp natural yoghurt (*dahi*)

2 tbsp finely grated fresh ginger (*adrak*)

¾ cup fresh coriander leaves, finely chopped (*hari dhania*)

1 tsp freshly ground *garam masala* (see page 17)

2 tsp salt, or to taste (*namak*)

1 dsp grated unripe green papaya (optional) (*hara papita*)

For the garnish

sliced tomatoes (*timatar*)

onion rings (*pyaz*)

sliced green peppers (*simla ki mirch*)

strips of fresh ginger (*adrak*)

green chillies (*hari mirch*)

Fry the onions in the oil, together with the whole red chillies, until they turn a honey brown. Lift the onions and chillies out of the frying pan with a perforated spoon and blend them to a smooth consistency in a food processor. Dry-roast the *gram* flour in a heavy cast-iron or non-stick frying pan, moving it around all the time and scraping it off as it sticks to the bottom, so you achieve an even colour a few shades darker than when you began. Dry-roast the coriander and poppy seeds in the same way, then grind them to a fine powder.

With the exception of the cooking oil, mix together all the ingredients with the minced meat and knead thoroughly with your hands to obtain a paste-like texture. Lightly grease your hands with cooking oil to prevent the mixture from sticking to them and wrap some meat around the top end of a skewer so that it is about 3–5 in./7·5–12·5 cm long. *Seekh kababs* come in a variety of thicknesses so you can choose whether you would rather make lots of slim *kababs* or fewer plumper ones.

If you are grilling the *kababs* over live coals on a barbecue, keep turning them so they cook evenly. If the meat is very lean you might want to smear some clarified butter or cooking oil on the *kababs* as they cook to prevent them from drying out. If you are using your grill at home, then remove the wire rack and line your grill tray with foil, to catch the dripping grease. Cook the *kababs* under low heat to start with, raising the flame to brown them when they are almost done. If you cannot fit the skewers into your grill tray or do not have enough, then carefully ease off the meat wrapped around each skewer. I find it is quite simple to gently slide the *kababs* off the front of the skewer and lay them directly on the foil lining the grill tray. With this method you really only need one skewer to prepare all the *kababs*. Grill as before, turning the *kababs* over when they are done on one side so they cook all round. Serve immediately.

If you want, you can do most of the work beforehand so that your *kababs* are cooked quickly when your guests arrive. In this case, half cook the *kababs*, carefully place them in a container and keep them in the fridge until just before you need them. *Seekh kababs* freeze extremely well. It is a good idea to half-cook them first and then finish them off after defrosting, when you are ready to eat.

Garnish with finely sliced tomatoes and green peppers and onion rings. Serve with tamarind chutney, fine long strips of ginger and fresh green chillies.

Seekh Kabab II

2 lb/900 g lean beef, minced (*qeema*)

2 tbsp *gram* flour (*besan*)

1 tbsp ground coriander (*dhania*)

2 tsp ground white cumin (*safeid zeera*)

6 oz/175 g onions, peeled and finely chopped (*pyaz*)

1 tsp red chilli powder (*lal mirch*)

1 tbsp crushed garlic (*lehsun*)

1 tbsp finely grated fresh ginger (*adrak*)

1 tbsp finely grated unripe green papaya (*hara papita*) (optional)

salt to taste (*namak*)

clarified butter (*asli ghee*) (optional)

In a heavy cast-iron or non-stick frying pan dry-roast the *gram* flour, stirring it around continuously and scraping it off the bottom as it sticks, until it turns a few shades darker. Dry-roast the ground coriander and cumin in the same way, separately, one after another. Mix together all the ingredients listed, except the clarified butter, and knead thoroughly for at least 5 minutes. Although it is not essential, if you have the time, allow the meat mixture to marinate for an hour to allow the flavour of the spices to be well combined. You can make the *kababs* right away if you like, just delay the cooking.

Refer to the previous recipe for instructions on how to wrap the mince around the skewers or on how to proceed without skewers when cooking the *kababs* on a barbecue or indoors under a grill.

Dhangar kay Seekh Kabab III

It is a highly prized delicacy to capture, in certain dishes, the special smoked aroma that comes from real coal. Yet it is becoming more and more rare for people to bother with this sort of traditional detail that could make the food just that little bit more unusual. I love the smoky fragrance of these *kababs* and hope you will agree that they are well worth taking a small amount of trouble over now and again.

1 × *seekh kabab* recipe (I or II)	2 garlic cloves, crushed (*lehsun*)
a piece of onion skin (*pyaz ka chilka*)	a piece of coal (*koyla*)
	cooking oil (*tail*)

Prepare the *kabab* mixture and leave it to marinate for the prescribed length of time.

To smoke the minced meat, put the prepared mixture in a saucepan, clearing a round hole in the centre. Place a piece of onion skin in this hole and put the crushed garlic on it. Take a red-hot, live coal and, lifting it carefully with tongs, gently drop it on top of the garlic. Immediately pour a spoonful of oil directly on top of the coal and quickly cover the saucepan with a tightly fitting lid. Wait for the coal to cool and stop smoking. Discard the coal, onion skin and garlic. Wrap the mince around the skewers and proceed as previously described on page 99.

Maghaz
(Brain Masala)

Use the same recipe for both lamb's as well as calf's brains. Calf's brains have a finer flavour but, for some reason, are not as readily available as lamb's brains. While you may not easily be able to buy calf's brains over the counter, I have found most butchers will take an order and bring them in if given a few days' notice.

Brain is a popular Indian dish which has not acquired the elite status of being a rare delicacy that it seems to hold in the West. This extremely tasty dish is quite quick and simple to cook. The most difficult and time-consuming part lies in removing the fine membrane that covers the brain.

2 calf's brains (*bheja*)
salt to taste (*namak*)
4–6 fl. oz/120–175 ml cooking oil (*tail*)
4 oz/100 g onions, peeled and finely chopped (*pyaz*)
½ tsp fenugreek seeds (*methi dana*)
1 dsp crushed garlic (*lehsun*)
1 dsp finely grated fresh ginger (*adrak*)

½ tsp turmeric (*haldi*)
½ tsp red chilli powder (*lal mirch*)
¼ tsp ground coriander (*dhania*)
1 cup fresh coriander leaves, finely chopped (*hara dhania*)
2–3 green chillies, finely chopped (*hari mirch*)

Soak the brains in cold water, with 1 teaspoon salt added, for an hour. Wash well and remove the fine membrane and any bone splinters you may find. Those who feel squeamish about handling uncooked brains can, when they have been washed, put the brains in a saucepan of water and bring it to one quick boil. Throw out the water and then tackle removing the membrane. You will lose some meat if you choose to follow this second method.

Heat the oil and fry the finely chopped onions until golden brown. Turn the heat down and throw in the fenugreek seeds, closely followed by the garlic and ginger. Half a minute later add the ground spices and fry this mixture for about another minute. Add the brains and some salt and continue to fry over low heat, breaking them up, sort of like scrambled eggs. In a few minutes when the colour turns brown and you smell the aroma, add the coriander leaves and green chillies. Stir for a few more minutes and it is ready.

VEGETABLE DISHES

· Vegetable Dishes ·

These days it surprises me to recall that as a child I hated to eat any vegetable more uncommon than a potato. I have vivid and traumatic memories of the most punishing experiences of being encouraged, scolded, enticed and bullied to try the various vegetable dishes that would appear, through the efficient operation of some bad magic, on our table at each meal. I became extremely proficient at finding new ways of disposing of the vegetables I was forced to take on to my plate and would go to many lengths to escape swallowing hateful French beans or any wretched relative of those beans which were, to my young mind, parental instruments of torture. I had, in any case, a deep-seated mistrust of my parents' eating habits and was privately convinced that it was just another grown-up fetish to willingly eat and enjoy *tinda*, *loki*, *kaddu*, *bhindi* or *karelay* – names that made me wince and the very sounds of which sent distasteful shudders through the taste buds in my tongue.

I was impatient to grow up and enjoy the pleasures of freedom I believed it would bring. I can still remember dreaming about the day when I could go out without permission or decide not to go to school any more. But the best fantasy of all was the one in which I was old enough not to be forced into eating revolting foods and to finally be recognized as someone who had the capacity to choose for herself. It seems ironical, but no sooner had I entered this phase of my life when fate, or some other similar subversive force, took control and cheated me out of keeping my childhood promises to myself. Rather disloyally I denounced my earlier beliefs as youthful revolt, and shamelessly followed in the footsteps of those others before me who had similarly and happily recanted and learned to eat and enjoy all those dreaded vegetables which were the bane of their early years. Being prone to extremes I didn't just begin to eat and enjoy what to me were new tastes; I fell passionately in love with all things that grow and are edible. It has been exciting for me to discover new ways of cooking different vegetables and settling on some favourites.

Many things make me grateful for being born Indian. Food must figure high on that list. Indian cuisine emanates from a rich and complex culinary tradition in which vegetable dishes are greatly cherished and not in any way treated as the poor relation. This may have as much to do with economics as it clearly has with religious diktat. I believe that the recent surge of interest in Indian food in the West is intimately linked with the present-day preoccupation of many western people with vegetarianism and the comparatively recent recognition of the enormous potential benefits of such diets to our health and well-being. What finally tips the scales for me is the added bonus of the comparatively short time in which a vegetarian meal can be prepared, cooked and served. I think the fact that our vegetarian dishes are not just an accompaniment to the main meat or fish course, but have been conceived as whole dishes, with the ability to stand independently, each distinctive in its own right, inspires cooks to take greater care. Hence many styles of cooking have developed for every single vegetable in the market.

I remember when I first started cooking in England I was terribly impressed with the quality of fresh fruit and vegetables available at the greengrocers and even in the supermarkets. I felt greatly inspired by the near artificial perfection of the displays of fresh produce. Every cauliflower was perfectly formed and outsize. I could hardly believe the tomatoes so uniformly red and firm were real; even the onions were pure white and seemed to be wrapped in paper instead of skins. With the admiration of the once colonized, I told myself this was England. So comprehensive was the brainwashing that – to give you just one example – I never questioned for an instant whether the purple coloured onions we use in the subcontinent might be tastier than the 'made-in-England' brand.

On my first visit back to Karachi, I found that the vegetable dishes tasted infinitely better. At first I thought no more about it than to appreciate the difference between my mother's superior cooking and my own inexperience. Eventually I had to admit to myself that, though my mother's cooking could well be better than mine, the staggering difference came from the fact that the vegetables sold in Empress Market, Karachi, were fuller of natural flavour and goodness than their average European relative. They certainly looked smaller, dirtier and poorer in size and quality compared to the unblemished, polished vegetables and fruit we are used to seeing displayed in big cities in the West. These, however, have been grown with the help of chemical insecticides, nurtured by stimulants, and boosted with so much artificial fertilizer that they have sacrificed much of their taste purely for cosmetic improvement. The rumour is that this situation is even more critical in the United States which really is a sad comment on the price of development and a serious difficulty for all of us who live in the West. Yet it is not a problem most of us feel able to do anything about.

You can sometimes find organically grown fresh foods but these are not mass-produced, so they are hard to come by and are also much more expensive. While it may be best to grow our own, not all of us have the space, time or inclination to become vegetable gardeners. I do believe that farmers and growers are beginning, slowly, to respond to the ever-increasing demand for more naturally grown produce, and the signs are promising that a major change could be on the way.

It seems to me that it is even more difficult to cook vegetables well than meat. The fate of any vegetable dish could be irretrievably sealed at the greengrocers at the stage of selection and purchase. English greengrocers do not like you to touch their produce and pick your own which makes it very hard for someone like me. In Pakistan and India, where people are quite relaxed about this kind of thing, shopping can be more fun. You can, if you like, hand pick every fruit and vegetable and rummage through the heap and bring out the juicy ones hidden at the bottom, so knowing exactly what you are buying. While prime-quality meat makes life much simpler for the cook, there are ways in which you can marinate, tenderize and cook meat to compensate for and disguise many shortcomings in quality. It's nearly impossible to do this with poor quality vegetables.

I always buy tender, fresh vegetables. Their size is sometimes an indication of age. I find it best to cook with vegetables that are not so immature that their flavour is as yet undeveloped, nor so old as to be past it. If you do buy middle-aged vegetables or they grow old sitting in your fridge waiting to be cooked, add a teaspoon of sugar to them which will renew some loss of colour and flavour. It is also useful to remember that most goodness in a vegetable is concentrated in that part which lies closest to its skin. If a recipe calls for the skin to be removed, beware not to pare away all the vitamins and minerals in the process.

It is difficult to divide up vegetables into those more commonly available or less commonly available. That will vary greatly depending on what corner of this world you live in. In the selection of recipes for this chapter I made a conscious decision to include some of those indigenous subcontinental vegetables which are now imported into Britain, although you may need to make a small effort to buy them. I did this in part for those of you who are perhaps curious to encounter something altogether new, but also because to have done otherwise would have been restrictive, with too many important omissions from the range of Indian vegetarian cookery. I hope I have succeeded in finding the right balance between both the hard-to-find and easily available vegetables.

Whether or not one should use frozen vegetables really is a personal decision. I would never attempt to hunt out frozen vegetables out of preference as there is no denying the simple truth that nothing tastes so good as fresh. There are some vegetables such as spinach which I regularly bought frozen until not so long ago, when one day, quite accidentally, I bought the real thing. I had completely forgotten just how delicious fresh spinach can be and it was as thrilling as discovering a new vegetable or being reunited with an old friend after a long time. I am well aware that not all of us have the time to shop for and cook with fresh vegetables all the time. Reluctantly I have suggested the option of using frozen vegetables, for expediency, where I don't think it will hurt the recipe too much.

Our finest vegetable dishes are the creations of a light hand, where great care is taken to ensure that the natural flavour of the vegetable is enhanced by the cooking, and not smothered. Achieving the correct texture and colour of a dish is also essential and it is worth paying as much attention to these aspects of cooking as to the balance of ingredients. It is learning the sense of these finer details that will distinguish you from, and set you above, more ordinary cooks who may be using the same recipe. It doesn't require some inspirational touch or take any longer to cook well, but simply calls for some mild concentration on what you are doing until you acquire an instinct for what is right.

If you are planning a vegetarian meal, pay attention to mixing a variety of different tastes, colours and textures in the dishes you select. If you are serving rice, then it's nice to have at least one wet dish with lots of gravy. If you prefer, a moist *daal* dish could be substituted for this purpose and can be combined with more dry or crisply prepared vegetables. I try to avoid choosing too many dishes of the same colour for one meal. For instance, I would never serve spinach with okra and green lentils – it would look supremely boring on the table. Since it is customary to lay out all the food at the same time, much of the pleasure is derived from being able to dip into several different tastes. I like to serve something spicy with something mild and perhaps something sour or sharp as well. When eating Indian food, I get the greatest satisfaction from taking two or three different items on to my plate at the same time so I can eat morsels in different combinations. The larger the variety to indulge such eating habits, the greater is the gourmet's pleasure. Sadly, since most of us have a few things we enjoy in our lives besides eating, it is not always possible to spread out fifty-one dishes to trifle with at each meal. Still, even if you do have a more modest lifestyle, the principle is still the same.

POTATOES

I have never understood why the poor old potato is universally treated so badly when so many of us love and eat it all the time. Times have changed a little now, but I can clearly remember the days when there was vociferous anti-potato propaganda in the West which made us believe that it was terribly harmful to our health. Strange things can happen to a person writing a cookery book. I find myself wanting to take up the cause of the potato, not only to defend it against its attackers, but to protest about how we have come to treat it with a certain disregard and lack of respect.

In Indian cookery, potatoes are important and the many excitingly different potato dishes are tangible proof of at least this culture's guilt-free relish for the vegetable. It is absolutely true that if I were to write them all down they would easily take over the book. I find it very useful to know several potato recipes, not only because I am partial to their taste but because they are cheap, easy to cook, readily available all the year round and can be stored for long periods.

Aloo Zeera
(Sauté Potatoes with Cumin Seeds)

No selection of potato dishes would be complete that did not include at least one version of this recipe. I have found it hard to resist the temptation to tell you several ways of cooking *aloo zeera* and must admit to feeling a degree of frustration at having to choose between several favourites.

I like to use a wok for this dish because it gives me the freedom to stir-fry comfortably without little pieces of potatoes continually falling out of the pan.

2 lb/900 g potatoes, scrubbed (*aloo*)
cooking oil (*tail*)
5–6 whole dried red chillies (*sabut lal mirch*)
½ tsp turmeric (*haldi*)

salt to taste (*namak*)
2 tsp white cumin seeds (*sabut safeid zeera*)
2 tbsp fresh coriander leaves, finely chopped (*hara dhania*)

Boil the potatoes in their skins until they are slightly less than half done, and set them aside to cool. Once they are completely cool, peel and cut them into ½ in./1·2 cm pieces. Using only a little oil, start off by frying the potatoes over a high heat, turning them over occasionally so they cook evenly.

Break up the red chillies into three or four pieces each and when the potatoes appear to be getting crisp and are beginning to brown, add these broken chillies, the turmeric and salt, and mix them well together. Stir-fry the potatoes until they are done, adding the cumin seeds only a few minutes before removing them from the heat. Garnish with fresh coriander and serve.

Panchphoran Aloo
(*Potatoes in Whole Spices*)

The combination of the particular five whole spices used in the next two recipes is a well-known one called *panchphoran*. It is a traditional Bengali spice mix which is used in different ways in several vegetarian dishes as well as in fish cookery. You can either make your own at home in the way described below or else you could buy the seeds ready mixed at most Indian spice stockists.

2 lb/900 g potatoes, peeled (*aloo*)
cooking oil (*tail*)
½ tsp turmeric (*haldi*)
½ tsp red chilli powder (*lal mirch*)
salt to taste (*namak*)

Panchphoran:
fenugreek seeds (*methi dana*)
nigella seeds (*kalonji*)
black mustard seeds (*rai*)
white cumin seeds (*sabut safeid zeera*)
fennel seeds (*sonf*)

Mix these in equal quantities. Use 2–3 tsp of mix for this recipe.

For the garnish
3–4 tbsp fresh coriander, finely chopped (*hara dhania*)

Slice the potatoes into ¼–½ in./6 mm–1·2 cm rounds, then dice these further into small, evenly sized cubes. Using a wok or other non-stick pan, take the minimum amount of oil needed and fry these cubed potatoes over high heat to start with and then turn the heat down and cover. When the potatoes are a little more than half done, add the turmeric, red chilli powder and some salt, closely followed by 2–3 teaspoons of the whole spice mixture. Stir to mix well and put the lid back on once again. When the potatoes are nearly ready (and you will need to be vigilant to ensure that they do not get too soft), take the lid off, turn the heat up and stir-fry to enable all the excess moisture to evaporate. Garnish with fresh coriander and serve.

Aloo Timatar Panchphoran
(Potatoes with Whole Spices in a Tomato Sauce)

This dish is made using the same whole spice mixture as the one above and is a hybrid of the previous one. The main difference between the two is that here the potatoes are cooked with onions and tomatoes as well, which makes it a more moist dish.

1 × recipe *Panchphoran Aloo*
1 medium onion, peeled and finely chopped (*pyaz*)

1 × 14 oz/400 g can peeled plum tomatoes in juice (*timatar*)

Fry the onions in some oil until golden. Add all the spices, both whole and ground, and fry for a few minutes. Add the potatoes and stir well so that the spices spread evenly through the dish. Then put in the peeled plum tomatoes and stir once more, breaking them up. Cover and simmer until the potatoes are cooked. Garnish liberally as above with fresh coriander before serving.

Harey Masalay kay Aloo
(Potatoes with Spring Onions and Fresh Coriander)

I find it easiest to make this recipe using a large non-stick frying pan that has a lid, as its dimensions make it possible to hold the potatoes almost in a single layer which helps them cook more evenly than if they were crowded into a saucepan.

1½ lb/700 g potatoes, peeled (*aloo*)
10 oz/275 g tomatoes (*timatar*)
6 oz/175 g spring onions, trimmed (*hari pyaz*)
2 garlic cloves, crushed (*lehsun*)
½ in./1·2 cm cube fresh ginger, finely grated or chopped (*adrak*)
4 fl. oz/120 ml cooking oil (*tail*)

¾ tsp turmeric (*haldi*)
1 tsp ground coriander (*dhania*)
1 tsp red chilli powder (*lal mirch*)
1 tsp salt, or to taste (*namak*)
½ tsp nigella seeds (*kalonji*)
½ cup fresh coriander leaves, finely chopped (*hara dhania*)

Dice the potatoes into tiny ½ in./1·2 cm cubes, and finely chop the tomatoes. Slice the hairy root tufts off the spring onion heads and, removing only the wilted leaves, chop the rest into fine rounds. Lightly brown the garlic and ginger in hot oil and add the ground spices. Stir-fry for a minute, then add the potatoes. Fry over high heat and mix well with the spices. Put in the tomatoes and salt, stir a few times, cover the pan and cook over low heat. Continue to give the occasional stir every now and then.

When the potatoes are on the verge of being done and most of the moisture has evaporated, stir in the nigella seeds and chopped spring onions. After a few minutes add the fresh coriander and stir-fry over medium to high heat for a minute or two and serve.

Aloo Achar
(Small Diced Potatoes with Lemon or Mango Pickle)

This dish is perfect for eating with hot *pooris* at a large Sunday breakfast or a simple family lunch. The recipe was given to me, on a recent visit home, by a friend who knows my weakness for all sorts of pickles. The idea once conceived sounds so obvious, yet it was completely new to me. This is certainly an unusual dish which calls for very little skill or effort.

1½ lb/700 g potatoes, peeled (*aloo*)
salt to taste (*namak*)
1 tsp turmeric (*haldi*)
1 tsp nigella seeds (*kalonji*)
½ cup fresh coriander leaves, finely chopped (*hara dhania*)

2 green chillies, finely sliced (*hari mirch*)
2–3 tbsp lemon or mango pickle (*achar*)

Dice the potatoes into ½ in./1·2 cm cubes and cook them in only a little water (such that it should have evaporated by the time they are done) with salt, turmeric and nigella seeds. When the potatoes are almost done stir in the fresh coriander and green chillies.

Chop up any large pieces of lemon or mango in the pickle and mix it with the potatoes about a minute or so before taking them off the heat to serve.

Aloo Methi

(Diced Potatoes with Fenugreek Leaves)

To obtain the authentic taste traditionally associated with this dish I suggest that you use pure mustard oil. Its distinctive aroma and flavour are very influential. Since fresh fenugreek leaves are not always easily available in the West, I have suggested that you buy a packet of dehydrated leaves which are quite commonly stocked at those shops selling Indian spices. It may be sold under its Indian name, *methi*.

1½ lb/700 g potatoes, peeled (*aloo*)

2 small garlic cloves (*lehsun*)

1½ tbsp dehydrated fenugreek leaves (*methi*)

2 tbsp pure mustard oil (*sarson ka tail*)

½ tsp turmeric (*haldi*)

salt to taste (*namak*)

3–4 whole dried large red chillies, or to taste (*sabut lal mirch*)

Chop the potatoes into pieces approximately ½ in./1·2 cm square. Peel and cut the garlic cloves across into very fine slices. Place the dehydrated fenugreek leaves in a fine sieve and wash in cold running water. Leave to soak by placing your strainer containing the leaves immersed in a bowl of cold water. This freshens the leaves and releases their aroma.

Heat the oil and fry the sliced garlic until medium brown. As soon as the garlic changes colour put in the turmeric, immediately followed by the potatoes, and stir them around for a short while over low heat. Add the salt and then the fenugreek leaves. You should not need to add any water as the leaves themselves will be moist from the soaking they were given. Cook slowly over low heat in a covered pan, stirring occasionally if you find the potatoes sticking to the bottom of the pan. Shortly before the potatoes are fully cooked, cut up the whole red chillies and throw them in.

This dish does not have a gravy. When it is finished the potatoes will be cooked through and the fenugreek leaves should be clinging to them. Delicious with plain *parathas* as a simple lunch or accompanying other dishes at a main meal.

Aloo Palak
(Diced Potatoes and Spinach)

1½ lb/700 g potatoes, scrubbed (*aloo*)

1 lb/450 g fresh spinach, weighed without stalks, or frozen leaf spinach (defrost before use) (*palak ka saag*)

1 medium onion, peeled and finely chopped (*pyaz*)

4–5 tbsp cooking oil (*tail*)

½ tbsp finely chopped or grated fresh ginger (*adrak*)

2 garlic cloves, crushed (*lehsun*)

¼ tsp turmeric (*haldi*)

1 tsp white cumin seeds (*sabut safeid zeera*)

½ tsp red chilli powder (*lal mirch*)

1 medium tomato, finely chopped (*timatar*)

Boil the potatoes in their jackets so that they are almost, but not quite, done and set them aside to cool. In the meantime wash the spinach. Without drying the leaves, place them in a covered saucepan and cook gently for 10 minutes until tender. Chop the spinach when it is cool enough to handle, and reserve.

Fry the onion in the oil until golden brown and then add the ginger and garlic and stir for a minute before adding the remaining spices. Stir-fry for a few minutes before adding the chopped tomato. Fry the tomato and spice mixture for another 3–5 minutes over a low to medium flame.

When the potatoes are completely cool, peel and dice them into small cubes. Add the potatoes to the spices and stir to mix well together. Add the spinach, and after you have stirred it in with the potatoes, cover the pan and simmer gently until ready. During this time you may need to open the pan once or twice to stir the vegetables around to prevent them from sticking to the bottom of the pan.

Aloo aur Simla ki Mirch
(Potatoes with Green Peppers)

In Urdu we call green peppers 'the chilli of Simla' and in Bangla I am told they are known as the 'foreign chilli'. The story is that they were first imported into the subcontinent by the British, who cultivated them in that popular colonial hill station of Simla because they found the native Indian chilli unbearably hot. Whatever the degree of accuracy of this tale, such dubious beginnings have certainly not harmed in any way the delicate flavour and mild wholesome appeal of this dish.

2 lb/900 g potatoes, peeled and finely diced (*aloo*)

12 oz/350 g green peppers, seeded and sliced into thin strips (*simla mirch*)

7 tbsp cooking oil (*tail*)

2 small onions, peeled and finely chopped (*pyaz*)

½ tsp fenugreek seeds (*methi dana*)

1 tsp white cumin seeds (*sabut safeid zeera*)

1 dsp crushed garlic (*lehsun*)

1 level tsp turmeric (*haldi*)

1 level tsp red chilli powder (*lal mirch*)

salt to taste (*namak*)

8 oz/225 g tomatoes, finely chopped (*timatar*)

½ cup fresh coriander, finely chopped (*hara dhania*)

Heat the oil in a saucepan and brown the onions. When they are golden add the fenugreek and cumin seeds and stir until they turn a shade or two darker. This will only take a few moments. Then add the garlic, turmeric, red chilli powder and salt and stir together for a few minutes, taking care that the spices do not burn and ruin both the flavour and colour of the dish.

Add the chopped potatoes and green peppers and simmer over low heat in a covered pan. After 5 minutes add the tomatoes, replace the lid and cook until both the potatoes and peppers are tender. Stir in the fresh coriander before removing from the heat to serve.

BHURTA

The word *bhurta* denotes a special type of preparation in which a vegetable has been cooked, mashed, seasoned and finally stir-fried. This technique is particularly suited to root vegetables and some others belonging to the family of squashes and marrows.

Several different methods can be employed during the first stage of the cooking prior to peeling off the skin and scooping out or mashing up the flesh. Traditionally vegetables like aubergines were roasted on a skewer held over a coal fire and their skins completely charred in the process. With root vegetables like potatoes, turnips and radishes it is generally considered to be both quicker and simpler if they are boiled.

Aloo ka Bhurta
(Spicy Mashed Potatoes)

Of all the *bhurtas* this one is probably the best known to most people as it is eaten, with some regional variations, right across the subcontinent. Recipes vary somewhat, not just regionally, but even from home to home. This is our family's standard *aloo bhurta* recipe which, even after eating several others, remains the one to which I feel most drawn. There may well be an element of partisanship in this view, my palate having been influenced early during its formative period, but it is quick and simple to make and the restrained use of only one or two spices produces a deliciously mellow flavour that goes well with any dishes that may accompany it. However, you may improvise if you wish by adding or substituting other spices such as garlic, ginger, fenugreek and nigella seeds which are quite commonly used in other *aloo bhurta* recipes.

For *aloo ka bhurta* the potatoes are boiled and then crudely mashed with a fork. The correct texture comes at the next stage, through the process of stirring and turning the potatoes as they are fried with spices and onions. This makes them smoother than they were to start with, but is not supposed to blend them into the creamy style of English mashed potatoes.

I find the generous proportions of the wok very comfortable to work with when making this dish.

2 lb/900 g potatoes, scrubbed (*aloo*)
1–1½ lb/450–700 g onions, peeled and coarsely chopped (*pyaz*)
4 fl. oz/120 ml cooking oil (*tail*)
2–3 tsp white cumin seeds (*sabut safeid zeera*)
salt to taste (*namak*)

1–1½ tsp red chilli powder, or to taste (*lal mirch*)
1 cup coriander leaves, finely chopped (*hara dhania*)
1–2 green chillies, finely chopped (*hari mirch*)

Boil the potatoes in their skins. When they are cooked, peel them and break them up well with a fork. While the potatoes are boiling, fry the onions in the oil until they are soft and translucent. Add the broken potatoes to the onions and fry them, mashing and mixing the two over a highish heat. When the potatoes are well mashed, sprinkle in the cumin seeds, salt and red chilli powder, and mix so they are spread evenly through the potatoes.

Once your potatoes have been sufficiently fried, put in the fresh coriander and green chillies and toss the ingredients together. Do this only shortly before you are ready to serve the dish so that the coriander and chillies retain their fresh green appearance and taste.

Baingan ka Bhurta
(*Aubergine Bhurta*)

Our mothers and great grandmothers would roast whole aubergines over an open charcoal fire until the skin was scorched all round and charred completely black. This was perfected to such a fine art that the danger of the aubergine occasionally bursting open and making an almighty mess seemed not even to occur to them. There are not many cooks nowadays who have easy access to charcoal fires and the loss of the smoked flavour, once considered such a delicacy, is only a small sacrifice to make for an otherwise very tasty dish.

1½ lb/700 g aubergines (*baingan*)

5 tbsp cooking oil (*tail*)

10 oz/275 g onions, peeled and chopped (*pyaz*)

1 in./2·5 cm cube fresh ginger, peeled and finely chopped or grated (*adrak*)

1 tsp red chilli powder, or to taste (*lal mirch*)

salt to taste (*namak*)

For sourness

2 tbsp tamarind pulp or thick juice extract (*imli*), see page 29

or 2 tbsp green mango, blended to paste (*kacha aam*)

or 2 tbsp lemon juice (*neeboo ka ras*)

To finish

2–3 tbsp fresh coriander leaves, finely chopped (*hara dhania*)

2 tbsp fresh mint leaves, finely chopped (*pudeena*)

2–3 green chillies or to taste, finely chopped, (*hari mirch*)

The first step is to cook the aubergines so as they can be mashed. You can either bake them in the oven wrapped in foil (400°F/200°C/Gas 6 for 30–40 minutes) or cook them in a heavy-bottomed saucepan with only a tiny bit of water, turning them over from time to time so that they cook evenly.

When the aubergines are completely tender, cut off the stems, peel away the skin and mash up the pulp. Heat the oil and fry the onions until they are soft and a translucent gold colour. Add the aubergine pulp to the onion and fry well for a minute or two before adding the ginger, red chilli powder and salt. Fry well until the spices are well absorbed by the aubergines and release their aroma. Then add the souring agent you have chosen and stir-fry some more over high heat for about 5 minutes. When the oil separates, sprinkle on the chopped coriander, mint and green chillies, stir in well and serve.

Shaljum ka Bhurta
(Turnip Bhurta)

1–1½ lb/450–700 g white turnips, peeled and halved or quartered (*shaljum*)

salt to taste (*namak*)

4–5 black peppercorns (*kali mirch*)

1 small cinnamon stick (*dalchini*)

1 large cardamom (*bari elaichee*)

cooking oil (*tail*)

8–10 oz/225–275 g onions, peeled and chopped (*pyaz*)

1 in./2·5 cm cube fresh ginger, peeled and finely chopped or grated (*adrak*)

1 tsp red chilli powder, or to taste (*lal mirch*)

For sourness (optional)

2 tbsp tamarind pulp or thick juice extract (*imli*), see page 29

or 2 tbsp green mango, blended to paste (*kacha aam*)

or 2 tbsp lemon juice (*neeboo ka ras*)

To finish

2–3 tbsp fresh coriander leaves, finely chopped (*hara dhania*)

2 tbsp fresh mint leaves, finely chopped (*pudeena*)

2–3 green chillies, finely chopped, or to taste (*hari mirch*)

Start by boiling the turnips in salty water with the peppercorns, cinnamon and cardamom, discarding them with the water once the turnips have cooked.

Heat some oil and fry the onions until they are soft and a translucent gold colour. Mash the turnips and add them to the onions and fry well for a minute or two before adding the ginger, red chilli powder and some salt. Fry the spices with the turnips over highish heat until they are well absorbed by the turnips and onions and begin to release their aroma. Then add the souring agent, if you have chosen to do so, and stir-fry some more, still over high heat. When the oil separates, sprinkle on the chopped coriander, mint and green chillies, stir in well and serve.

Loki ka Bhurta
(*Marrow Bhurta*)

You can use both the round marrow or the long ones but avoid large old marrows in preference for smaller young ones, as the seeds in the baby marrows are soft and delicious to eat, unlike those in the more mature vegetable. (Marrows can be bought almost all the year round at Indian greengrocers.)

1½ lb/700 g marrow (*loki*)
cooking oil (*tail*)
10 oz/275 g onions, peeled and chopped (*pyaz*)
1 tsp white cumin seeds (*sabut safeid zeera*)
1 in./2·5 cm cube fresh ginger, peeled and finely chopped or grated (*adrak*)

1 tsp red chilli powder (*lal mirch*)
salt to taste (*namak*)
2–4 tbsp fresh coriander leaves, finely chopped (*hara dhania*)
2–3 green chillies, finely chopped, or to taste (*hari mirch*)

Peel and cut up the marrow, then boil it, using just enough water for it to evaporate by the time the marrow is cooked (about 10–15 minutes). Heat the oil and fry the onion until soft and a translucent gold colour. Add the cumin seeds and briefly stir-fry with the onion before adding the mashed marrow. Continue to fry over a fairly high heat for a few minutes and then add the ginger, red chilli powder and some salt. Fry with the spices until they are well absorbed by the vegetables and release their aroma. When the oil separates, sprinkle on the chopped coriander and green chillies and stir in well.

Mooli ka Bhurta
(*Mashed White Radish Sautéed with Spices*)

It is becoming easier to find these radishes in ordinary fruit and vegetable shops and even in supermarkets. I am interested to see them being sold in England under the name *mooli*. In India we had always thought that the 'English' name for this vegetable was 'white radish'. In any case they are generally available at those Indian greengrocers who specialize in importing tropical fruits and vegetables. Sadly, this vegetable is usually sold here with its crown of fresh green leaves missing. If you are fortunate enough to find any *mooli* with its leaves still intact, do not hesitate to buy it as the pleasure of this dish will be doubled.

1–1½ lb/450–700 g long white
   radishes (*mooli*)
salt to taste (*namak*)
1 tsp red chilli powder, or to taste
   (*lal mirch*)
3 garlic cloves, crushed (*lehsun*)

1½ tbsp vegetable cooking oil (*tail*)
1 cup fresh coriander leaves, finely
chopped (*hara dhania*)
1–2 green chillies, finely chopped,
   or to taste (*hari mirch*)

Wash the radishes thoroughly and separate the roots from the leaves. Scrape and slice the radishes into rounds. Boil the chopped radishes, with their leaves and stems, in a saucepan with a little salted water for about 50 minutes until tender. Once they are cooked, mash the radishes well and mix in some salt, the red chilli powder and crushed garlic.

Heat the oil and fry the spicy mashed radishes over medium heat. When well sautéed, stir in the chopped coriander and green chillies, fry for another minute and serve.

Mooli ki Sabzi
(Diced White Radishes)

1–1½ lb/450–700 g white radishes
   with all their leaves (*mooli*)
3–4 tbsp cooking oil (*tail*)
8 oz/225 g onions, peeled and finely
   chopped (*pyaz*)
3–4 garlic cloves, crushed (*lehsun*)
1 dsp finely grated fresh ginger
   (*adrak*)

½ tsp turmeric (*haldi*)
½ tsp red chilli powder, or to taste
   (*lal mirch*)
salt to taste (*namak*)
1–2 green chillies, very finely sliced
   (*hari mirch*)
2 tbsp fresh coriander leaves, finely
   chopped (*hara dhania*)

If you have been able to find any *mooli* with its leaves still attached, then select the tender fresh green ones and after washing them well chop them up finely and reserve. Scrape the *mooli* as you would carrots, dice them and put them in a pan of water to boil. As soon as it comes to the first boil throw out the water, draining the *mooli* into a colander.

Heat the oil and fry the onions until brown, then add the garlic, ginger, turmeric, red chilli powder and some salt. Stir-fry for about a minute before adding the diced *mooli* and leaves. Stir to mix all the ingredients together, cover and cook over low heat until all the excess moisture has evaporated and the vegetables are tender. Turn the heat up and briskly stir-fry for a few minutes before taking it off the heat altogether. Garnish with green chillies and fresh coriander and serve.

Tali Hui Bhindi
(Deep-Fried Crispy Okra)

This delicious recipe is my most favourite way of eating okra. It is stupidly simple to make and has none of the characteristic slimy stickiness so many people associate with this vegetable. Quite to the contrary, the delicate small pieces of okra turn out wonderfully crunchy. The only catch is that it is a relatively expensive way of serving okra as it shrinks in size after being deep-fried; while you might start out with what looks like being a sufficient enough quantity double it, or you'll be sure to run short. You'll need 1 lb/450 g okra for two to three people.

1 lb/450 g okra (*bhindi*)	cooking oil (*tail*)
salt to taste (*namak*)	green chillies to taste, finely sliced
red chilli powder to taste (*lal mirch*)	(*hari mirch*)

Wash the okra and allow it to dry completely. Slice off the head and the tip of its tail and cut the pods into tiny $\frac{1}{4}$ in./6 mm pieces. Sprinkle the okra with salt and red chilli powder, allowing for a little loss of the spices during the deep-frying.

Using a deep fryer or saucepan, heat a generous quantity of oil. When it is crackling hot put in the pieces of okra with the green chillies to fry. Keep a close watch over them and lift them out of the pan, with a perforated spoon, when they have turned brown. Do not allow them to get too dark or burn.

Karhai Bhindi
(Stir-Fried Okra)

Okra (*bhindi*) is a good example of those vegetables that until recently were only available in the West in certain specialist shops and which are now much more visible on account of their growing popularity.

The best okra, and in my opinion the only kind worth using, are young, crisp and tender. Look for small to medium pods as neither the very large nor the fully ripe variety taste much good. They are tough and stringy and, inevitably, the seeds have grown overly big and hard.

When okra is stir-fried in a wok it doesn't shrink in size as it does when it is deep-fried, but nor is it quite as crunchy. Although they may appear similar it's unfair and misleading to compare the two as they are quite distinct from each other in flavour and texture.

1 lb/450 g tender, young, small or medium-sized okra (*bhindi*)

cooking oil (*tail*)

½ tsp red chilli powder (*lal mirch*)

2–3 whole dried red chillies (*sabut lal mirch*)

½ tsp turmeric (*haldi*)

salt to taste (*namak*)

Wash and dry the okra. Slice off the head and the tip of its tail and cut the pods into small ½ in./1·2 cm size pieces. Using a wok or a non-stick pan, heat a little oil and add the red chilli powder, whole dried red chillies, turmeric and some salt. Almost immediately add the chopped okra and stir to mix well so that the oil and spices are evenly spread. Continue to stir-fry over a medium flame. A stringy glue-like white substance will come from the okra. In Urdu we call this *lace*. Carry on stirring over a gentle heat until the *lace* disappears.

You may if you like cover the wok and leave it to cook over low heat for approximately 10 minutes. Once the okra seems tender, turn up the heat and briskly stir-fry over high heat until the okra browns a little.

Pyaz aur Timatar Main Bhindi
(Okra with Onions and Tomatoes)

This recipe does not have a sauce or gravy but, since it also uses onions and tomatoes, does stretch further than the previous one. Onions are used twice, at different stages of the cooking – once right at the beginning when they are fried to form the base of the *masala* and, again, right towards the end when finely sliced onion rings are tossed together with the okra.

1 lb/450 g tender young small or medium-sized okra (*bhindi*)

8 oz/225 g onions, peeled and sliced into rings or half rings (*pyaz*)

4 oz/100 g fresh tomatoes, finely chopped (*timatar*)

4–5 tbsp vegetable cooking oil (*tail*)

½ tsp mustard seeds (*rai*)

2–3 medium garlic cloves, crushed (*lehsun*)

1 dsp finely chopped or grated fresh ginger (*adrak*)

½ tsp turmeric (*haldi*)

½ tsp red chilli powder (*lal mirch*)

1 tsp ground coriander (*dhania*)

1 tsp salt, or to taste (*namak*)

2 green chillies, finely sliced (optional) (*hari mirch*)

For the garnish
finely chopped raw onions

Wash and dry the okra. Slice off their heads and the tips of their tails and cut them into approximately 1–1½ in./2·5–3·8 cm pieces.

Using a wok or a large non-stick frying pan, heat the oil and fry half the onions until golden brown. Then add the mustard seeds closely followed by the garlic, ginger, turmeric, red chilli powder, coriander and salt. Stir-fry over low heat for a minute or two before adding the okra. Once you put in the okra, mix it well with the spices. The okra may give out a gluey substance. Cover and cook over gentle heat for 5 minutes, then add the chopped tomatoes. Replace the lid to hold in the steam and cook for about a further 10 minutes over low heat.

During this time uncover it two or three times and give a quick stir to ensure that the spices do not stick to the bottom of the pan. Then add the remaining onion and the green chillies if using any, cover and cook gently for a final 5 minutes. At the end, take off the lid, turn the heat up and briskly stir-fry until the okra is tender and ready to be served. Garnish with finely chopped raw onions.

Bhagarey Baingan
(*Hyderabadi Aubergines*)

This dish is a fine example of the wonderful cuisine that evolved in Hyderabad, Deccan, once the influence of Mughlai cooking made its mark deep in the south of India. The easy availability of spices such as mustard seeds and red chillies, the practice of using *karri* leaves, coconut and tamarind which characterizes Southern Indian cookery, radically transformed the North Indian style Mughlai cooking to create a new culinary tradition that is peculiarly Hyderabadi and is recognized as being one of the finest regional cuisines of the subcontinent.

This is quite a complicated recipe calling for a wide range of spices and ingredients. Tackle it if you are in the mood to take on a challenge which offers as its reward the world's best aubergine dish. If you follow the steps carefully it is not that difficult to cook, although it can at first appear a little daunting. In the subcontinent you get a variety of aubergine that is much smaller than that normally seen in the West, giving you around six to eight aubergines to 1 lb/450 g in weight. The smallest aubergines I have come across in the West weigh, on average, no less than two per lb/450 g. The classic recipe for *bhagarey baingan* naturally assumes the availability of the small aubergine which is easier to stuff and simpler to handle. Although the small variety is imported to England from Kenya and is available at Indian greengrocers, I have written this recipe keeping in mind the sort indigenous to Europe. However, do try and buy them as small as you can find them and avoid at all costs getting the exceptionally large ones for this dish.

1 lb/450 g small aubergines (*baingan*)
2 medium onions, peeled (*pyaz*)
½ tsp turmeric (*haldi*)
1 tbsp ground coriander (*dhania*)
1 tsp red chilli powder (*lal mirch*)
1 dsp crushed garlic (*lehsun*)
1 dsp finely grated fresh ginger (*adrak*)
salt to taste (*namak*)
pure mustard oil (*sarson ka tail*), or any vegetable cooking oil (*tail*)
4–6 *karri* leaves (*karri patta*)
5–6 tbsp thick tamarind juice (*imli*) see page 29

For the garnish
½ cup fresh coriander leaves, finely chopped (*hara dhania*)

Dry roasted and ground to a powder (see 2. below)
2 tbsp desiccated coconut (*naryal*)
2 tbsp white cumin seeds (*sabut safeid zeera*)
2 tbsp sesame seeds (*til*)
2 oz/50 g peanuts (*moomphalli*)

Whole spices
1 tsp white cumin seeds (*sabut safeid zeera*)
1 tsp black mustard seeds (*rai*)
1 tsp nigella seeds (*kalonji*)
1 tsp fenugreek seeds (*methi dana*)

1. Measure out all the ingredients.
2. To dry-roast ingredients, mix them together and, using a *tava* or cast-iron pan, start off over medium heat, turning down the flame once it is sufficiently hot. Keep stirring and moving the ingredients around so they roast evenly. As soon as they release their aroma and turn a shade darker take them off the heat. Grind
3. Slice 1 onion into fine rings or half rings. Blend the other one to a paste.
4. Wash the aubergines and cut them open making four incisions lengthwise, taking care that they remain attached at the stem.
5. Mix all the powdered spices, the roasted and ground ingredients, the garlic, ginger, onion paste and some salt. Rub *half* this paste liberally into the cuts so the aubergines are well filled with the mixture.
6. Heat some oil in a heavy-bottomed saucepan. Add the finely sliced onion rings and stir-fry until they are *pale* golden but no darker. Put in the whole spices – all the seeds – with the *karri* leaves, and stir-fry. Within a minute the seeds will begin to pop and turn a shade darker. Then add the remaining half of the spice mixture, and stir-fry until it browns a little. Carefully place the stuffed aubergines in this saucepan, turn the heat down low, add 2 fl. oz/50 ml water, cover and cook gently, turning the aubergines over from time to time so they are done evenly.

This is where your own judgement is of critical importance. You will probably need to continue adding a little water, about 2 fl. oz/50 ml at a time, to prevent the spices from sticking to the bottom of the pan. The art lies in not adding too much water at a time which would only serve to stew the vegetable. Spoon some hot oil and spice mixture into the gashes to help brown the stuffing. It is inevitable that some of the filling will fall out.

When the aubergines appear to be tender, pour in the tamarind juice, with a few additional drops of water if necessary, and cook over extremely low heat for a further 5 minutes. Transfer the aubergines carefully to a serving dish and pour the thick spicy sauce over them. Garnish with fresh coriander. This dish is eaten both hot as well as at room temperature.

Pyazwaley Karelay
(Bitter Gourds with Onions)

Connoisseurs of this vegetable claim that the more bitter the taste of this dish the greater is their pleasure. By this yardstick, my own appreciation is clearly very unsophisticated. I have found that I do not enjoy an overpoweringly bitter flavour. The greatest concentration of bitterness in the *karela* is contained in its knobbly scale-like outer skin and seeds. Unlike 'stuffed karela', in which the vegetable is kept intact, in this recipe the skin is scraped off, the seeds thrown away and the bitter gourd liberally rubbed with salt. This reduces the bitterness leaving only a mild pleasant trace of its original flavour.

Buy fresh, young, medium-sized *karelay* in which the seeds are not fully ripe and are still soft. Most specialist Indian grocers stock these bitter gourds and although they are not generally available at your ordinary greengrocers, they are not hard to find.

1 lb/450 g bitter gourds (*karelay*)	8 oz/225 g tomatoes, finely chopped (*timatar*)
salt to taste (*namak*)	
1 lb/450 g onions, peeled (*pyaz*)	
cooking oil (*tail*)	*For the garnish*
½ tsp turmeric (*haldi*)	2 tbsp fresh coriander leaves, finely chopped (*hara dhania*)
1 tsp red chilli powder (*lal mirch*)	

Scrape off the outer skin from the *karelay*, slit them open lengthwise and remove their seeds. Cut into thin slices across the width to create open rings. Rub with salt and leave to one side for about an hour. At the end of the hour wash well and squeeze out the water. Shallow-fry these *karela* rings in some oil until they are a crisp golden brown, and lift them out with a slotted spoon.

Coarsely chop half the onions and fry them to a deep golden brown in the same oil. Add turmeric, red chilli powder and some salt, and stir-fry for another few seconds. Then put the crisply fried bitter gourds into the spice and onion mixture, together with the finely chopped tomatoes and the remaining raw onions sliced into thin rings. Cover with a loosely fitting lid that allows some moisture to escape. After a few minutes, when the onion rings look soft and cooked and most of the water given off by them has evaporated, your dish is ready. Garnish with fresh coriander when serving.

Hyderabadi Timatar Cut
(Hot and Sour Tomatoes from Hyderabad)

This dish is not exactly a chutney, yet it can be eaten and enjoyed as a chutney straight from the fridge or at room temperature. It can also be served piping hot and is quite properly a dish in its own right which, in true Hyderabadi style, has incorporated the best essence of a chutney needing no relish to accompany or enhance its spectacular taste. In my experience it is an extremely successful side dish which has a strong hot and sour flavour that never fails to make an impact even on the most bored palate.

8 oz/225 g onions, peeled and coarsely chopped (*pyaz*)

2 × 14 oz/400 g cans peeled plum tomatoes in juice (*teen kay timatar*)

1 tbsp finely grated fresh ginger (*adrak*)

3–4 large garlic cloves, crushed (*lehsun*)

1 tsp red chilli powder, or to taste (*lal mirch*)

½ tsp turmeric (*haldi*)

20 *karri* leaves (*karri patta*)

4 whole green chillies (*hari mirch*)

salt to taste (*namak*)

8 fl. oz/250 ml thick tamarind juice (*imli*), see page 29

4 tbsp vegetable cooking oil (*tail*)

1 tsp white cumin seeds (*sabut safeid zeera*)

3 whole dried red chillies (*sabut lal mirch*)

Mix the onions with the tomatoes in a saucepan. Add 16 fl. oz/475 ml water and put on the stove to cook. Now add the ginger, garlic, red chilli powder, turmeric, half the *karri* leaves, the four whole green chillies and some salt, and stir these ingredients well together. After bringing the contents of the pan to a quick boil, cover and simmer over low heat until the tomatoes and onions are completely soft. You may need to squash the tomatoes with a wooden spoon to break them up.

While the onions and tomatoes are cooking pour the tamarind water into the tomato mixture and continue to cook slowly until it thickens. Remove from the heat.

In a frying pan heat the oil and fry the cumin seeds, whole red chillies and remaining *karri* leaves until they turn a shade darker. Pour this sizzling mixture with the hot oil over the tomatoes, and serve hot.

Phool Gobi ki Bhujiya
(Fried Cauliflower with Cumin and Sesame Seeds)

I find using a large wok, preferably one that is non-stick, by far the most convenient way in which to cook this cauliflower recipe. The reason for this is that while the vegetable is still raw and the florets are quite bulky they fit effortlessly into its wide comfortable shape.

You will notice that no ground spices, not even chilli powder, are used in this recipe. This omission is deliberate as the cauliflower is therefore able, without interference, to absorb the golden colour and flavour of the fried onions, and the gentle combination of cumin and sesame seeds is just delightful. The dried red chilli is less hot but has a fuller flavour, and is a great improvement on the commercially sold red chilli powders.

2–2½ lb/900 g–1·1 kg cauliflower, weighed after removing outer leaves (*phool gobi*)

10 oz/275 g onions, peeled and sliced into fine rings or half rings (*pyaz*)

cooking oil (*tail*)

5–8 dried red chillies (*sabut lal mirch*)

salt to taste (*namak*)

2–2½ tsp cumin seeds (*sabut safeid zeera*)

1–1½ dsp sesame seeds (*til*)

3 tbsp fresh coriander leaves, finely chopped (*hara dhania*)

1 in./2·5 cm cube fresh ginger, peeled and extremely finely diced (*adrak*)

2–3 green chillies, according to taste and size (*hari mirch*)

Wash the cauliflower and separate it into large florets; also chop up the central stem and those stalks that are long or bulky. Fry the onions in a little oil until they are a very pale gold. Break each of the dried red chillies into three or four pieces, add them to the onions and stir-fry for a few moments before putting in the cauliflower and some salt. Mix the ingredients well, close the lid and cook over low heat until the cauliflower appears to be tender. You will need to open the lid from time to time to stir things around so it all cooks evenly. As the cauliflower softens you should gently divide it into smaller, more delicate florets, with the edge of your wooden spoon.

When you see that the cauliflower is almost cooked, turn up the heat and add the cumin seeds closely followed by the sesame seeds, and briskly stir-fry to remove any excess moisture or sogginess, leaving the cauliflower a crisp brown.

Shortly before lifting it off the heat, add the chopped fresh coriander, finely diced fresh ginger and chopped green chillies and stir them in well. Serve immediately while the coriander leaves are still a fresh green, thus providing an attractive contrast.

Masalaydar Gajar aur Palak
(Spicy Carrots in a Sea of Spinach)

A colourful dish that looks exceedingly attractive on the dinner table and while the combination may be familiar to Europeans, it is one which would strike many Indians as being something out of the ordinary.

1 lb/450 g carrots, scrubbed and sliced into thin rounds (*gajar*)

1½ lb/700 g fresh spinach, washed and chopped (*palak ka saag*)

4 oz/100 g onions, peeled and finely chopped (*pyaz*)

5–6 tbsp cooking oil (*tail*)

3 garlic cloves, crushed (*lehsun*)

1 in./2·5 cm cube fresh ginger, peeled and grated (*adrak*)

1½ tsp ground coriander (*dhania*)

½ tsp ground white cumin (*safeid zeera*)

1 level tsp turmeric (*haldi*)

1 tsp red chilli powder, or to taste (*lal mirch*)

6 oz/175 g tomatoes, finely chopped (*timatar*)

salt to taste (*namak*)

Fry the onions in the oil until they turn a pale honey colour. Add the garlic and ginger and stir-fry for a minute. Turn the heat down and add the remaining spices, closely followed by finely chopped tomatoes. Fry this mixture for a few minutes, adding a few drops of water if necessary to prevent the spices from burning or sticking to the bottom of the pan.

Add the carrot rounds to the spicy mixture, and fry with the spices for a few minutes. Add about 4 fl. oz/120 ml (or a little more) water and simmer over low heat. When the carrots are half done, add the spinach. Cook gently until the carrots are quite tender. At this point take the lid off the saucepan, and turn the heat up so the excess moisture can evaporate. Stir more or less continuously at this stage so that the vegetables don't burn at the bottom of the pan.

Bund Gobi ki Tarkari
(Fried Spicy Cabbage)

1–1½ lb/450–700 g white cabbage (*bund gobi*)
cooking oil (*tail*)
½ tsp nigella seeds (*kalonji*)
½ tsp mustard seeds (*rai*)
½ tsp fennel seeds (*sonf*)
1 lb/450 g onions, peeled and finely chopped (*pyaz*)
3–4 green chillies or to taste, finely chopped (*hari mirch*)

2 garlic cloves, crushed (*lehsun*)
1 tsp finely grated fresh ginger (*adrak*)
½ tsp turmeric (*haldi*)
½ tsp red chilli powder (*lal mirch*)
1 tsp white cumin seeds (*sabut safeid zeera*)
salt to taste (*namak*)
2 tbsp fresh coriander leaves, finely chopped (*hara dhania*)

Wash the cabbage, remove its stem and hard core, and chop it up finely. Heat a very little oil, and add the nigella, mustard and fennel seeds, immediately followed by the finely chopped onions, green chillies and remaining spices, seeds and salt.

Stir them around for a minute to mix well and then add the chopped cabbage. Stir some more to mix the cabbage with the other ingredients, then turn the heat down low, cover the saucepan and leave to cook gently. The dish should be ready in about 15–20 minutes. During this time stir it occasionally to make sure it is not sticking to the bottom of the pan. Stir in the chopped coriander leaves and serve.

Bavli Handya ki Tarkeeb
(A Dish of Mixed Vegetables)

The name of this recipe in translation would read something like 'how to make a crazy dish'. I suspect that this name caught on amongst UP *wallahs* because it was the only way they knew of dealing with a dish that seemed to defy all their strict conventions of cookery which dictate what may or may not be cooked together.

There is a tradition that such a dish is fed to a new mother on the sixth day after the birth of her child to renew her strength and so she may taste many good things. In Bengal there are several similar dishes of mixed vegetables such as 'rainy season vegetables', 'autumn vegetables' or 'winter vegetables' which are cooked in celebration of the changing seasons. I have chosen some of the more common vegetables for this 'sample' recipe to which you may add or substitute other favourites.

cooking oil (*tail*)
8 oz/225 g onions, peeled and finely chopped (*pyaz*)
3 garlic cloves, crushed (*lehsun*)
½ tsp turmeric (*haldi*)
2 tsp ground coriander (*dhania*)
1 tsp red chilli powder (*lal mirch*)
salt to taste (*namak*)
8 oz/225 g tomatoes, chopped (*timatar*)
1 × 10 oz/275 g packet mixed frozen cauliflower, peas and carrots (*gobi, matar, gajar*)

1 lb/450 g potatoes, peeled and diced small (*aloo*)
8 oz/225 g aubergines, diced in small cubes (*baingan*)
2–3 green chillies or to taste, finely chopped, (*hari mirch*)
½ cup coriander leaves, finely chopped (*hara dhania*)
1 tsp finely chopped fresh ginger (*adrak*)

Heat some oil and lightly brown the chopped onions. Turn the heat down low, add the garlic, turmeric, coriander, red chilli powder and some salt, and stir for a few moments. Put in all the vegetables and stir to mix well with the spices.

Cover the pan with a well fitting lid and cook slowly until the vegetables are done, stirring a few times. Right at the end when your vegetables are cooked, turn the heat up and stir-fry them well for a few minutes before sprinkling in the chopped green chillies, fresh coriander and ginger.

Turai ki Sabzi
(Braised Courgettes with Cumin and Broken Chillies)

Turai, also called *tori* or *ghia*, is an Indian vegetable that closely resembles the courgette. I like to cook tender baby courgettes in which the seeds have as yet barely formed. In India it is customary to peel the *turai* in preparation for cooking, but if the courgettes are young enough, I prefer to slice them into rounds without removing their skins. In Indian cookery courgettes are cooked a little more than is the European practice, but care should be taken that they do not get so soft that the pieces just begin to dissolve. Use the minimum amount of oil possible as the courgettes easily absorb it and can then appear overly greasy.

1½ lb/700 g courgettes (*turai*)
6 dried whole red chillies, or to taste (*sabut lal mirch*)
8 oz/225 g onions, peeled and finely chopped (*pyaz*)
5 tbsp cooking oil (*tail*)
2–3 tsp white cumin seeds (*sabut safeid zeera*)

salt to taste (*namak*)
½ cup fresh coriander leaves, finely chopped (*hara dhania*)
2 green chillies, sliced (optional) (*hari mirch*)

Slice the courgettes into slim rounds. Give the whole red chillies a couple of short whirrs in an electric grinder so they are coarsely crushed rather than ground to a fine powder.

Fry the onions in the oil until a golden colour, then throw in the cumin seeds and crushed red chillies, and stir-fry for a minute before adding the sliced courgettes. Mix well together and stir-fry for a further few minutes. Add some salt, then turn the heat down very low. Cover the wok or pan and let the courgettes cook in their own steam until they are quite tender. During this period stir several times, turning the vegetables over to prevent them burning at the bottom of the pan.

Just before serving add the chopped coriander and green chillies and stir fry for a few more minutes.

·LENTIL DISHES·
(Daal)

· Lentil Dishes ·
(Daal)

Daal occupies a central place in Indian cuisine – its following drawn from all classes, castes and religions – yet more often than not we take it for granted and treat it as though it were only marginal to our diet. Let me give you an example: say I have cooked three dishes – *kofta*, *bhindi* and a *daal*. On being asked what there was for dinner I would be very likely to mention only the meat and the vegetable, not thinking it was necessary to specify the lentils. Looking at it superficially you may conclude that *daal* is denied any status. Yet to do so would be to miss the point. It is an intrinsic part of almost every meal we eat. The usual idiomatic way of extending a lunch or dinner invitation to a friend would be to ask them to eat *daal-chawal* or *daal-roti*, which means 'lentils and rice' or 'lentils and bread'.

There are several varieties of lentils or *daals*. Some, like *masoor* and *moong*, cook extremely quickly; others, like *channa*, *urad* and *arhar*, take longer. There are also many different techniques for cooking *daals*. They may be pre-soaked or cooked straight after being washed; they may be fried in onions and/or spices before the water is added or else water may be added to the *daal* even before the spices; once cooked they may simply be garnished with fresh mint or coriander or perhaps seasoned with hot oil and a great variety of things such as browned onions or cumin seeds fried in this oil. The particular technique used is determined as much by tradition as by the nature of the *daal*. For example, with *arhar* and *kabli channa* it is essential to pre-soak the *daals* for a long time as otherwise they can take forever to cook.

There are basically two consistencies to aim for when making your *daals*. One is similar to a thick soup and the other is drier and more like rice, where each grain of *daal* is separately visible, yet is plump, moist and perfectly soft. *Daal* is also cooked with different vegetables in delicious original and unusual combinations. *Daal-gosht* is traditionally cooked with lamb and *channa daal*; *haleem* or *khichra* is cooked using several different *daals* all together with meat, whole wheat and rice. The variety of dishes that could be listed under the single word *daal* is vast. I have found that most people settle on one or two favourite *daals* which they eat regularly, only cooking any others for occasional variety. My everyday favourite is a 'wet' *daal* dish made with *masoor*. I can eat it day after day, meal after meal, without it occurring to me that this is a boring thing to do. After all we eat rice and bread with every meal too. I also like *sookhi mash ki daal* – a preparation in which the *daal* is lightly spiced and cooked dry.

There are a couple of things to bear in mind when choosing which *daal* to cook. Firstly think about the other dishes you are planning to cook. If they are mostly without a gravy then select a wet *daal* recipe; conversely if you have several dishes with gravy then a dry *daal* may be more welcome. Secondly, pay some attention to the colour of the *daal* so it complements the other food. In this respect a *daal* dish is very much seen as accompanying the other dishes and though important, will seldom be the main focus of the meal.

WET DAALS

In the selection that follows you will find some recipes for wet *daal* dishes. Although they are each different and made using various different lentils there are some cooking hints common to all that you may find useful.

There are basically two techniques you can employ to produce the desired texture for those *daal* dishes which should be akin to a thick soup.

1) In the first method, you add a lot more water than your *daal* will need to allow for evaporation during cooking. Using an 8 fl. oz/225 ml cup, add about 3 cups of water to each cup of *daal* and, after adding your spices, bring it rapidly to a boil over high heat. As soon as it reaches boiling point turn the flame right down and simmer slowly over very low heat. If the water evaporates before the *daal* is completely soft (and this will vary from *daal* to *daal*) add another cup or two of water, stir to mix and continue cooking on an extremely low heat until the *daal* is completely mushy. With this method the *daal* needs a little more time but it virtually cooks itself and hardly needs any of your attention.

2) In the second method, you need to start with less water, say about 2 cups of water to every cup of *daal*, and after bringing it to a quick boil, turn the heat down and simmer slowly, making sure you leave the lid of the saucepan a little ajar or the *daal* tends to boil over. Once the water has been absorbed by the grains of *daal*, take a wooden cooking spoon and stir briskly round and round the saucepan to break down the grains and blend the *daal*. This process is called *ghontna* in Urdu and is a quicker method of bringing the *daal* to the correct consistency than the previous one (where the breaking down of the grains was done by the steam and a slow cooking process). Once the *daal* grains have been sufficiently broken up, add some more water, stir to mix evenly, and simmer for a short time more.

BHAGAR OR TARKA

Many *daal* dishes are seasoned with sizzling hot *asli ghee* or oil containing onions, garlic, cumin seeds etc. This is known as the *bhagar* or the *tarka*. The cooked *daal* is ladled out into a serving dish and the hot oil and seasonings are poured over it *just* before it is served.

Lal Masoor ki Daal I
(Red Masoor Lentils)

Split and husked *masoor daal* is probably the most commonly available of the Indian pulses. It is easily identifiable by its tiny round peach-coloured grains. It is the *daal* I cook most often because it needs no pre-soaking, is quick, easily digestible, and its mild flavour goes well with everything else. If you like you can swap around the *bhagar* for the two recipes below.

The whole red chillies used in the *bhagar* are not supposed to be eaten. They will not make the dish any hotter but will add to its flavour. Also take care when frying the cumin seeds that they do not turn too dark or burn, or else they will ruin the taste of the *daal*.

8 oz/225 g/1 cup red split *masoor* lentils (*lal masoor ki daal*)
1 tsp red chilli powder (*lal mirch*)
½ tsp turmeric (*haldi*)
3 whole green chillies (*hari mirch*)
2 oz/50 g tomatoes, chopped (*timatar*)
1 tsp salt or to taste (*namak*)
1 tbsp fresh coriander leaves, finely chopped (*hara dhania*)

For the bhagar
4 tbsp cooking oil (*tail*)
2 tsp white cumin seeds (*sabut safeid zeera*)
4–6 *karri* leaves, preferable though not essential (*karri patta*)
4–5 dried red chillies (optional) (*sabut lal mirch*)

Pick over and thoroughly wash the lentils. Add all the ingredients except for the coriander and cook in water using one of the two methods described on pages 138–139.

When the *daal* is quite soft and well blended, pour it into a serving dish and stir in the fresh coriander.

To make the *bhagar*, heat the cooking oil in a frying pan and put in the cumin seeds, *karri* leaves and red chillies. In a few seconds the cumin seeds will begin to pop and crackle and turn a shade darker. Quickly pour the mixture over the *daal*. Do not stir to mix as the *bhagar* of hot oil also serves as a garnish.

Lal Masoor ki Daal II
(Red Masoor Lentils)

The raw green mango used in this recipe adds a wonderfully sour taste to the *daal* that is much sought after. It is not always easy to find it at regular western supermarkets, but it is normally available at Indian greengrocers. Don't worry if you are unable to get it, as the recipe works perfectly well without.

8 oz/225 g/1 cup red split *masoor* lentils (*lal masoor ki daal*)

1 garlic clove, crushed (*lehsun*)

1 small onion, peeled and chopped (*pyaz*)

½ small green mango, peeled and chopped (*kacha aam*)

1 tsp red chilli powder (*lal mirch*)

½ tsp turmeric (*haldi*)

½ tsp salt, or to taste (*namak*)

For the bhagar

4 tbsp cooking oil or clarified butter (*tail/asli ghee*)

1 small onion, peeled and finely chopped into rings or half rings (*pyaz*)

1 small garlic clove, peeled and finely sliced (*lehsun*)

Pick over and thoroughly wash the *lentils*. Add all the other ingredients to the *daal* and cook in water using one of the two methods described on pages 138–139. When the *daal* is cooked and smoothly blended, ladle it out into a deep serving dish.

To make the *bhagar*, heat the cooking oil or *asli ghee* and fry the chopped onion. When soft and translucent, on the point of turning golden, add the sliced garlic. Continue stirring and frying until both the onions and garlic are a golden brown and immediately pour this sizzling mixture on to the *daal*. Do not stir to mix as the *bhagar* of hot oil also serves as a garnish.

Lal Masoor ki Daal ka Bhurta
(Bhurta of Red Masoor Lentils)

In this recipe the *daal* is first cooked to a somewhat dryish consistency and is then stir-fried with a combination of fried and raw onions, green chillies and fresh coriander. It is frequently made out of leftovers from many different lentils, but most popularly from *moong* and *masoor*.

8 oz/225 g/1 cup red split *masoor* lentils (*lal masoor ki daal*)

1 tsp salt, or to taste (*namak*)

1 tsp red chilli powder (*lal mirch*)

½ tsp turmeric (*haldi*)

10 oz/275 g onions, peeled and finely chopped (*pyaz*)

3 tbsp vegetable cooking oil (*tail*) or clarified butter (*asli ghee*)

3 green chillies or to taste, sliced, (*hari mirch*)

2–3 tbsp fresh coriander leaves, finely chopped (*hara dhania*)

Pick over and wash the lentils thoroughly in several changes of water. Add 2 cups water to the lentils with the salt, red chilli powder and turmeric. Bring it rapidly to a boil over high heat. Once the *daal* is boiling turn the heat down as low as possible and simmer slowly until all the water has evaporated. You should cover the saucepan with a lid but leave it slightly ajar. When the *daal* is cooked soft and is fairly dry (not soupy), with no excess moisture visible, take it off the stove.

Fry half the onions to a rich golden colour in the oil or *ghee*, and pour the contents of the pan into the saucepan containing the *daal*. Turn the heat back on under the lentils and stir-fry them over high heat. Add the remaining chopped raw onion, green chillies and fresh coriancer and continue to stir-fry for just another 30–60 seconds.

The flavour of the green chillies adds quite a lot to the dish. If you prefer it to be less chilli hot then remove the seeds from the chillies which will reduce their potency.

Khari Kali Masoor ki Daal
(Whole Masoor Lentils)

This dish is made with whole *masoor* lentils in which the small, round peach-coloured grains are still covered with their dark skins and are full of natural goodness. It is delicious when eaten with plain boiled rice and *achar* (pickles).

8 oz/225 g/1 cup whole *masoor* lentils (*kali masoor daal*)

1 small onion, peeled and blended to a smooth paste (*pyaz*)

½ tsp red chilli powder, or to taste (*lal mirch*)

¼ tsp turmeric (*haldi*)

1 tsp ground coriander (*dhania*)

small pat butter (*makhan*) or 1 tbsp cooking oil (*tail*)

salt to taste (*namak*)

2–3 tbsp thick tamarind juice (*imli*) (see page 29) *or* lemon juice (*neeboo ka ras*)

1 dsp finely chopped fresh ginger (*adrak*)

2 green chillies or to taste, finely chopped (*hari mirch*)

1 tbsp fresh mint leaves, finely chopped (*pudeena*)

For the bhagar
cooking oil (*tail*)

1 small onion, peeled and chopped into fine rings or half rings (*pyaz*)

2 small garlic cloves, finely sliced into rounds (*lehsun*)

For the garnish
1 dsp mint leaves, finely chopped (*pudeena*)

Carefully pick over the lentils and wash thoroughly in several changes of water. Put them in a saucepan with 3 cups water. Add the onion paste, red chilli powder, turmeric, coriander, the oil and some salt and rapidly bring to the boil. Once it reaches boiling point turn the heat right down, cover the saucepan and cook slowly for about 45 minutes until the *daal* is tender. When the *daal* has softened, use a wooden spoon and stir vigorously in a circular motion a few times. Only if the water has evaporated and the lentils are almost dry should you add another ½ cup water at this stage. Put in the tamarind or lemon juice, ginger, green chillies and half the mint and cook in a covered saucepan over low heat for another 10 minutes.

For the *bhagar*, heat a little oil in a frying pan and fry the onion. Just as it is about to turn brown, add the sliced garlic. As soon as both the onions and garlic turn golden pour the whole sizzling mixture over the *daal*. Garnish with fresh mint and serve.

Dhulli Moong ki Patli Daal
(*Split Moong Lentils*)

Moong daal is available whole, or simply split, or both husked as well as split. It is amazing how, on being cooked, each of them can taste so completely different. In Urdu we call the whole *moong hari moong ki daal* or 'green' *moong*; the split variety is *chilkon wali moong* or, in translation, 'the *moong* with the skin'; and the split and husked *daal* is called *dhulli hui moong*, 'washed *moong*'.

The *moong daal* in this recipe is made with the split and husked variety of *moong*, which has small, oval, irregularly shaped grains, and are a pale lemon in colour. This spicy wet *daal* dish is equally welcome when served as part of a simple everyday meal as at more special occasions. You can, for variety, make it equally well using equal quantities of *moong* and *masoor* together.

8 oz/225 g/1 cup yellow split *moong* lentils (*dhulli hui moong daal*)

1 tsp turmeric (*haldi*)

½ tsp red chilli powder, or to taste (*lal mirch*)

2–3 garlic cloves, crushed (*lehsun*)

½ tsp ground coriander (*dhania*)

1 tsp salt, or to taste (*namak*)

1 dsp finely chopped fresh ginger (*adrak*)

2 green chillies, finely sliced (*hari mirch*)

1 cup mint leaves, finely chopped (*pudeena*)

½ tsp freshly ground *garam masala* (see page 17)

5–6 tbsp cooking oil (*tail*)

1 small onion, peeled and finely chopped (*pyaz*)

Carefully pick over the lentils for any bits of grit, and wash thoroughly in several changes of water. Add 3 cups cold water, the turmeric, red chilli powder, crushed garlic, coriander and salt and bring to a boil. Turn the heat right down, cover the saucepan, leaving the lid open a crack, and simmer for about half an hour or until the *daal* is soft. Then use a wooden spoon and stir it vigorously round and round the saucepan to blend the *daal*. Add another cup of water and bring it to the boil once again, cover, turn the heat down and cook for about 10 minutes. Add the ginger, green chillies and mint leaves. Stir them in well and leave the *daal* to simmer gently in a covered saucepan over very low heat for a further 5 minutes.

When the *daal* is ready transfer it to a serving dish and then sprinkle the freshly ground *garam masala* over its surface. Heat the oil in a frying pan and fry the finely chopped onions until golden. Immediately pour the hot oil and onions over the *daal* and serve.

Bhunni Hui Dhulli Moong
(Spicy Fried Split Yellow Moong)

Although this is not a recipe for a dry *daal*, here the grains of the lentils are not blended to a smooth consistency but should remain somewhat visible after cooking. This is why you need to fry the spices and *daal* well together before adding the water.

8 oz/225 g/1 cup split yellow *moong* lentils (*dhulli hui moong daal*)

3–4 tbsp cooking oil (*tail*)

1 small onion, peeled and finely chopped (*pyaz*)

½ tsp red chilli powder, or to taste (*lal mirch*)

½ tsp turmeric (*haldi*)

½ tsp white cumin seeds (*sabut safeid zeera*)

½ tsp freshly ground *garam masala* (see page 17)

salt to taste (*namak*)

1 dsp finely chopped fresh ginger (*adrak*)

2 green chillies, finely chopped (*hari mirch*)

For the garnish
cooking oil (*tail*)

1 small onion, peeled and cut into fine rings or half rings (*pyaz*)

2 dsp fresh coriander leaves, finely chopped (*hara dhania*)

Carefully pick over and wash the lentils thoroughly, strain and reserve. Heat the oil and fry the finely chopped onion until golden brown. Add the red chilli powder, turmeric, cumin, *garam masala* and some salt, and fry for a minute or two. Add the lentils and continue to fry with the spices for a few more minutes. Add 1 pint/600 ml water, cover the saucepan and, leaving the lid open a little, cook slowly. After about half an hour you should check to see whether the *daal* is tender. Add some more water if necessary and cook until the grains are soft. Once the *daal* is cooked stir in the ginger and green chillies and simmer gently for another 5 minutes. Transfer to a serving dish.

Heat some oil in a frying pan and fry the onion until golden brown. Lift out of the pan on to a kitchen towel and blot any excess oil. Garnish the *daal* with these crisp fried onions and the fresh coriander.

Khilli Moong Masalay Main
(*Sprouted Whole Moong Daal in Spices*)

Both *khari moong* (whole *moong* lentils) and *kala channa* (black chickpeas) are cooked and eaten after being sprouted. Not only are they delicious to eat in this way, they are also bursting with goodness. Unless you can find sprouted *moong daal* in health-food shops or specialist Indian shops, you will have to sprout them yourself at home. It is simple enough to do but in this case you will need to plan a couple of days ahead to make this dish.

8 oz/225 g/1 cup whole green *moong* lentils (*hari moong*)

4 fl. oz/120 ml cooking oil (*tail*)

4 *karri* leaves (*karri patta*)

1 dsp containing equal quantities of whole white cumin, fenugreek, mustard and fennel seeds (*sabut safeid zeera, methi, rai, sonf*)

3 garlic cloves, very finely chopped (*lehsun*)

¼ tsp turmeric (*haldi*)

½ tsp red chilli powder (*lal mirch*)

salt to taste (*namak*)

2 tbsp lemon juice (*neeboo ka ras*)

1 tbsp fresh coriander, finely chopped (*hara dhania*)

4 green chillies, finely sliced (*hari mirch*)

1 small onion, peeled and finely chopped (*pyaz*)

To sprout the lentils, pick over and wash them well, and place in a dish. Add enough tepid water to completely cover the grains, and leave, covered, in a dark place or alternatively in a closed box or other container which will keep out all light. Check after every 24 hours, and if the lentils have drunk all the water add some more to cover the grains again. If kept at room temperature the lentils should sprout in a couple of days. Once sprouted, rinse in running cold water but do not rub with your fingers as you may damage the sprouts.

To make the recipe, heat the oil and add the *karri* leaves and the mixed whole seeds. After a minute add the garlic, turmeric, red chilli powder and salt. Stir-fry for another minute before putting in the lentils. Do not fry the spices for too long as the mustard and fenugreek seeds will get bitter if they burn. Stir the lentils gently to mix them with the spices, add 8 fl. oz/250 ml water and cook slowly in a covered pan over low heat. Check after a while and if the *daal* appears too dry add a little more water. When the *daal* is cooked, squeeze in the lemon juice and stir in the chopped coriander, finely sliced green chillies, chopped raw onion and serve.

Moong Daal aur Methi ka Saag
(*Yellow Split Moong with Fenugreek Greens*)

This is a recipe for a 'dry' *daal* dish in which the yellow *moong* and green fenugreek complement each other, each highlighting the other in colour and taste. It is a classical recipe for an attractive and appetizing dish that will go well with any meat, chicken, fish or vegetable dishes on your table. Remember, though, that if you are serving rice, you will need at least one other dish with a gravy.

I am aware that fenugreek greens are not yet easily available at high street supermarkets and corner grocery shops, and that the English are not, therefore, usually familiar with them. Fresh fenugreek is, however, imported regularly into England and is stocked by Indian greengrocers as it is very popular with the British Asian community who would take some trouble to hunt it out. Ask for *methi ka saag*.

8 oz/225 g/1 cup split yellow *moong* lentils (*dhulli moong*)

2 oz/50 g fenugreek greens, or to taste (*methi ka saag*)

3 tbsp cooking oil (*tail*)

1 dsp crushed garlic (*lehsun*)

1 tsp red chilli powder (*lal mirch*)

½ tsp turmeric (*haldi*)

salt to taste (*namak*)

1 dsp finely grated fresh ginger (*adrak*)

1–2 green chillies, finely sliced (seeded if desired) (*hari mirch*)

For the bhagar

2 tbsp cooking oil (*tail*)

1 garlic clove, finely sliced (*lehsun*)

Carefully pick out any grit and wash and strain the lentils. Heat the oil and fry the garlic, red chilli powder and turmeric for a minute before adding the lentils. Stir the lentils with the spices for a further 2 minutes. Add 16 fl. oz/475 ml water and some salt, and after rapidly bringing it to the boil, immediately turn the heat down low. Cover the saucepan and cook for approximately 20 minutes, by which time the *daal* should be tender and the water absorbed. Check to see that this is so.

Wash and break off the fenugreek leaves, discarding the thick stalks, and add to the *daal* once it is tender. Stir well to mix. After 5 minutes stir in the ginger and green chillies, cover tightly to trap in the steam, and cook for 5 more minutes. Transfer to your serving dish. For the *bhagar*, heat the oil in a frying pan and fry the finely sliced rounds of garlic until pale golden. Pour this sizzling hot over the *daal* and serve immediately.

Chilkon vali Moong aur Dhulli Moong

(Split Green and Yellow Moong)

This recipe is unusual, not only because you get to taste two forms of the same *daal* in one dish, but the use of fresh tomatoes and green chillies in the *bhagar* is also extremely uncommon.

4 oz/100 g/½ cup split yellow *moong* lentils (*dhulli moong daal*)

4 oz/100 g/½ cup split green *moong* lentils (*chilkon vali moong daal*)

1 tsp salt, or to taste (*namak*)

1 tsp red chilli powder, or to taste (*lal mirch*)

1 small pat butter (*makhan*)

1 cup fresh coriander leaves, finely chopped (*hara dhania*)

1 tbsp finely chopped fresh ginger (*adrak*)

For the bhagar

3–4 tbsp cooking oil (*tail*)

1 small onion, peeled and finely sliced (*pyaz*)

1 medium tomato, finely chopped (*timatar*)

2–3 green chillies, finely sliced (*hari mirch*)

Mix the two types of lentils in a saucepan and wash them thoroughly. Add 1¼ pints (750 ml) water, the salt and red chilli powder, and after quickly bringing the lentils to a boil, simmer over low heat in a covered saucepan until thick and soft. Using a wooden spoon blend the grains by stirring vigorously round and round for a few minutes. If the *daal* appears too thick, add some more water to bring it to the correct consistency which should be similar, if you can imagine it, to a pea porridge. Stir in the butter, fresh coriander and ginger and take off the heat. Transfer to a serving dish and keep covered while preparing the *bhagar*.

Heat the oil in a frying pan and fry the onion, tomato and green chillies until soft. Pour them and the hot oil over the lentils immediately. Do not stir to mix.

Panchmel
(Five Daals)

This is a delicious, old, traditional North Indian recipe in which these particular five *daals* are cooked together in their split form.

2 oz/50 g/¼ cup split *channa* lentils (*channa daal*)

2 oz/50 g/¼ cup split *arhar* lentils (*arhar daal*)

2 oz/50 g/¼ cup split *mash/urad* lentils (*mash/urad daal*)

2 oz/50 g/¼ cup split *moong* lentils (*moong daal*)

2 oz/50 g/¼ cup split *masoor* lentils (*lal masoor daal*)

4–5 whole dried red chillies, broken (*sabut lal mirch*), or 1 tsp red chilli powder (*lal mirch*)

¼ tsp turmeric (*haldi*)

½ small onion, peeled and chopped (*pyaz*)

salt to taste (*namak*)

1 tbsp finely chopped fresh ginger (*adrak*)

1 small green chilli, finely chopped (*hari mirch*)

1–2 tbsp fresh coriander and/or mint leaves, finely chopped (*hara dhania* and/or *pudeena*)

1 tsp *garam masala* (see page 17)

For the bhagar

3–4 tbsp cooking oil (*tail*)

2 garlic cloves, finely sliced (*lehsun*)

1 dsp white cumin seeds (*sabut safeid zeera*)

For the garnish

fresh mint or coriander, chopped (*pudeena* or *dhania*)

For convenience you can mix the *channa* and *arhar daals* and wash them together. Mix the other three together in a separate utensil and also wash them well. Place the *channa* and *arhar daals* in a saucepan with the broken red chillies, turmeric, chopped onion, salt and 1 pint/600 ml water, and cook first, as these *daals* take longer to become tender. After bringing to a boil, turn the heat down and simmer gently in a covered saucepan for about 20 minutes before adding the remaining three *daals*. When you have added all the *daals* also pour in another ½ pint/300 ml water and continue to cook over low heat in a covered pan stirring occasionally. It is important not to stir too often so reducing the *daals* to a smooth consistency; one of the beauties of this dish is that the different sizes and shapes of the grains should remain visible. When the lentils are tender and have a thick soupy consistency, add the ginger, green chilli, fresh herbs and *garam masala* and cook for just another 5 minutes. Remove from the heat.

For the *bhagar*, heat the oil and brown the garlic and cumin seeds, and pour, still sizzling, over the *daal*. Garnish with fresh mint or coriander.

Dhulli Hui Urad ya Mash ki Daal Khari

(*Split White Mash* or *Urad Lentils*)

This *daal* dish comes from the heart of the best kitchens in Uttar Pradesh. It is known amongst UP *wallahs* as *dastarkhan ki zeenat* or 'the beauty of the dinner table'. However, the important thing to achieve in this recipe, before the dish may qualify for such high praise, is to cook it so that each grain of *daal* is soft, plump and separate and not in the least bit mushy. Such finesse is harder to achieve than you might believe from a glance at this deceptively simple recipe. Although I have suggested how much water should be needed, you must also remain vigilant yourself, adjusting the heat up or down as necessary. The creamy coloured grains of this split *mash daal*, if cooked correctly, look like tiny pearls and the vision is made all the more attractive by the ruby red chillies scattered amongst them. It has such a delicate flavour that to appreciate it fully it needs to be spiced with great restraint, as you will see from the recipe below.

8 oz/225 g/1 cup split white *urad* or *mash* lentils (*dhulli hui urad/mash daal*)

salt to taste (*namak*)

1 tbsp cooking oil (*tail*)

4–5 whole dried red chillies (*sabut lal mirch*)

1½ tbsp peeled and finely sliced strips fresh ginger (*adrak*)

2–3 green chillies, finely sliced (*hari mirch*)

For the bhagar

3–4 tbsp cooking oil or clarified butter (*tail/asli ghee*)

1 small onion, peeled and finely chopped (*pyaz*)

1 dsp white cumin seeds (*sabut safeid zeera*)

For the garnish

2–3 tbsp fresh mint leaves, finely chopped (*pudeena*)

Pick over the lentils for any bits of grit and rinse once or twice. Soak for a couple of hours in water and then wash again thoroughly, discarding the odd few skins that will have come loose. Drain out all the water. Put the lentils in a saucepan with some salt, the cooking oil, whole red chillies and 1½ cups water. Cover and bring rapidly to a boil over high heat, then immediately turn the heat right down and cook until the water has all been absorbed and the lentils are tender. Stir in the ginger and green chillies and cook for another 2 minutes. Transfer the *daal* to a serving dish.

For the *bhagar*, heat the oil in a frying pan and brown the chopped onion. When almost golden add the cumin seeds and fry for another few minutes. Pour this sizzling mixture over the *daal*. Garnish liberally with chopped mint.

Urad/Mash Daal aur Palak
(Split Mash Lentils with Fresh Spinach)

This recipe is doubly delicious when served with a side dish of *mooli* (white radish).

8 oz/225 g/1 cup lentils (*mash/urad daal*)

8 oz/225 g fresh spinach, weighed without stalks (*palak ka saag*), or frozen leaf spinach

1 tsp crushed garlic (*lehsun*)

½ tsp red chilli powder (*lal mirch*)

salt to taste (*namak*)

1 dsp finely chopped fresh ginger (*adrak*)

2 green chillies, finely chopped, or to taste (*hari mirch*)

For the bhagar

cooking oil or clarified butter (*tail/asli ghee*)

1 small onion, peeled and finely chopped (*pyaz*)

2 garlic cloves, finely sliced (*lehsun*)

1–2 green chillies or to taste, finely sliced, (*hari mirch*)

Carefully pick over and wash the lentils. Wash and chop the spinach. Put the lentils in a saucepan with 3 cups water, the crushed garlic, red chilli powder and some salt and after bringing to a rapid boil turn the heat down and simmer in a covered pan until the *daal* is tender. Stir with a spoon to *ghonto* or blend the lentils. Add the chopped spinach with the ginger and green chillies and mix well with the *daal*. Cover the saucepan and cook over a tiny flame for another few minutes until the spinach is tender. Transfer to a serving dish.

For the *bhagar*, heat a little clarified butter or cooking oil in a frying pan and fry the onion, garlic and green chillies. When the onions are golden brown pour this sizzling mixture over the *daal* and serve.

Split Arhar ki Daal I
(Split Arhar Lentils)

This is a rather beautiful looking *daal*, clearly distinct from all the others, with large shiny mustardy-gold grains. It is somewhat sweet tasting and it is therefore usual to serve with it some sour limes or other contrasting tastes, such as raw onion rings or fresh mint leaves, on the side.

8 oz/225 g/1 cup split *arhar* lentils
  (*arhar ki daal*)
½ tsp turmeric (*haldi*)
salt to taste (*namak*)
2 medium garlic cloves, crushed
  (*lehsun*)

1 tsp red chilli powder (*lal mirch*)
2–3 whole green chillies (*hari mirch*)

For the bhagar
3 tbsp cooking oil (*tail*)
1 garlic clove, finely sliced (*lehsun*)

Soak the lentils for an hour. Cook them in a covered pan in 1 pint/600 ml water, adding just the turmeric and some salt. When the *daal* is almost tender and most of the water has evaporated, add the crushed garlic, and red chilli powder. Stir vigorously with a wooden spoon to break down the grains and blend the *daal*. Then throw in the whole green chillies, add some more water if necessary, and after stirring to mix all the ingredients, cover the saucepan and cook for another few minutes.

For the *bhagar*, heat the oil in a frying pan and fry the garlic slices until golden. Pour the hot oil and garlic over the *daal* and serve.

Split Arhar ki Daal II
(Split Arhar Lentils)

This recipe can also be made with three parts *arhar daal* and one part split *urad/mash daal*.

8 oz/225 g/1 cup split *arhar* lentils (*arhar ki daal*)

3 whole large dried red chillies (*sabut lal mirch*)

salt to taste (*namak*)

1 dsp finely chopped fresh ginger (*adrak*)

2 green chillies, finely chopped (*hari mirch*)

2 tbsp fresh mint, finely chopped (*pudeena*)

For the bhagar

1 small onion, peeled (*pyaz*)

3–4 tbsp cooking oil (*tail*)

Soak the lentils for an hour. Cook in a covered pan with 1 pint/600 ml water, adding the dried chillies and some salt. Stir gently only now and again until the *daal* is very tender. Add the ginger, green chillies and fresh mint and stir to mix.

For the *bhagar*, either finely chop the onion or cut into rings, and fry in the oil until golden brown. Pour this over the lentils and serve.

Channa Daal
(Split Yellow Channa Lentils)

There are other varieties of *channa daal* such as *kabli channa* or *chola* as well as *kala channa*, but when we refer to *channa daal* or *channay ki daal*, we mean those golden yellow lentils which also belong to the chickpea family whose nearest relative familiar to westerners is the yellow split chickpea, which is very similar but not exactly the same. Indian *channa daal* is readily available at all Indian grocers which stock lentils. This *daal* has been hulled and split and has large round grains.

Channay ki daal is rich and more nutritious than *masoor* and *moong*. It needs to be pre-soaked, takes longer to cook, and is harder work for the stomach to digest. On account of the fullness of its flavour it is frequently referred to as a meat substitute or sometimes praised for being 'even tastier than meat'. It can be cooked on its own and also with meat or vegetables. I have never quite understood why it is so seldom eaten at homely everyday meals, but is reserved for more special occasions.

8 oz/225 g/1 cup split *channa* lentils or yellow split chickpeas (*channa daal*)

1 tsp salt, or to taste (*namak*)

1 tbsp crushed garlic (*lehsun*)

½ tsp ground white cumin (*safeid zeera*)

½ tsp turmeric (*haldi*)

1 tsp red chilli powder (*lal mirch*)

1 tsp freshly ground *garam masala* (see page 17)

fresh coriander leaves, finely chopped (*hara dhania*)

1–2 green chillies, finely sliced (*hari mirch*)

For the bhagar

3–4 tbsp cooking oil (*tail*)

1 small onion, peeled and sliced into fine rings or half rings (*pyaz*)

1 tsp white cumin seeds (*sabut safeid zeera*)

For the garnish

1 tbsp fine strips peeled fresh ginger (*adrak*)

1–2 green chillies, finely sliced (optional) (*hari mirch*)

1 tbsp fresh coriander leaves, finely chopped (*hara dhania*)

lemon wedges (*neeboo*)

Thoroughly wash the *channa* and pre-soak for 1–2 hours before cooking. Add 1 pint (600 ml) water and some salt, and after bringing it to the boil, turn down the heat and simmer gently for approximately 20 minutes, by which time the *daal* should be half done. Then add the garlic, cumin, turmeric and red chilli powder, and cook in a covered pan over low heat until the *daal* is soft. Take off the heat and using a wooden spoon stir vigorously round and round to *ghonto* or blend the *daal*. Do not blend completely as in this *daal* the grains should remain somewhat visible. Cook again over low heat for 10 minutes, adding the *garam masala*, fresh coriander and green chillies. Transfer the *daal* to a serving dish.

For the *bhagar*, heat the oil and brown the sliced onions. Add the white cumin seeds just as the onions are beginning to turn colour. Pour the browned onions, cumin seeds and hot oil over the *daal*. Garnish liberally with fine strips of fresh ginger, chopped green chillies and fresh coriander. Serve with lemon wedges on the side as it is popular to squeeze some fresh lemon juice over this *daal* when eating.

Channa Daal aur Karelay
(Split Chickpeas and Bitter Gourds)

1 lb/450 g/2 cups split *channa* lentils or yellow chickpeas (*channa daal*)
1 lb/450 g bitter gourds (*karelay*)
salt to taste (*namak*)
8 oz/225 g onions, peeled and finely sliced into rings or half rings (*pyaz*)
mustard oil (*sarson ka tail*)
3 medium garlic cloves, crushed (*lehsun*)
1½ tsp finely grated fresh ginger (*adrak*)

1 tsp turmeric (*haldi*)
1 tsp red chilli powder (*lal mirch*)
½ tsp ground coriander (*dhania*)
¼ tsp each of nigella, fennel, white cumin and mustard seeds (*kalonji, sonf, sabut safeid zeera* and *rai*)
1 tbsp lemon juice (*neeboo ka ras*)

For the bhagar
mustard oil (*sarson ka tail*)
2 oz/150 g onion rings (*pyaz*)
1 garlic clove, finely sliced (*lehsun*)

Pick over the *channa* and wash them in several changes of water and keep to one side. Peel away the knobbly scale-like outer skin of the bitter gourds, slit them open down one side and scoop out their seeds. Cut them horizontally across into fine rounds. Rub with salt and leave for 15 minutes. Wash them in cold water, strain and set aside.

Fry the onions in about 5 tablespoons hot oil until brown then, using a slotted spoon, lift them out and reserve. In this same oil, over low heat, now fry the garlic and ginger for 1 minute, and then add the ground spices closely followed by the seeds and fry for about another minute. Put in the lentils and stir to mix with the spices. Add some salt and 28 fl. oz (825 ml) water, and after bringing to a rapid boil cook in a covered pan over low heat. Check after some time and see if you need to add any more water.

In a separate pan heat some oil and fry the sliced gourds until they are lightly browned. Lift them out of the oil with a perforated spoon and put them to one side with the onions fried earlier.

When the *daal* is almost tender, add the fried gourds and onions together with the lemon juice, cover once again and leave on very low heat for a few more minutes until the lentils are completely done. Do not stir too vigorously as the grains of *daal* should retain their shape in this dish.

For the *bhagar*, heat 2–3 tablespoons oil and fry the onion rings and sliced garlic. When golden brown pour over the *daal* and serve.

Karhi

If I had the power I would make it mandatory for anyone who has never known *karhi* to try this dish. I have only your best interests at heart and am convinced that the experience would gladden your palates and awaken even the most indulged and tired senses to an exquisitely unusual and new taste.

Karhi (pictured on the cover) is a lemon-yellow, creamy, yoghurt-based dish, which is thickened by being gently simmered for some time with gram flour, and in which deep-fried golden brown *pakoras* (made from the same spicy flour) are immersed. (This flour is called *besan* and is made from chickpeas. It is sold in Indian shops, sometimes under the name of gram flour.) Finally the dish is garnished and seasoned with crispy brown onions and whole spices still sizzling in hot oil. This is a Punjabi recipe and is somewhat different to the *karhi* eaten by Gujerati people. It is a simple, healthy vegetarian dish which is usually served with plain boiled rice and some other vegetable on the side.

For the karhi
1 lb/450 g natural yoghurt (*dahi*)
4 oz/100 g gram flour (*besan*)
3 oz/75 g onion, peeled and chopped (*pyaz*)
½ tsp turmeric (*haldi*)
1 tsp red chilli powder (*lal mirch*)
1 tsp ground coriander (*dhania*)
1 dsp crushed garlic (*lehsun*)
1 dsp grated fresh ginger (*adrak*)
1 tsp salt, or to taste (*namak*)
5–6 *karri* leaves (*karri patta*)

For the pakoras
6 oz/175 g gram flour (*besan*)
6 fl oz/175 ml water
2 garlic cloves, crushed (*lehsun*)
½ tsp red chilli powder (*lal mirch*)
1 green chilli (*hari mirch*)
1 tsp ground white cumin (*safeid zeera*)

2 tbsp fresh coriander leaves, finely chopped (*hara dhania*)
salt to taste (*namak*)
plenty of cooking oil (*tail*)

For the bhagar
4 fl. oz cooking oil (*tail*)
1 medium onion, peeled and sliced into fine rings or half rings (*pyaz*)
2 tsp white cumin seeds (*sabut safeid zeera*)
½ tsp fenugreek seeds (*methi dana*)
½ tsp black mustard seeds (*rai*)
5–6 *karri* leaves (*karri patta*)

For the garnish
2 tbsp fresh coriander leaves, finely chopped (*hara dhania*)
1–2 green chillies, finely sliced (*hari mirch*)

Stage One

If you have an electric blender, use it, as it makes life much easier when making this dish.

To make the *karhi*, whisk the yoghurt, and mix in the *gram* flour, a little at a time, so that it blends smoothly. Purée the chopped onion in the blender so that it is evenly mixed in with the yoghurt. Add the other ground spices and the garlic and ginger, and whisk all the ingredients thoroughly. Do not add salt at this stage as the yoghurt may curdle.

Pour the mixture into a saucepan and add $2\frac{1}{2}$–3 pints/1·5–1·75 litres water. Bring it to a boil over medium heat, stirring all the time. As soon as it comes to the boil, turn the heat down very low and place a saucer upside down in the centre of the saucepan. This is to prevent the *karhi* from boiling over. Simmer gently over very low heat for half an hour, then add the salt and *karri* leaves. Continue to simmer for another hour by which time the *karhi* will be a thick soupy consistency.

Do not put a lid on the saucepan while the *karhi* is simmering. However you will probably need to cover it with a wire net anti-splatter device, if you have one, as every now and again the *karhi* is liable to leap-frog right out of the pan. If you are not careful, your cooker and the surrounding area will get awfully messy.

Stage Two

The next step is to make the *pakoras* and immerse them in the cooked *karhi*. Mix the gram flour with water to make a smooth batter, about the consistency of a coating batter. Add to this all the other ingredients except for the oil.

Heat a generous quantity of oil, at least half the depth of a large frying pan and drop in a dessertspoonful of batter at a time. If the oil is sufficiently hot, each spoonful should first sink then immediately float up to the surface again. Turn each *pakora* over so it browns evenly on both sides. Fry as many at one time as you can manage, but in any case don't do any more than the pan will hold in a single layer. Fry several batches if necessary, lifting them out of the oil with a slotted spoon and laying them on absorbent paper to soak up any extra grease. The *pakoras* should be well fried to a deep brown, so that they do not disintegrate when soaked in the *karhi*. Only immerse them in the *karhi* about an hour before you are ready to eat. Reheat well before serving, transfer to deep dish and proceed to next stage.

Stage Three

For the *bhagar*, heat the oil in a frying pan and brown the onions. Just as the onions are turning golden, add the seeds and *karri* leaves and stir-fry for another minute. Pour this sizzling hot mixture into the dish containing the *karhi* and *pakoras*. Garnish with the finely chopped fresh coriander and green chillies and serve.

POULTRY AND GAME DISHES

· Poultry and Game Dishes ·

'My children only eat chicken,' my father would remark sarcastically to emphasize just how thoroughly spoilt he thought we were. In the subcontinent chicken is the most expensive meat available, and has become synonymous with good living, hospitality and privilege. Almost all the regional languages use chicken as a metaphor to describe affluence and indulgence. To honour your guests properly, there must be at least one chicken dish on the table. To avoid this, and still appear welcoming, could prove both more expensive and troublesome. For an adequate substitute, a traditional sense of Indian hospitality would require a main dish of the calibre of a *biryani* or *haleem* or, at the very minimum, a much greater than usual selection of dishes to acknowledge the special nature of the occasion.

My father is an intelligent and complex man and so it was inevitable that he would develop a complicated relationship with chickens. The inherent difficulty he has in making simple decisions simply made it impossible for him either to give up, or to relish openly, the varied and wonderful chicken dishes my mother spread before him. Almost like grace before a meal, he would mutter and grumble about how chicken was a highly over-rated bird with no merit which he had to suffer only because it was a favourite with the rest of us. Sadly for him, none of his offspring were sufficiently obliging or well-mannered to let him get away with so transparent a subterfuge. We would lie silently in wait until the end of the meal when we pounced triumphantly to confiscate the heap of tiny, perfectly chewed bones which were to be our exhibits 'A' to 'D' and conclusive proof of his secret passion. While the corners of his mouth may have lifted just a fraction in a give-away smile, his legal training and stubborn nature never allowed him to change his plea to guilty.

Most of us no longer have any memory of how good a chicken can taste. Our children growing up in the cities have probably never had the privilege of eating free-range chickens. Poultry farming is such big business that the few lone chickens that are allowed to roam free are very much the odd hens out; the once fun-loving rooster that enjoyed natural competition is no more than a machine devised by industry to provide the necessary stimulus for the reproductive process; and those poor chicks so berated by my father, the end product of this ghastly tale, are deprived of any taste of real grain and fed from birth on specially prepared fish meal to speed up their growth and encourage weight gain. It is no surprise then that they taste little better than bland copies of some forgotten original. But there may be hope for those of us carnivores who feel cheated and hanker for the taste of 'real meat': the trendsetters in the business are making efforts to meet changing customer demand by rearing more free-range chickens and feeding birds on pure grain, such as corn.

To cook or not to cook chicken for an important dinner party is a common dilemma shared by many 'new Britons' or other displaced people living and entertaining in different countries of the West, whose journeys began in India, Pakistan or Bangladesh. It illustrates well the difficulties of transferring an entire culinary tradition to a new culture. Having always known chicken to be the most expensive and highly prized meat, and beef to be the cheapest and least valued, on coming here people at first avoid chicken and buy beef to economize. They are then justifiably confused and are left wondering how they would afford to eat any meat if even beef was being sold at these prices. Similarly you can no longer buy what you have always known to be the commonest vegetables, as here in the West, they are exotic imported luxuries to indulge yourself with at the same price as meat or when homesickness blues are deepest. Once the new realities are discovered and the initial confusions resolved, it finally sinks in that there is nothing for it but to topple over in a swift somersault all those preconceptions formed under different geographic and economic conditions, and to invent new eating habits and codes of hospitality better suited to the new habitat. The beauty of the trick is that the cuisine is no less authentic or divorced from its traditions despite these difficulties of migration.

Personally I was very pleased to find chickens put in their place in the West. It is true that I have always been fond of chicken, but the pomp and snobbery surrounding it in the subcontinent did make it a little hard to swallow. The good news is that, because it holds this highly elevated position in Indian cookery, there are chicken dishes that are nothing short of being creations of genius. Several of these dishes are extremely simple and quick to make, which they have to be as any chicken worth the name cooks so easily that it will not survive lengthy cooking techniques.

In Indian cookery all poultry is skinned before being cooked. Except in those recipes which ask you to keep the chicken whole or to cut it into quarters or into small pieces off the bone, there is a standard technique used for jointing chickens. Skin the chicken, cut the leg joints into two, thigh and drumstick, separate the wings and cut each breast into two or three pieces, depending on the size of the chicken.

In many of the recipes that follow, the chicken will need to be cut into ten or twelve pieces in the manner described above. Where the recipe is not specific about the length of time needed to cook these, you should estimate about 45 minutes to an hour. Where the chicken is cooked whole, it is likely to take an hour to an hour and a half to be well cooked.

Sabut Murghi Dahi Main
(Whole Chicken in Yoghurt)

I love the gentle seasoning and mild flavour of this dish in which the chicken is marinated in an abundance of yoghurt, delicately spiced with black pepper and cumin, before it is braised in a *kachoomar* of onions, fresh tomatoes, coriander leaves and green chillies. My over-riding sense of this recipe is one of goodness and well-being that comes from its use of fresh wholesome ingredients.

1 medium roasting chicken, skinned but whole (*murghi*)

3 eggs (*unday*)

4 cups fresh coriander leaves, finely chopped (*hara dhania*)

8 oz/225 g tomatoes, finely chopped (*timatar*)

5 green chillies (a mild variety if you wish), finely chopped (*hari mirch*)

lemon juice (*neboo ka ras*)

salt to taste (*namak*)

½ tsp ground white cumin (*safeid zeera*)

½ tsp freshly ground black pepper (*kali mirch*)

1½ lb/700 g natural yoghurt (*dahi*)

clarified butter or cooking oil (*asli ghee/tail*)

1 medium onion, peeled and coarsely chopped (*pyaz*)

1 tsp red chilli powder (*lal mirch*)

¼ tsp turmeric (*haldi*)

4 medium potatoes, peeled and halved (*aloo*)

Hard-boil and peel the eggs. Mix the chopped fresh coriander, tomatoes and green chillies together with a generous squeeze of lemon juice and a sprinkling of salt. Carefully place the hard-boiled eggs and about half of the above mixture in the stomach of the chicken and tie it firmly so it stays in place. Put the chicken in a bowl. Mix the cumin, black pepper and some salt into the yoghurt, pour this over the chicken and set aside to marinate for an hour or two.

When you are ready to cook the chicken, first heat the *asli ghee* or oil in a saucepan large enough to hold the chicken and fry the onion until golden. Add the red chilli powder and turmeric followed by the remaining tomato, coriander and green chilli mixture, and stir-fry all these ingredients together. After a few minutes add the potatoes and chicken in its marinade. Cover the saucepan and cook over a slow flame until tender. Add 8 fl. oz/250 ml or less water to make a gravy and to prevent the spices from sticking to the bottom of the pan. You may want to turn the chicken over a few times while it cooks so it can brown evenly all around.

Murgh Irani
(Chicken with Fresh Cream, Saffron and Green Cardamoms)

It was at first very deflating for my ego to find that a dish which I took great pride in as being my own invention was in fact so similar to one that has always existed and is known to many by this name. The experience served to remind me that there really is not that much that is unique or original any more in cookery. Small variations and experienced cooks can make the same recipe taste new in their handling of it.

I suspect that this dish is called *Irani* because of the generous use of saffron and green cardamoms. These are luxury spices in the subcontinent and you will find that most North Indian recipes which call for their use are named something *Mughlai* or, as in this case, *Irani*, as an acknowledgement of the Persian influence.

2–2½ lb/900 g–1·1 kg roasting chicken, skinned and cut into pieces (see page 163) (*murghi*)

2½ medium onions, peeled and chopped (*pyaz*)

clarified butter (*asli ghee*) or cooking oil (*tail*)

6–8 medium garlic cloves, crushed (*lehsun*)

1 tbsp finely grated fresh ginger (*adrak*)

1 tsp red chilli powder (*lal mirch*)

½ tsp ground black cumin (*kala zeera*)

10 black peppercorns, ground (*kali mirch*)

8 oz/225 g natural yoghurt (*dahi*)

4 fl. oz/120 ml single cream (*malai*)

salt to taste (*namak*)

10–12 small green cardamoms (*choti elaichee*)

1 tsp saffron (*zafran*)

1 tbsp slivered blanched almonds (*badam*)

Fry the onions in some *asli ghee* (preferably) until a rich golden brown, then lift out with a perforated spoon and set aside for the moment. Fry the chicken pieces in this same *ghee* over a medium high heat to seal in the juices.

Once this is done, lower the heat a little and add the garlic and ginger. After allowing them to fry for a minute, add the red chilli powder followed a couple of minutes later by the ground cumin and pepper. When the chicken has been well fried in these spices, pour in the yoghurt and cream, which should be whisked together. Stir finally to mix all the ingredients evenly, add a little salt, then cover the saucepan with a lid and leave to simmer slowly. The chicken should cook in its own juices and the moisture released by the yoghurt and cream.

While the chicken is cooking, crush the green cardamoms in an electric grinder and mix them with the fried onions set aside earlier. Lightly roast the saffron in a frying pan over low heat and crumble it over the onion and cardamoms. At the stage when the chicken is about three-quarters cooked you should put in the saffron–onion–cardamom mixture as well as the almonds and after mixing them in well, cover the saucepan once again and let it simmer until the chicken is quite tender.

Dhaniyay ki Murghi
(Lemon Coriander Chicken)

The special flavour of this dish comes from the fresh coriander which is commonly seen only in tiny quantities as a garnish but is used here with great generosity and treated almost as though it were a vegetable rather than a herb. Combined with this, the sour tang of lemons that makes itself felt through the spices adds the perfect finishing touch to an undeniably appetizing dish. Take care only to add the coriander leaves right at the end as you might hurt both its flavour and good looks if you cook it for too long.

The flavour of green chillies is important to the recipe and I have suggested the use of the large Spanish chilli as it is relatively mild. For those of you who want to enjoy the flavour but get no pleasure at all from the sting of the chilli, it is probably advisable to remove the seeds which is where the real danger lies.

Although you can cook this dish in any conventionally shaped saucepan or cooking pot that is handy, in my experience the *karhai* or wok is the most comfortable shape to use, as it enables you to stir the chicken pieces and comfortably turn them without danger of their breaking.

2–2½ lb/900 g–1·1 kg roasting chicken, skinned and cut into 8–10 pieces (see page 163) (*murghi*)

2 medium onions, peeled and coarsely chopped (*pyaz*)

vegetable oil or clarified butter (*tail/asli ghee*)

1 level tsp turmeric (*haldi*)

5 medium garlic cloves, crushed (*lehsun*)

1 dsp finely grated fresh ginger (*adrak*)

1 tsp red chilli powder (*lal mirch*)

salt to taste (*namak*)

5 oz/150 g natural yoghurt, lightly whisked (*dahi*)

2–3 large Spanish green chillies, finely chopped (*hari mirch*)

3–4 cups fresh coriander leaves, finely chopped (*hara dhania*)

4 tbsp lemon juice, or to taste (*neeboo ka ras*)

Fry the onions in the *asli ghee* or cooking oil until they turn a deep almondy colour. At this stage add the turmeric, garlic, ginger, red chilli powder and some salt, and stir-fry these spices together for a few seconds before putting in the chicken pieces. Continue stirring and gently frying the chicken and spices together for a few minutes until they are well mixed and the chicken is a pale golden brown. Now add the yoghurt, a little at a time, and stir it into the pot until it is smoothly blended with the spices. Turn the heat down to low, cover and allow it to simmer for 20–30 minutes. When the chicken is almost completely cooked, add the chopped green chillies, coriander leaves and lemon juice and stir well together. Replace the lid and simmer until tender.

Kali Mirch ki Murghi
(Black Pepper Chicken)

In this recipe, chicken is fried in clarified butter simply with some browned onions and natural yoghurt until it is almost completely cooked. At the last minute coarsely ground peppercorns are scattered into the saucepan, instantly infusing the dish with their rich flavour and aroma. It is important to add the black pepper only right at the end, both to preserve the freshness of the spice and also because adding the pepper too early would ruin the delicate colour of the chicken.

2½–3 lb/1·1–1·4 kg roasting chicken, skinned and cut into pieces (see page 163 (*murghi*)
lemon juice (*neeboo ka ras*)
12 oz/350 g onion, peeled and finely chopped (*pyaz*)
clarified butter (*asli ghee*)

8 oz/225 g natural yoghurt, whisked (*dahi*)
salt to taste (*namak*)
1 heaped tsp black peppercorns, coarsely ground (*sabut kali mirch*)
lemon wedges (*neeboo*)

Drench the chicken pieces in lemon juice and leave for 3–4 hours.

Take a large heavy-bottomed saucepan and fry the finely chopped onion in a generous quantity of clarified butter until golden brown. Add the chicken pieces, discarding the lemon juice and any moisture that may have been released. Fry over high heat for a few minutes until the chicken loses its raw appearance, then pour in the whisked yoghurt and some salt, and stir to mix well. Turn the heat down, cover the pan and cook until almost tender.

When the chicken is close to being ready, take the lid off the saucepan, turn the heat up and add the ground black pepper. Stir-fry over high heat and mix the pepper evenly with the chicken. After a few minutes turn the heat down again, cover the saucepan and cook over gentle heat until the chicken is ready. Serve with wedges of lemon.

Hyderabadi Murgh Qorma
(Chicken Qorma Hyderabadi Style)

Just knowing that a particular dish is cooked in the Hyderabadi style arouses in me feelings of eager anticipation and pleasure in the certainty that it will be delicious. It was with this complete trust in my own weakness for Hyderabadi food in general, and the inspirational use of almonds, coconut and poppy seeds in the preparation of this dish in particular, that I accepted, without question, the present of this recipe from my mother's friend Tehniat Baig, promising her to use it in this book. At the time I had neither tried nor tasted it but it was an excellent decision and a promise it gives me pleasure to keep.

3 lb/1·4 kg roasting chicken, skinned and cut into 8–10 pieces (see page 163) (*murghi*)

salt to taste (*namak*)

1 tbsp finely grated fresh ginger (*adrak*)

1 tbsp crushed garlic (*lehsun*)

8 oz/225 g natural yoghurt (*dahi*)

2 tsp poppy seeds (*khas khas*)

2 oz/50 g almonds (*badam*)

2 tbsp desiccated coconut (*naryal*)

6 small cardamoms (*choti elaichee*)

2–3 large cardamoms (*bari elaichee*)

½ tsp black cumin seeds (*sabut kala zeera*)

½ in./1·2 cm cinnamon stick (*dalchini*)

1 tsp red chilli powder (*lal mirch*)

1 tsp turmeric (*haldi*)

8–10 oz/225–275 g onions, peeled and finely chopped (*pyaz*)

4 oz/100 g clarified butter (*asli ghee*) or cooking oil (*tail*)

3 tbsp fresh coriander leaves, finely chopped (*hara dhania*)

1 green chilli, finely chopped (*hari mirch*)

Whisk the salt, ginger and garlic with the yoghurt and marinate the chicken pieces in it for at least an hour. In the meantime dry-roast the poppy seeds, almonds and coconut on a *tava*, cast-iron skillet or non-stick frying pan, and reduce to powder in an electric grinder. Also freshly grind the small and large cardamoms, black cumin seeds and cinnamon. Combine the ground ingredients with the red chilli powder and turmeric.

Fry the onions in the *asli ghee* or oil, lifting them out when they are golden brown. Crush these fried onions with a few short whizzes of your electric blender and mix them in with the dry spices.

Using the same oil in which you fried the onions, now fry the chicken pieces in their marinade over a fairly high heat for a few minutes, and then add the onion and spice mixture. Stir well until all the ingredients are evenly mixed and then turn the heat down and cook gently until the chicken is tender. When almost completely done, add the fresh coriander and green chilli, cover again and simmer for a few more minutes.

Murghi ka Tikka
(Grilled or Barbecued Chicken Tikka)

Your may choose to make this recipe by cutting up a chicken into the usual pieces (see page 163) or you can, if you prefer, just buy drumsticks or breast pieces instead. you could also just as easily use this same recipe to skewer much smaller pieces off the bone. This is such a simple yet tasty way to eat chicken, and I have found it particularly useful either for summer barbecues or for large parties where I may want as many as three or four chickens. The marinade can be prepared with the minimum of fuss after which all that remains is to grill the chicken slowly shortly before you are ready to serve the meal. I prefer not to use artificial food colouring to give it that bright red appearance that has become associated with shop- or restaurant-bought *tikkas* and *tandoori* cooking.

2–2½ lb/900 g–1·1 kg pieces of chicken, skinned (*murghi*)

4 oz/125 g natural yoghurt (or lemon juice) (*dahi* or *neeboo ka ras*)

4 medium garlic cloves, crushed (*lehsun*)

1 fat 1 in./2·5 cm cube fresh ginger, peeled and finely grated (*adrak*)

1 tsp red chilli powder, or to taste (*lal mirch*)

1 tsp ground coriander (*dhania*)

½ tsp ground white cumin (*safeid zeera*)

salt to taste (*namak*)

Add the yoghurt (or lemon juice) to the other ingredients, and mix well with a fork. Prick the pieces of chicken with a fork, coat in the spicy marinade and set aside for at least 2 hours.

If making the *tikkas* indoors under a grill then spread some foil over the bottom of your grill pan and arrange the chicken pieces over it. Grill under medium to low heat turning the pieces over from time to time to ensure that they cook evenly all around. If cooking on an outdoor barbecue the procedure is the same except that you will place your chicken over coals. Serve when the meat is quite tender.

Murgh Fry I
(Fried Chicken)

Fried chicken is a popular choice, equally welcome as the main dish at a big meal or simply with a green salad or yoghurt *raita* for lunch. Be sure to buy only small, young birds as they are best for frying.

Here you have two recipes to choose from which are quite different to each other. The first is for a moist dish which has a small amount of gravy clinging to the chicken pieces, whereas in the second (see below) the chicken is first cooked just with a few cloves and some garlic and then dipped in beaten eggs and coated with highly seasoned *gram* flour before being crisply fried.

I find it easiest to make this dish in a wok as it has the space to hold the pieces of chicken in a single layer which makes frying them more comfortable and efficient.

2½ lb/1·1 kg chicken, skinned and cut into pieces (see page 163) (*murghi*)

4 fl. oz/120 ml cooking oil (*tail*)

6–8 oz/175–225 g onions, peeled and finely chopped (*pyaz*)

1 tsp crushed garlic (*lehsun*)

2 tomatoes, very finely chopped (*timatar*)

4–6 green chillies, finely chopped, or to taste (*hari mirch*)

2–3 tbsp fresh coriander leaves, finely chopped (*hara dhania*)

salt to taste (*namak*)

1 tsp freshly ground black pepper (*kali mirch*)

For the garnish
fresh sliced tomatoes (*timatar*)

Heat the cooking oil and fry the onions just until they become soft and translucent. Then add the garlic, tomatoes, green chillies, fresh coriander and salt and stir-fry over high heat for a minute before adding the pieces of chicken. Start by frying the chicken over medium to high heat until the pieces are lightly browned and the ingredients are all mixed together, then turn the heat down and cook until tender (about 30 minutes). Allow all excess moisture to evaporate by the time the chicken is cooked which may mean taking the lid off at the end and turning the heat up for a short while. As a final gesture stir-fry over high heat for a few moments before taking the chicken off the heat. Sprinkle with freshly ground black pepper, garnish with sliced fresh tomatoes and serve.

Murgh Fry II
(Crispy Fried Chicken)

2–2½ lb/900 g–1·1 kg chicken,
    skinned and cut into pieces (see
    page 163 (*murghi*)
6 garlic cloves, peeled (*lehsun*)
2 cloves (*laung*)
salt to taste (*namak*)

either
Grind together
¼ tsp white cumin seeds (*sabut safeid
    zeera*)
¼ tsp black cumin seeds (*sabut kala
    zeera*)
¼ tsp coriander seeds (*sabut dhania*)
5 black peppercorns (*sabut kali
    mirch*)
2 cloves (*laung*)
2 large cardamoms (*bari elaichee*)
1 in./2·5 cm cinnamon stick (*dalchini*)

or
2 tsp freshly ground *garam masala*
    (see page 17)

½ tsp red chilli powder (*lal mirch*)
1 cup *gram* flour (*besan*)
3 eggs (*unday*)
4 fl. oz/120 ml cooking oil (*tail*)

Cook the chicken pieces with the whole garlic cloves, some salt and just enough water that by the time the chicken is tender, about 30–45 minutes, the water should have evaporated. Spread the chicken pieces out to cool.

Using *either* the whole freshly ground spices *or* the 2 teaspoons freshly ground *garam masala*, mix with the red chilli powder, *gram* flour and some salt. Beat the eggs well and dip each piece of chicken first in egg and then coat it with the seasoned *gram* flour.

When all the chicken has been prepared in this way, heat the oil and fry quickly until a crispy brown. Do not fry any more at one time than you can handle comfortably or than the pan will hold in a single layer.

Desi Roast Murgh
(Indian Roast Chicken)

This mildly spiced roast chicken sits just as comfortably on an Indian table as it does at a European meal. In fact it was one of our favourite 'English foods' when we were growing up in Bombay. In my mother's kitchen, as in most Indian kitchens, this roast is usually made on top of the stove in a large heavy-bottomed saucepan and not, for some reason, in the oven. I have myself carried on the same tradition out of habit, although I am sure there is no reason why you should not cook it in the oven if you prefer. This chicken is also very tasty eaten cold or made into a chicken salad.

1 medium roasting chicken, whole but skinned (*murghi*)
4 fat garlic cloves, crushed (*lehsun*)
1 × 2 in./5 cm cube fresh ginger, peeled and finely grated (*adrak*)
salt (*namak*)

1 tsp red chilli powder (*lal mirch*)
8 oz/225 g natural yoghurt (*dahi*)
cooking oil or clarified butter (*tail/asli ghee*)
2 large cardamoms (*bari elaichee*)

Mix the crushed garlic, finely grated ginger, some salt and the red chilli powder, with the yoghurt, and whisk with a fork. Smother the chicken with this mixture and set aside for at least an hour.

When the chicken has marinated long enough, heat plenty of oil or *asli ghee* in a saucepan. (This is especially important if you are making it on top of the cooker; you can drain away the excess oil before serving and though that might sound a bit wasteful it does cook better in a lot of oil.) Throw the large cardamoms into the hot oil, followed closely by the chicken smothered in marinade. Fry over a fairly high flame, slowly turning to cook on all sides. When it has been fried all around, turn down the heat, cover and cook slowly until tender. While the chicken is cooking you should also turn it over a few times so it browns evenly on all sides.

Once the chicken is tender, lift it out and place it on a serving dish. Spoon off the extra oil from the gravy in the saucepan and pour the rich brown sauce over the chicken and serve.

Karhai Chicken

(Stir-Fried Chicken with Onions, Tomatoes and Peppers)

A *karhai* is a heavy cast-iron cooking utensil which is similar to a wok, but rounder and deeper. It is most commonly used for deep-frying Indian sweets, *pooris*, *pakoras* and so on. In this dish its use for stir-frying small pieces of chicken with onion rings, tomatoes and green peppers has become traditional although it is perhaps a little uncharacteristic.

Karhai chicken is one of those dishes that has gained such widespread popularity that it is difficult to place it any more within one distinct regional cuisine. Some say that it originated in Afghanistan from where it travelled over the border to the North-West Frontier province in Pakistan, and was later appropriated by Punjab and Sindh.

5 boneless chicken breast fillets, skinned, weighing approximately 1½ lb/700 g, cut into small 1 in./2·5 cm pieces (*murghi*)
3 garlic cloves, peeled (*lehsun*)
1 × 1 in./2·5 cm cube fresh ginger, peeled and cut in half (*adrak*)
cooking oil (*tail*)
1 lb/450 g onions, peeled and cut into rings (*pyaz*)

1 lb/450 g tomatoes, roughly chopped (*timatar*)
salt to taste (*namak*)
1 tsp red chilli powder (*lal mirch*)
½ tsp nigella seeds (*kalonji*)
½ lb/225 g green peppers, seeded and sliced into strips (*simla ki mirch*)
2 green chillies, cut in half (*hari mirch*)

Cook the chicken pieces in a very small quantity of water with the garlic and ginger. When the meat is about three-quarters cooked, throw out any water that has not already evaporated, and also discard the garlic and ginger.

Heat a little oil in a *karhai* or wok and add the onions, tomatoes, and chicken pieces with a little salt. Cook over gentle heat for a while, stirring occasionally. When the onions and tomatoes are half cooked and the chicken is almost tender, add the red chilli powder, nigella seeds, green peppers and the halved green chillies. Turn the heat up and stir-fry to brown the chicken and cook the peppers. When the chicken is cooked and the colour of the dish blossoms out and smells peppery, you will know it is ready.

Chicken Cocktail Snacks or Starters

Serve these small delectable morsels of chicken at a party with drinks or as appetizers before a meal.

3–4 chicken breast fillets, skinned, weighing approx. 12 oz/350 g (*murghi*)

4 tbsp lemon juice (*neeboo ka ras*)

1 tbsp crushed garlic (*lehsun*)

1 tbsp finely grated fresh ginger (*adrak*)

cooking oil (*tail*)

4–5 whole dried red chillies, coarsely ground (*sabut lal mirch*)

a pinch of turmeric (*haldi*)

½ tsp ground coriander (*dhania*)

salt to taste (*namak*)

1 cup coriander leaves, finely chopped (*hara dhania*)

1 oz/25 g butter (*makhan*)

Cut the chicken breasts into small ½ in./1·2 cm cubes, and marinate them with the lemon juice, garlic and ginger for an hour. Lift the pieces of chicken out of the lemon juice, saving it for later, and fry them in the least possible quantity of oil, preferably using a wok or large non-stick frying pan with a lid.

After frying the chicken for some 10 minutes over medium heat add the ground red chillies, turmeric, coriander, some salt and remaining lemon juice, and stir to mix well. Cover and cook very gently over low heat for another 10–15 minutes, stirring now and again, until the chicken is tender. Add the fresh coriander and stir-fry briskly for a few minutes right at the end. Melt in the butter which will add a delicious fragrance to the dish.

Murghi ka Salan
(*Chicken in a Gravy*)

No selection of chicken recipes would be complete without this dish which is perhaps the most common and, consequently, the one most easily overlooked. When I miss my mother's cooking, living thousands of miles away in London as I do, it's the homely spicing and plentiful gravy of simple unpretentious dishes such as this that I long for most. Serve it with plain boiled rice or a *pullao* to derive maximum pleasure from the gravy.

3–3½ lb/1·4–1·6 kg roasting chicken, skinned and cut into pieces (see page 163) (*murghi*)

12 oz/350 g onions, peeled and finely chopped (*pyaz*)

5 tbsp vegetable cooking oil, or clarified butter (*tail/asli ghee*)

4–5 medium garlic cloves, crushed (*lehsun*)

1 in./2·5 cm cube fresh ginger, finely grated (*adrak*)

2 tsp ground coriander (*dhania*)

1 tsp turmeric (*haldi*)

1 tsp red chilli powder (*lal mirch*)

8 oz/225 g natural yoghurt (*dahi*)

9 oz/250 g ripe tomatoes, finely chopped (*timatar*)

salt to taste (*namak*)

3 tbsp fresh coriander leaves, finely chopped (*hara dhania*)

Fry the onions in the oil or *ghee* until golden. Add the garlic and ginger and stir-fry for a minute before adding the other ground spices. Cook together, taking care that the spices do not burn, for about another minute. Add the chicken pieces. When the chicken is well mixed in with the spice mixture, whisk the yoghurt with a fork and slowly pour it on to the chicken, stirring all the time.

Turn the heat down low, cover the saucepan and cook gently for 15 minutes. Add the chopped tomatoes, 16 fl. oz/475 ml water and some salt, and cook slowly until the chicken is tender. Before taking the pan off the heat, stir in the fresh coriander.

Dhaniyay-Zeeray ki Sabut Murghi
(Chicken Baked with Roasted Coriander and Cumin)

The powerful flavours of freshly roasted and ground cumin and coriander seeds penetrate deep into the chicken which releases the most tantalizing aroma as it cooks in the oven.

2½–3 lb/1·1–1·4 kg roasting chicken, skinned but kept whole (*murghi*)

2 tsp coriander seeds (*dhania*)

2 tsp white cumin seeds (*sabut safeid zeera*)

5–6 whole large dried red chillies, or to taste (*sabut lal mirch*)

salt to taste (*namak*)

3–4 tbsp natural yoghurt (*dahi*)

clarified butter (*asli ghee*)

Dry-roast the coriander and cumin seeds and red chillies on a *tava* (or cast-iron or non-stick frying pan) over medium heat, stirring them around all the time. As soon as they begin to crackle and pop and you smell their distinctive aroma, take them off the heat, being careful that they do not get too dark or burnt. Crush them in an electric grinder but only briefly so they retain some texture and are not too finely powdered. Mix these spices and some salt with the yoghurt to make a paste. Use only as much yoghurt as you need to make a thick paste as yoghurt releases a lot of moisture which you want to avoid.

Cut deep diagonal slashes across the chicken breasts and legs. Rub this paste well over the chicken, pushing some into the cuts. Brush generously with clarified butter and place in a pan, also well greased with clarified butter, roast in a pre-heated oven – at 375°F/190°C/gas 5 – until the chicken is tender, basting several times.

Kharey Masalay ki Murghi
(Sautéed Chicken in Whole Spices)

There are several recipes you could follow to make this dish including the one listed for *Lamb in Whole Spices* (see page 57) which works equally well with chicken. However, unlike that recipe which uses tomatoes, onions and yoghurt to produce a more moist dish, here you simply fry the chicken and toss it together with an assortment of whole spices and fresh coriander. This recipe is one that I use a lot as it has all the attributes of my favourite type of cooking, being quick, effortless and truly delicious.

2–2½ lb/900 g–1·1 kg chicken, skinned and cut into 8–10 pieces (see page 163) (*murghi*)

cooking oil or clarified butter (*tail/asli ghee*)

1–1½ in./2·5–3·8 cm cube fresh ginger, peeled and finely chopped (*adrak*)

5–6 medium garlic cloves, sliced (*lehsun*)

5–8 large whole dried red chillies, cut in half (*sabut lal mirch*)

2 tsp white cumin seeds (*sabut safeid zeera*)

¾ tsp nigella seeds (*kalonji*)

½ tsp fenugreek seeds (*methi dana*)

salt to taste (*namak*)

1 cup fresh coriander leaves, finely chopped (*hara dhania*)

Use a generous amount of cooking oil or clarified butter to be able to fry the chicken pieces well. (You can always remove some with a spoon before the next stage when adding the spices.) Using a wok if possible, heat the oil and fry the chicken over low to medium heat until it is half cooked (about 20–30 minutes). Add the ginger, garlic, chillies, seeds and salt, and stir-fry for a few minutes over high heat. Then turn the heat right down, cover the wok or other pan and cook gently on *dum*, in the trapped steam, until the chicken is tender. At this stage, or just before serving if you are not planning to eat right away, add the fresh coriander and stir-fry briskly over high heat for another few minutes to brown the pieces of chicken.

Masalaydar Battakh
(Braised Duck in a Spicy Sauce)

In our home, duck was not a regular feature by any means. Just once or twice a year, in the winter months, my mother would serve us with duck and therefore it always felt like a special occasion. The aromatic thick sauce of this dish goes extremely well with the rich dark meat of the bird.

4 lb/1·8 kg duck, jointed into quarters (*battakh*)
lemon juice (*neeboo ka ras*)
1 tbsp crushed garlic (*lehsun*)
1 dsp finely grated fresh ginger (*adrak*)
1 tsp red chilli powder (*lal mirch*)
1 tsp freshly ground *garam masala* (see page 17)

1½ tsp ground coriander (*dhania*)
salt to taste (*namak*)
8 oz/225 g natural yoghurt (*dahi*)
8 oz/225 g onions, peeled and chopped (*pyaz*)
5–6 tbsp clarified butter (*asli ghee*)
6 small cardamoms, coarsely ground (*choti elaichee*)

Skin the duck joints and remove all the fat. Wash in cold water, then douse generously with lemon juice and set aside for a couple of hours. At the end of this period discard the lemon juice and any moisture that may have been released by the meat. Mix the garlic, ginger, red chilli powder, *garam masala*, ground coriander and salt with the yoghurt, and spread all over the duck joints. Leave to marinate for another hour.

Fry the onions in clarified butter until they are a rich golden brown. Put the clarified butter and fried onions into an electric blender and reduce to a smooth paste.

Pre-heat the oven to 350°F/180°C/Gas 4, and grease a roasting tin with more clarified butter. Place the four joints and their yoghurt marinade in the pan, spread some fried-onion paste over each joint, and then sprinkle the ground cardamoms on top.

Place the duck on the middle shelf of your oven. Baste after 15 minutes, and after a further 10 minutes add 8 fl. oz/250 ml water which will make a delicious gravy with the yoghurt, onions, spices and juices from the duck. How much water you may add depends on how much and how thick you want the gravy, so use your discretion. Continue to cook until the meat is tender, turning the pieces a few times, about every 10–15 minutes, to keep the joints moist as they brown. It should be ready in about 1½ hours.

Teetar aur Batair
(Partridges and Quail)

In India partridges and quail were a rare delight to greedily indulge oneself with, perhaps once or twice, in the short *shikar* season. Life in London has made them an even rarer sight on our table as they are available only from exclusive butchers and at phenomenal prices. I still think it's worth the indulgence to get them for a special celebration, even if you only allow yourself the luxury very seldom.

Quails are such tiny birds that they should be cooked whole; you can halve the partridges to make them more manageable if you wish. Skin the birds, taking care to remove all the feathers. Drench them in lemon juice and leave to marinate overnight to kill their gamey smell. About 3–4 hours before cooking, chuck out the lemon juice and any liquid that may have been released.

The two recipes here work equally well for both partridge and quail.

The basic difference between them is that one has a gravy made by adding onions and yoghurt; in the other, the birds are simply cooked in their own moisture and are served without any sauce or gravy, but are a golden brown colour on the outside and succulent and juicy on the inside with a hint of lemon. I personally prefer the second recipe but tastes vary and they really are both very good.

1. In a Sauce

3 partridges or 6 quail (*teetar, batair*), skinned

8 fl. oz/250 ml lemon juice (*neeboo ka ras*)

8 oz/225 g natural yoghurt (*dahi*)

1 tsp red chilli powder, or to taste (*lal mirch*)

6–8 medium garlic cloves, crushed (*lehsun*)

1 in./2·5 cm cube fresh ginger, peeled and finely grated (*adrak*)

salt to taste (*namak*)

2 medium onions, peeled and finely chopped (*pyaz*)

cooking oil (*tail*)

For the garnish

crisply fried onion rings (*pyaz*)

lemon slices (*neeboo*)

tomato slices (*timatar*)

After the birds have been left to soak in lemon juice overnight and the excess moisture has all been thrown out, there is one further stage of marinating. Whisk the yoghurt and mix in the red chilli powder, crushed garlic, grated ginger and salt and rub this mixture well over the partridges or quail. Leave for 3–4 hours so the spices may be well absorbed. You may even prick holes with a fork all over the birds to enable the spices to enter more easily.

When you finally come to cook them, first fry the onions in some oil over high heat, stirring continuously. When soft and translucent (but not yet browned) add the partridge or quail with all the yoghurt marinade. Fry for a few minutes over high heat, turning over once. Then turn the heat right down, cover with a tightly fitting lid and simmer gently for an hour to an hour and a half until completely tender. (It is difficult to be precise about cooking time, so be prepared for them to take slightly longer.) Garnish with crisply fried onion rings, fresh slices of lemon and tomatoes.

2. Without a Sauce

Use the same ingredients as above except that you should leave out the onions altogether and use only 1 tablespoon of marinating yoghurt at the very most. Make a paste of the garlic, ginger and red chilli powder with this yoghurt and rub over the birds (after they have been soaked in lemon juice overnight) and set them aside for a further 3–4 hours.

At the end of this time, using a wok or other utensil that will hold the birds in a single layer, fry them over high heat initially to seal in their juices. Then turn the heat down, cover the pan, and simmer slowly until cooked. Once the meat is tender and before serving, brown the birds over high heat and evaporate any excess moisture in the pan.

FISH AND
PRAWN DISHES

· Fish and Prawn Dishes ·

When I was growing up in Bombay, the only fish that I was completely unafraid of was pomfret. This fish was so delectable and satisfying that nothing and no-one could convince me that it was worth trying any other. It is probably quite a damning confession for a cookery writer to make, but I grew up with a very limited experience of eating most fish and an overdeveloped sense of loyalty to this one. Falling in love changed all this. I married a Bengali man whose love for fish transcends all other loves and inspires more lyrical expression than even his love for me. I knew I must overcome my shyness with fish and cut short my monogamous relationship with the pomfret (*pamplet*) or risk being left out in the cold.

Having accepted the challenge thrown at me by my husband and his fish, I cautiously set out to learn. I started to hunt out recipes, experiment, invent and create fishy meals, with my husband as willing adviser and consultant. At least he knew what the end result should be.

I drew the line at cleaning, gutting or scaling fish which remains to this day an honour shared by my husband and the fishmonger. Like all important chefs, I enter the kitchen when the unsightly mess has been completely cleared away and the fish, thoroughly rinsed in turmeric water, lies peacefully waiting to be transformed by my touch. (I can only guess that fish are traditionally rinsed in turmeric water because of the antiseptic properties of the spice.)

In our home we often cook fish imported from Bengal, many of which are readily available at specialist Indian shops. Fish such as *papda*, *ruhu* and *ilish* are particular favourites. When I find Bombay pomfret, my original love, it is a very special treat and remains for me the finest fish in the world. Although these fish have to be frozen on account of their long journeys, they are of choice quality, probably better than those available in the fish markets of the subcontinent – the best of the haul having unfairly been selected for export. Choosing from the fish freshly available in England I find that we eat mostly trout, sole, plaice, cod, halibut, haddock, occasionally salmon and, of course, plenty of prawns.

Fish cookery is very important in the subcontinent. People place a lot of importance on the freshness of fish and really prefer to see it alive and moving before they buy it. The beauty of a fish cooked moments after it has been caught is unsurpassed. Fish also plays an important role in the cultural, religious and spiritual life of many Indian communities and is an important symbol of fertility.

Despite all this, Indian restaurants in the West seldom, if ever, offer even a single item of fish on their menus. This is as true of the inexpensive high-street take-away place as it is of the more sophisticated restaurant. To be fair, I should admit that very recently I have seen some of the more upmarket restaurants include perhaps one fish dish in their *à la carte* selection. This, I suspect, is motivated more by a search for originality, in a business saturated with so much of the same, than by any genuine desire to attempt to provide a better representation of the cuisine. While it is true that Indian restaurants have played an important role in popularizing our food in the West, it hurts me terribly that they have felt, for the most part, so little pride in presenting the genuine article. Fish has suffered most by neglect. I have so often found myself in the ridiculous position of attempting to persuade sceptics, whose sole knowledge of Indian food is derived from eating in restaurants, that not only do we frequently eat fish but that it is the staple diet in many regions of the subcontinent.

Just as North Indians have always known that pure butter *ghee* is the best cooking medium for a true *qorma* or *biryani*, in Bengal they understood a long time ago that you cannot improve upon the taste of fish cooked or fried in pure mustard oil. In many of my recipes I have listed pure mustard oil amongst the ingredients, hoping to encourage you to get some and taste for yourself the difference it makes. If, however, on a particular occasion this is not possible, you may substitute sunflower oil, corn oil or any other general vegetable oil that may be handy.

As far as prawns are concerned, I have found that it is next to impossible to buy them fresh but uncooked in England. I understand that they are boiled alive by fishermen even before the haul is brought in. Since prawns should only be cooked for a few minutes and extended cooking only makes them tough and chewy, the quality of the ready-cooked prawns can vary greatly according to the length of time they were boiled before reaching the shops. Fresh prawns may be bought shelled or unshelled and are easily available all the year around. Frozen prawns are sold ready cooked and are almost invariably shelled, with the exception of Pacific king prawns which I have often seen being sold unshelled. Certain varieties of freshwater prawns, imported from Bangladesh, are frozen raw and are sold still a bluey-green colour. As we find ourselves with little choice other than to use ready-cooked prawns, it is necessary to be extra cautious and not overcook them. In the recipes that follow, the prawns go in last and are braised or fried with spices, vegetables and other ingredients for a few brief moments before they are taken off the heat.

Halibut Seasoned with Ground Mustard in a Rich Gravy

Halibut figures high on the list of my most favourite fish. If I could afford to, I would eat it much more often than I do. The distinctive flavour of this dish comes from the use of ground mustard seeds and pure mustard oil which is an outstanding combination, and so beautifully absorbed by the firm white flaky flesh of the halibut. The rich gravy of ground onions sautéed with garlic, ginger and coriander needs no reliance on yoghurt or tomatoes for flavour or body as is the case in so many other fish recipes.

1–1½ lb/450–700 g halibut (*machli*)
1½ tsp white cumin seeds (*sabut safeid zeera*)
¾ tsp mustard seeds (*rai*)
2–3 whole dried red chillies, or to taste (*sabut lal mirch*)
lemon juice (*neeboo ka ras*)
salt to taste (*namak*)
pure mustard oil (*sarson ka tail*)
1 medium onion, peeled and roughly chopped (*pyaz*)

½ tsp fenugreek seeds (*methi dana*)
3–4 medium garlic cloves, crushed (*lehsun*)
1 in./2·5 cm cube fresh ginger, peeled and finely grated (*adrak*)
½ tsp turmeric (*haldi*)
1 tsp ground coriander (*dhania*)
½ tsp red chilli powder (*lal mirch*)
2–3 green chillies, or to taste (*hari mirch*)

Remove the dark olive skin of the halibut, but leave the white skin on the other side. Cut the fish into $2\frac{1}{2}$ in./6·3 cm steaks or cutlets. In an electric coffee mill grind the cumin seeds, mustard seeds and whole red chillies to a powder; then mix them with a little lemon juice and salt to make a paste. Rub this paste well over the pieces of halibut, and leave them to marinate for an hour.

Heat some oil in a frying pan and over medium heat shallow-fry the fish very quickly on both sides, taking care that it does not cook completely. Lift out the pieces of fish with a slotted spoon and set them aside. Discard this cooking oil.

Now blend the raw onion to a smooth paste, and prepare and measure out the remaining spices. In a wok or other wide cooking utensil, heat a few tablespoons of mustard oil until it is crackling (but not smoking) hot, and then add the fenugreek seeds. They will almost immediately darken and pop a little, so turn the heat down quickly, and put in the onion paste. (A word of warning: do not allow the fenugreek seeds to darken too much or they will burn and taste bitter.) Stir-fry the onion paste well. As the onions begin to turn yellow you may add a tablespoon of water at a time, to enable you to carry on frying for a while longer without danger of the onions or spices burning. Once the onions have been well fried, add the garlic, ginger, turmeric, ground coriander, red chilli powder and some salt, and stir-fry for a while more. Add 8 fl. oz/250 ml water and bring it to a boil so that all the ingredients are well bonded together in a thick gravy. Continue to cook until the gravy turns from a yellow to a brown, which should take a few minutes. Then add the fried pieces of halibut, arranging them in a single layer in the gravy and top them with the whole green chillies. Simmer gently, perhaps turning the fish over just once, spooning the sauce over the pieces every now and again, until the fish is done.

Haddock in a Spicy Onion Sauce with Fresh Green Chillies and Coriander

You may cook this dish with any firm white fish of your choice. I have chosen haddock as its fillets are firm and chunky, holding together well even when the fish has been skinned.

1 lb/450 g skinless fillets of haddock (*haddock machli*)

salt to taste (*namak*)

lemon juice (*neeboo ka ras*)

2 medium onions, peeled and finely chopped (*pyaz*)

pure mustard oil (*sarson ka tail*), or any vegetable oil

4 garlic cloves, crushed (*lehsun*)

½ tsp red chilli powder (*lal mirch*)

1 tsp turmeric (*haldi*)

4 oz/100 g natural yoghurt, whisked (*dahi*)

2 cups fresh coriander leaves, finely chopped (*hara dhania*)

3–4 green chillies, finely chopped (*hari mirch*)

Cut the fish fillets into approximately 2 in./5 cm pieces. Rub them with salt and lemon juice and set aside for an hour. Fry the onions in some oil until they are a rich golden colour, lift them out with a perforated spoon, and blend to a smooth paste.

Using the same oil in which you browned the onions, fry the garlic, red chilli powder and turmeric for 30 seconds. Put in the onion paste and fry the mixture for a further couple of minutes. Now add the whisked yoghurt slowly, and stir to integrate well with the spices. Fry for a few more minutes over medium heat until the oil separates.

In a separate pan shallow-fry the fillets of fish in a little oil and lightly brown them on both sides, taking care that they are not fully cooked in the process. When all the pieces have been fried, carefully arrange them in a single layer in the pan holding the gravy. Add 8 fl. oz/250 ml water and quickly bring to a boil. Immediately add the chopped coriander leaves and green chillies and check that there is enough salt. Stir to mix the greens well with the sauce, taking care to handle the fish gently so it does not break. Cook gently for a few minutes until the fish is tender and flaky. Serve immediately.

Sabut Pamplet aur Hari Chutney
(Whole Pomfret Stuffed with Fresh Mint and Coriander Chutney)

These days it is not at all unusual to find pomfret in the West. It is flown in from India, Bangladesh or China and is available all the year around. Certainly, those specialist shops in Britain that import frozen fish from the subcontinent, order pomfret on a regular basis and seem always to have some in stock. Originally sought after only by the Chinese and Asian communities, a wider taste for this fish is developing as it gets better known, and I have seen pomfret lying on ice at local fishmongers side by side with more native varieties.

Pomfret is a flat, silvery, oval–shaped fish which weighs on average between 1–1½ lb/450–700 g. If it were available fresh I would have strongly urged you to prepare it for this dish simply by cleaning it and trimming its fins. With frozen fish it is probably wiser to cut off the head; although favoured by many as the tastiest part, it's not, I feel, safely eaten after being subjected to freezing.

1 pomfret, about 1–1½ lbs/450–700 g (*pamplet*)

2–3 green chillies (*hari mirch*)

1 cup fresh coriander leaves (*hara dhania*)

½ tsp red chilli powder (*lal mirch*)

3 tbsp natural yoghurt (*dahi*)

salt to taste (*namak*)

1 tbsp clarified butter (*asli ghee*)

Clean the fish, trim away the fins and tail, cut off its head, but otherwise leave whole. Wash thoroughly and pat dry.

In an electric blender make a chutney of the green chillies, fresh coriander, red chilli powder, yoghurt and salt. Make some deep incisions on both sides of the fish, taking care not to break it up. Rub the chutney all over the fish, into the cuts, and stuff some generously into the stomach cavity. Leave aside for an hour.

In a large frying pan heat the *asli ghee*, then put in the fish. Fry so gently that you are barely able to hear it cooking for about 10 minutes on each side and serve immediately.

Lemon Pepper Plaice in Breadcrumbs

Plaice fillets are ideal for this recipe. They are easily available both fresh and frozen from most supermarkets and fishmongers. The fillets are thin and fry up beautifully light and crisp, especially if made with finely ground home-made white breadcrumbs (so much more delicate in texture and flavour than the commercial varieties). I usually cut each fillet into smaller pieces, which is better suited to the way in which Indian food is eaten.

1 lb/450 g fillets of plaice (*plaice machli*)
6–8 small to medium garlic cloves, peeled (*lehsun*)
1 fat 1 in./2·5 cm cube fresh ginger, peeled (*adrak*)
½ tsp red chilli powder (*lal mirch*)
2 tbsp lemon juice (*neeboo ka ras*)
2 eggs (*unday*)
2 tsp freshly ground black pepper (*kali mirch*)
salt to taste (*namak*)
breadcrumbs (*double roti kay crumm*)
cooking oil (*tail*)

Blend the whole garlic, ginger and red chilli powder with the lemon juice in an electric blender to get a smooth paste. Trim away any fins from the fillets and cut each lengthwise down the middle into half and then across into four or six pieces. Rub the pieces of fish with the lemon and spice paste and leave to marinate for about 15 minutes.

Beat the eggs thoroughly and mix in the black pepper and salt. Use more black pepper than you think you will need as there is some wastage with quite a lot of the pepper getting left behind with all the beaten eggs not being utilized. You should therefore, perhaps, make an allowance for this in the amount of salt used as well. Dip each piece of fish first in the egg and then coat it with breadcrumbs.

When all the fish has been breaded, heat some oil in a frying pan and when it is good and hot fry the fish in batches so the pieces are golden brown on both sides. Serve immediately.

Braised Fillets of Sole with Mushrooms

Sole is given the lavish treatment it deserves in this recipe. For me the beauty of the dish lies in its cunning spicing and in the exquisite blend of fresh cream and saffron that bring out the natural flavour of the fish.

½ lb/225 g fillets of sole (*sole machli*)
lemon juice (*neeboo ka ras*)
7 garlic cloves, crushed (*lehsun*)
1 in./2·5 cm cube fresh ginger, peeled and finely grated (*adrak*)
1 tsp red chilli powder (*lal mirch*)
salt to taste (*namak*)
1 medium onion, peeled and chopped (*pyaz*)
pure mustard oil (*sarson ka tail*)
½ tsp turmeric (*haldi*)
1 heaped tsp ground white cumin (*safeid zeera*)

1 level tsp ground coriander (*dhania*)
3 small tomatoes, finely chopped (*timatar*)
8 oz/225 g mushrooms, finely sliced (*guchchian*)
4–6 fl. oz/120–175 ml single cream (*malai*)
1 tsp saffron threads (*zafran*)

For the garnish
2 tbsp fresh coriander leaves, finely chopped (*hara dhania*)

Cut each fillet across into two. Mix together a few tablespoons of lemon juice and half each of the garlic, ginger and red chilli powder with a little salt. Rub this mixture well over the fillets and leave them to absorb the flavours for about half an hour.

In the meantime fry the onion in some oil to a rich golden brown. Add the remaining garlic, ginger and red chilli powder, the turmeric, cumin and coriander and fry for a minute before adding the chopped tomatoes. Stir-fry the tomato and spice mixture over a medium to high heat for a couple of minutes, then add 4 fl. oz/120 ml water and cook for a further minute or until the tomatoes appear softer and the oil comes to the surface. Add the sliced mushrooms at this stage to the spice and tomato mixture and mix them in well. Turn the heat down and, stirring only occasionally, cook for about 10 minutes until the mushrooms are cooked and the oil separates.

Now heat some oil in another frying pan. Take the fillets one by one, with only as much marinade as clings to them naturally, and fry them for 1 minute on each side. When the fish has been fried pour the leftover marinade into the same oil and fry it for a few minutes until it turns brown and then add it to the mushrooms. Carefully arrange the fillets in the pan with the mushrooms and spoon some gravy and some mushrooms over them. Add 8 fl. oz/250 ml water, turn the heat up high to rapidly bring it to the boil, and cook for 2 minutes. Pour in the cream followed by the saffron and continue to cook until the fish is tender. This will only take a few minutes. Garnish with fresh coriander leaves and serve.

Masala Fried Cod

You may use any firm white fish similar to cod, such as haddock or halibut, that you please for this recipe. I frequently cook it with *rahu*, imported from Bangladesh, cut into thick cutlets or steaks. You may find it is easier to eat the fish boned and filleted; it is less easy to negotiate tiny bones when eating with knives and forks than when eating with one's hands, as we do.

2 lb/900 g white fish, cut into steaks or fillets (*machli*)
1 tbsp crushed garlic (*lehsun*)
1 dsp finely grated fresh ginger (*adrak*)
1 tsp ground white cumin (*safeid zeera*)
1½ tsp freshly ground *garam masala* (see page 17)
1 tsp red chilli powder (*lal mirch*)
1 tsp salt, or to taste (*namak*)
2 pinches *gram* flour (*besan*)
12 oz/350 g natural yoghurt (*dahi*)
pure mustard oil (*sarson ka tail*)
2 tsp fenugreek seeds (*methi dana*)

Add the garlic, ginger, cumin, *garam masala*, red chilli powder, salt and *gram* flour to the yoghurt and mix well. Marinate the fish in this mixture for an hour.

Heat 3 tablespoons of oil in a large frying pan, lift the fish out of the marinade with only as much of the spicy yoghurt as clings naturally, and shallow-fry, putting in only as many pieces as the pan will hold in a single layer. Keep the extra marinade aside for use later. At first fry the fish gently over low heat, turning the pieces over after they are done on one side. When the fish is cooked, turn the heat up and brown it on both sides before lifting out of the oil with a slotted spoon. When all the pieces have been fried, arrange them on a shallow serving dish or platter.

Take a clean frying pan and add 3 tablespoons of oil and fry the fenugreek seeds for a minute before pouring in the remaining marinade. Fry the marinade, stirring all the time until it browns and the oil separates. Spoon this sauce over the pieces of fish and serve.

Baked Trout with Seasoned Yoghurt

In this dish the trout are kept whole and, after being marinated for a time in a generous amount of natural yoghurt seasoned with freshly ground peppercorns and white cumin seeds, they are fried for a brief moment before being carefully laid out in a baking dish. In a separate pan some finely chopped tomatoes, coriander leaves and green chillies are fried with onions browned in pure mustard oil into which the remaining marinade is also stirred. This divine sauce fills the cavity of the trout as well as being poured over it. The fish is then placed in a preheated oven to be baked.

I like this dish best with salmon trout but have cooked it just as successfully with rainbow trout which is readily available all the year round. Serve with *saada pullao*, a *daal* and a vegetable of your choice.

1 lb/450 g trout (2 fish kept whole)

½ tsp white cumin seeds (*sabut safeid zeera*)

½ tsp black peppercorns (*sabut kali mirch*)

8 oz/225 g natural yoghurt (*dahi*)

½ tsp turmeric (*haldi*)

a pinch of red chilli powder (*lal mirch*)

salt to taste (*namak*)

pure mustard oil (*sarson ka tail*)

6 oz/175 g onion, peeled and finely chopped (*pyaz*)

8 oz/225 g tomatoes, finely chopped (*timatar*)

3 green chillies, finely chopped (*hari mirch*)

1 cup fresh coriander leaves, finely chopped (*hara dhania*)

Freshly grind the cumin seeds and peppercorns in an electric grinder and mix them with the yoghurt. Add the turmeric, red chilli powder and salt. Trim the fins and tail and scale the trout as well as you can. Wash the fish and immerse them, whole, in the spicy yoghurt marinade for at least 1 hour.

Heat some oil in a frying pan and fry the finely chopped onions until a golden brown, then add the finely chopped tomatoes, green chillies and fresh coriander. Fry them together until the tomatoes are completely soft. Keep to one side.

When the trout have marinated long enough, lift them out of the yoghurt with only as much of the marinade as clings naturally, and shallow-fry them briefly for no longer than half a minute on each side; carefully place them in a baking dish.

Pour the remaining marinade in with the tomato and onion mixture and stir-fry them together for a couple of minutes. Fill a little of this sauce in to each trout and pour the rest over them. Cover the dish with aluminium foil and put it in a preheated oven at 425°F/220°C/Gas 7 for 10 minutes. Then remove the foil, turn the oven up high and let it bake for about 5 more minutes.

Prawns with Coconut and Poppy Seeds

I like to think of this recipe as a hybrid; it incorporates some of my favourite elements of two completely different regional cuisines, those of North and South India. The use of coconut in meat and fish dishes, so commonplace in the south, is virtually unheard of in the north. Similarly, southern cookery seldom uses poppy seeds, which are a familiar ingredient in many North Indian dishes. Here the two traditions fuse together quite naturally and are seen to be beautifully compatible.

1 lb/450 g peeled and pre-cooked fresh or frozen prawns (*jhinga*)

2–4 tbsp desiccated coconut, or to taste (*naryal*)

2 tbsp white poppy seeds (*khas khas*)

2 tsp white cumin seeds (*sabut safeid zeera*)

4 fl. oz/120 ml pure mustard oil (*sarson ka tail*)

6 oz/175 g onions, peeled and finely chopped (*pyaz*)

1 tbsp crushed garlic (*lehsun*)

1 dsp finely grated fresh ginger (*adrak*)

½ tsp turmeric (*haldi*)

1 tsp red chilli powder, or to taste (*lal mirch*)

10 oz/275 g tomatoes, finely chopped (*timatar*)

salt to taste (*namak*)

½ cup fresh coriander leaves, finely chopped (*hara dhania*)

In a cast-iron *tava* or other heavy or non-stick frying pan, dry-roast the coconut, poppy seeds and cumin seeds over a low heat, stirring continuously. As soon as they begin to crackle and turn a shade darker remove them from the heat and grind them to a fine powder in a spice or coffee grinder.

Heat the oil and fry the chopped onions until golden brown, then first add the garlic and ginger, followed a minute later by the freshly ground poppy and cumin seeds, tumeric, red chilli powder and coconut. Stir them together and almost immediately add the finely chopped tomatoes and fry the mixture together for a few more minutes, adding a little water to prevent the spices from burning or becoming too dark. Once the tomatoes are soft and fairly well cooked, and the mixture has been well fried, add the prawns and salt and stir-fry over medium heat for a short while by which time the excess liquid will have evaporated. Stir in the fresh coriander and serve.

Chingri Aloo Palong Shak
(Prawns with Fresh Spinach and Diced Potatoes)

Those of you who know that *chingri* is the Bengali word for prawn will already have identified the origins of this recipe. At one time in Bangladesh such food was humble fare and this would have been a common household dish, easily within the reach of most people. This changed when demands from foreign markets awakened realization amongst entrepreneurs of the untapped earning potential that lay in the delicious estuary prawns found in the deltaic regions of Bengal. Huge quantities were frozen and packaged for export and local prices rose almost overnight as these once abundantly available prawns became a scarce and cherished commodity.

The combination of prawns with spinach and potatoes is nothing short of inspirational; they complement one another to perfection, bringing out the best in taste, colour and texture. Even for those of us who live in the West, prawns are a relatively expensive option. Yet cooked in this way they can be made to go much further and prove to be more economical than some other recipes I can think of. This is delicious served with plain boiled rice and some *masoor daal*.

1 lb/450 g fresh or frozen prawns, peeled and pre-cooked (*jhinga*)

1 lb/450 g fresh spinach (or frozen leaf spinach if fresh is unavailable or out of season) (*palak ka saag*)

7 tbsp pure mustard oil (*sarson ka tail*), or any vegetable oil (*tail*)

½ lb/225 g onions, peeled and finely chopped (*pyaz*)

1 tsp mustard seeds (*rai*)

1 tsp fenugreek seeds (*methi dana*)

1 tbsp crushed garlic (*lehsun*)

1 tbsp grated fresh ginger (*adrak*)

1 tsp red chilli powder (*lal mirch*)

1 tsp white cumin powder (*safeid zeera*)

½ tsp ground coriander (*dhania*)

½ tsp turmeric (*haldi*)

1 tsp salt (*namak*), or to taste

½ lb/225 g tomatoes, finely chopped (*timatar*)

1 lb/450 g potatoes, peeled and cut into ½ in./1·2 cm cubes (*aloo*)

1 green chilli, finely chopped (optional) (*hari mirch*)

If you are using frozen prawns, defrost them completely and pat dry. Thoroughly wash and finely chop the spinach, discarding the thick stalks. Peel and chop other ingredients as required and keep them ready.

Heat the oil in a wok or frying pan and fry the onions until golden brown. Add the mustard and fenugreek seeds and stir for 30 seconds before adding the garlic and ginger. Keeping the heat at about medium, stir-fry the spices together for another minute and then put in the ground spices and salt followed a minute or so later by the tomatoes. Continue to stir-fry the spice and tomato mixture but add a tablespoon or two of water at a time, if necessary, to prevent it from burning. When the tomatoes have softened, after approximately 10–15 minutes, put in the potatoes and stir to mix well with the sauce.

Cover and leave to cook over gentle heat for 10 minutes; then add the spinach. Do not worry if it looks a lot at this stages as it will soon wilt and reduce greatly. Stir in the spinach, cover once again and cook over low heat until the potatoes are ready. Stir a few more times during this process. Different varieties of potato cook at different speeds so it's hard to say precisely how long this will take. Once your potatoes are cooked but still firm add the prawns and stir them in well so they are evenly spread through the dish. Cover and cook gently for no more than 2–3 minutes. Just before finally taking them off the heat, add the finely chopped green chilli, turn up the flame and stir-fry for a minute.

Spicy Stir-fried Prawns with _Spring Onions and Fresh Coriander_

One great advantage of this recipe is that it takes no time at all to make and does not require any elaborate preparation. It is even possible to cook this dish with frozen prawns straight from the freezer. They thaw in seconds and, because they are pre-cooked, only need to be stirred around in the *masala* to be light *bhunoed*.

1 lb/450 g peeled and pre-cooked fresh or frozen prawns (*jhinga*)
pure mustard oil (*sarson ka tail*)
6 oz/175 g onions, peeled and finely chopped (*pyaz*)
1 dsp finely grated fresh ginger (*adrak*)
1 tsp crushed garlic (*lehsun*)
½ tsp turmeric (*haldi*)
1 tsp ground white cumin (*safeid zeera*)

1 tsp ground coriander (*dhania*)
1 tsp red chilli powder (*lal mirch*)
3 small tomatoes, chopped (*timatar*)
salt to taste (*namak*)
1 bunch spring onions, trimmed and sliced into slim rounds, green and white (*hari pyaz*)
5 tbsp fresh coriander leaves, finely chopped (*hara dhania*)

Heat some oil in a large frying pan and fry the chopped onions until they turn a rich golden brown. Add all the spices and stir for a few seconds until they lose their raw quality and release their aroma. Put in the chopped tomatoes and stir-fry until you have a well blended mixture of tomatoes and spices. Pour in a little water at this stage and simmer until the tomatoes are well softened. Then add the prawns and salt and stir-fry all the ingredients for about 5 minutes over medium heat.

If you are using prawns that are still frozen keep the heat high as they will release a lot of moisture which must evaporate. When most of the moisture has evaporated and you have a thick rich sauce clinging to the prawns your dish is almost ready. Stir the spring onions and fresh coriander into the prawns, and serve.

Besan Main Talay Huay Jhingay
(Prawns Fried in Spicy Gram Flour Batter)

This recipe and the one following, are extremely simple to make and are wonderful to eat either as appetizers or as one of a selection of dishes at your table. Whether dipped in *gram* flour or breadcrumbs, the delightfully light and crisp coating greatly improves the pleasure of the soft, tastily seasoned prawns they conceal. Always serve crispy hot for maximum pleasure, almost straight off the stove.

The sort of prawns you choose may vary with the occasion. It is probably wisest to use medium prawns, although there is no doubt that the more commonly available smaller prawns also turn out very successfully except that they do make more work for the cook. A dish of Pacific king prawns can make quite an impression and never fails to attract lavish praise. If you want to serve fan-tailed prawns, which can look very decorative, then buy them still in their shells and, twisting off the head, peel away the soft shell around the body right up to the last feeler-like claw, leaving just the tail.

1 lb/450 g pre-cooked prawns in their shells or 8 oz shelled prawns (*jhinga*)
1 cup *gram* flour (*besan*)
1 tsp white cumin seeds (*sabut safeid zeera*)
½ tsp ground coriander (*dhania*)
½ tsp red chilli powder (*lal mirch*)
2 garlic cloves, crushed (*lehsun*)
2–3 green chillies, finely chopped (*hari mirch*)
1 tbsp coriander leaves, finely chopped (*hara dhania*)
a pinch of baking soda
salt to taste (*namak*)
cooking oil (*tail*)

Blend the *gram* flour with about 8 fl. oz/250 ml water to make a smooth batter; the consistency should be heavier than a pancake batter, though not quite as thick as coating batter. If you have an electric blender it makes this task very painless; if doing it by hand, then add the water slowly, taking care not to let it get lumpy. When it is smoothly mixed add all the other ingredients, with the exception of the prawns and cooking oil, and whisk well with a fork. Put all the prawns into the spicy batter, shelling if necessary.

Pour a generous amount of cooking oil into your frying pan and heat it well. When the oil is crackling hot, turn the heat down to medium and, lifting the prawns out of the batter one at a time, drop them carefully into the hot oil. Fry only a few at a time so they are easy to handle; do not tackle any more than the pan can hold in a single layer. After a minute or two turn them over, to brown them on the other side. As the batter turns golden lift them out of the hot oil with a slotted spoon and put them on a plate covered with absorbent paper to soak up the excess oil.

If you are making this recipe with fan-tailed prawns, then it's probably best to lift them out of the batter with your fingers and drop them into the hot oil with just as much batter coating them as clings naturally. If, however, you are using shelled prawns, you could if you prefer, lift them out of the bowl in a spoonful of the tasty batter and fry them as delicious *pakoras* with a prawn concealed in each. This second method is probably more cost effective as it gives you a more substantial and filling dish for the same weight of prawns.

Fried Prawns in Breadcrumbs

Here again you can use pre-cooked prawns either shelled or with fan tails.

1 lb/450 g pre-cooked and shelled prawns (*jhinga*)
breadcrumbs (*double roti kay crumm*)
½ tsp red chilli powder (*lal mirch*)
½ tsp ground black pepper (*kali mirch*)
½ tsp ground white cumin (*safeid zeera*)

3 garlic cloves, crushed (*lehsun*)
2 tsp fresh coriander leaves, coarsely ground (*hara dhania*)
salt to taste (*namak*)
4 tbsp lemon juice (*neeboo ka ras*)
beaten egg (*unday*)
cooking oil (*tail*)

I like to make my own breadcrumbs at home, preferably using white bread, as the crumbs turn out a prettier gold than they do with brown bread. Leave some slices of bread to dry out in a warm place and crush them finely. Add the spices, garlic, fresh coriander and salt to the lemon juice and marinate the prawns in it for 15–30 minutes. Dip the prawns first in the beaten egg and then in the breadcrumbs, so they are all well coated. Collect them on a plate until they have all been prepared.

Heat the oil well and fry as many at a time as you can manage in a single layer. Using a slotted spoon, lift them out when they are golden brown all over and serve them crisp and hot.

RICE DISHES AND BREAD

· Rice Dishes and Bread ·

Indian food is always eaten with either rice or bread. The subcontinent could be neatly carved up into a map of rice-eating regions and wheat-eating regions. This is not to say that there would be no overlap or that people never eat both. But most of us would almost certainly first classify ourselves as *chawal* eaters or *roti* eaters, and once our primary allegiance was established, we might enjoy the second option for the variety it provided. Yet such an alternative, however pleasing, could never replace or adequately serve as a substitute for our staple diet.

In recent years rice has become comparatively scarce and is easily the more expensive of the two. There is evidence that this has had an impact on eating habits in South India, Bengal and Punjab which have always been solid rice-eating areas, but where today most people can no longer afford to eat rice at every meal.

In places where people eat both, etiquette varies about whether the rice should be served first or the bread. The convention that everyone agrees on is that you must not have them together. The sight of someone eating *chawal* with *roti* is considered a flagrant display of bad manners, and the person committing this act is the subject of universal mirth and ridicule. I have learnt to rise above such well-mannered laughter as I just cannot resist wrapping some *biryani* or *pullao* into my *chapatti* and popping the tasty but forbidden morsel into my mouth. Yet even I would not be tempted to eat plain boiled rice with *chapatti* or *paratha*. I firmly believe, though, that the secret of pleasurable eating is not to feel constrained by rules, especially those invented by 'polite society', whatever its ethnicity.

In Indian cookery it is generally assumed that rice means white rice. There are several kinds available in the shops, ranging from fine quality Basmati (from Pakistan and Dehradun) and Patna rice to American long-grain rice and pre-cooked minute rice. In my opinion there is nothing in the world to beat the flavour and tantalizing aroma of Basmati rice. The next best would be Patna closely followed by any long-grain rice. Take a tip from me and do not touch the pre-cooked variety.

It is important to remember that rice needs to be washed very thoroughly before being cooked. Take care though that you do not break the delicate grains as you rub them between your fingers. Use only cold or tepid water to wash rice. Hot water kills its taste. There is no exact count of how many changes of water will be necessary but on average between five and seven should be sufficient to wash a cup or two of rice. With each successive change you will notice the water getting less cloudy. Carry on until the water runs clear. Getting rid of this excess starch is important because the finished rice could otherwise be too sticky.

Indians, Pakistanis and Bangladeshis are all equally finicky about the final texture of the cooked rice. Each grain should have swollen to its maximum or it will be considered to be undercooked; yet care must be taken that the rice should remain dry and fluffy with the grains all separate and not the slightest bit soggy or mushy. Where rice is concerned there is only a fine line between 'done to perfection' and 'overdone'. In my recipes I have tried to give you some pointers on how to get your rice perfect. At first, the quality you produce may be a little erratic but if you persevere and remain attentive to what is happening, rather than just following the recipe blindly, you will soon perfect the art.

Standard formulas stipulating the ratio of rice to water seldom work to perfection. The length of cooking time as well as the proportion of rice and water may have to be varied depending on how starchy you find the rice, on whether it is new or old, or even on how hard or soft the water in your area is. As a general rule the older the rice the better it cooks.

There are basically two techniques for making rice in Indian cooking. Most rice dishes are made by the *dum* method in which all the water is absorbed by the grains during the cooking process. For this you need to learn not only the correct proportion of rice to water but its relationship to the degree of heat over which it is cooked. By turning the flame up or down at different stages while it is cooking, you can make last-minute adjustments which may save your dish from disaster. Precision and understanding are critical for *dum* cooking because for the main part the saucepan is tightly sealed to enable the rice to cook in the steam trapped inside. If you have a *tava* or heat diffuser you will find it invaluable for leaving the rice to *dum* on, as it eliminates the danger of it sticking to the bottom of the saucepan and burning. Just to be awkward I should say that in some circles a thin layer of burnt crisp rice called *khurchan* is favoured as a delicacy.

In the second method you can afford to be much less precise about the proportion of water you need as in the end you will throw it out and drain the rice into a colander. I favour this method for plain boiled rice because it gets rid of the excess starch and also it makes it much easier to judge with accuracy when the rice is ready. Here you need much less expertise or practice to be successful and a novice can test the grains several times while the rice is cooking to guarantee its eventual quality. Rice is also cooked in this way when making those *biryanis* in which the rice is first half-cooked in boiling water with whole spices, then drained before it is arranged in layers with meat or chicken for the final *dum*.

With so many rice dishes to choose from it may seem confusing to know how to pick the right one. In the main there are no hard and fast rules but traditionally certain dishes are thought to go well together. For instance, most people like to eat plain boiled rice with fish dishes, *koftay*, *karhi* and those other dishes which have an ample gravy. Meat and chicken *biryanis* are normally considered as being sufficiently elaborate in themselves to be the main focus of the meal and do not require much more than a *raita* to accompany them. If you want to entertain more lavishly, then *kababs*, especially *shami kababs* go very well with *biryanis*. For a simple, quick everyday meal I like to cook plain boiled rice, partly because it is painless to make and partly because it is not fattening or heavy on the stomach. If, however, I'm not in the mood to make several dishes I might decide on a vegetable *biryani* which demands only a little more work than plain rice, but frees me from the burden of cooking anything more complicated than a *daal* to accompany it. A plain *pullao* or *matar pullao* always livens up an ordinary meal; I also tend to rely on one or other of them when cooking for a dinner party or may instead choose a prawn *pullao* if I want the rice dish to be particularly special.

In this chapter I have given you recipes for three kinds of bread which are most commonly eaten with Indian food. In my parents' home hot *chapattis* or *phulkas* are served at every meal. We may have *pooris* for a Sunday lunch or brunch with spicy potatoes or we may be given the occasional *paratha* for breakfast or as a special treat with lunch or dinner. In my own home in London, I seldom make any kind of fresh *roti*. There is no doubt that the pleasure of an Indian meal is doubled if served with fresh bread but it really is a question of how much you can be bothered to take the extra trouble. For me, it is unthinkable to knead dough and cook fresh *chapattis, parathas* or *pooris* after a day's work. I have tried preparing a week's supply of *chapatti* dough and keeping it in the fridge to see if that makes the prospect of cooking fresh *chapattis* any less daunting. Quite honestly, when I finish cleaning the layer of flour dust that finds its way into every crevice of my hob, worktop and kitchen floor, I think less about the real pleasure of eating fresh *chapattis* than about the punishment which is its price. I usually serve only freshly heated packaged *pitta* bread or butter *naans* which are good substitutes, considering the headache they spare me. Once in a while when I feel strong withdrawal symptoms and the craving is intolerable, I will cook *chapattis, parathas* or *pooris* depending on my mood. It is not my intention to put off any of you who want to try and make the occasional *chapatti*. You may not even find it as much of a chore as I have led you to believe. Of course the catch in all this is that the more often you do it, the better you get and the easier it seems. Making good *roti* effortlessly is quite an art perfected only by years of practice.

Khushka
(Plain Boiled Rice)

The satisfaction and pleasure of a meal eaten with good quality boiled rice is like time spent in the company of an old friend, hugely enjoyable but completely taken for granted. We can eat and enjoy the most sensational *biryanis* and *pullaos* for a while but in a short time the real rice eaters amongst us would begin to hanker for the more familiar taste of perfectly plain boiled rice.

Basmati rice: Taking a cup (8 oz/225 g) as your measure, use as many cups as required. I usually estimate $\frac{3}{4}$–1 cup per person when cooking for Asian friends and $\frac{1}{2}$ cup for westerners. This is quite a generous calculation which means I always have enough and there may be some left over. (Depending on what else you are serving, you could well find that 2 cups of rice is plenty for up to six people.)

Water: Allow at least 4 cups of water to each cup of rice.

Salt: I usually do not add any salt at all to my boiled rice. If you want salt then remember that in this recipe about half the quantity of water will be absorbed by the rice and half thrown out.

Wash the rice thoroughly in several changes of cold or tepid water, gently rubbing the grains with the tips of your fingers until the water runs clear. Pour the required measure of water into a large open saucepan with the washed rice and set it to boil over high heat. When the water reaches boiling point, turn the heat down to a level where it keeps boiling but is not going to boil over. Check every few minutes until you feel that the rice is nine-tenths cooked; lift a few grains out at a time and test them to see that they have swollen to their maximum but still have a slim hard core. At this point, immediately take the saucepan of rice off the heat and drain it into a colander, leaving the empty saucepan turned upside down over the colander containing the rice. Leave undisturbed for a few minutes during which time the excess water will completely drain away and the steam trapped by the overturned saucepan will be absorbed by the rice thus completing the process.

If you add a slice of lemon to the rice as it boils it will help prevent the grains from sticking together.

Saada Pullao
(Plain Pullao)

The main difference between a *pullao* and a *biryani* is that a *pullao* is less rich and more lightly spiced with whole spices such as cardamoms, cumin, cinnamon and peppercorns and flavoured by onions and the clarified butter in which they are fried. I highly recommend pure butter *ghee* if you are not under any dietary restrictions, as the added flavour it brings to a *pullao* is just unsurpassable.

This recipe is made by *dum* cooking which means the rice is cooked by trapped steam in a tightly sealed saucepan. I have interrupted myself at several points to give reasons for certain steps or explain the process to you. Once you have mastered the technique you can then follow the same basic method for making *matar pullao*, *prawn pullao* or *tehri (vegetable biryani)*. I realize that at first glance it appears more long-winded than simply giving exact measurements but I feel strongly that without this it is not possible to learn how to make perfect rice every time. I am certain that you will ultimately agree that it makes the job easier to tackle with confidence.

1½ lb/700 g/3 cups Basmati rice
  (*basmati chawal*)
8 oz/225 g onions, peeled and finely
  chopped (*pyaz*)
3 tbsp clarified butter (*asli ghee*) or
  cooking oil (*tail*)
4 cloves (*laung*)
4 large cardamoms (*bari elaichee*)
2 in./5 cm cinnamon stick (*dalchini*)
2 bay leaves (*tejpatta*)

¾ tsp black cumin seeds (*sabut kala
  zeera*)
1 tsp black peppercorns (*sabut kali
  mirch*)
a pinch of nutmeg (optional)
  (*jaiphal*)
salt to taste (*namak*)

For the garnish
crisply fried onions (*pyaz*)

Wash the rice thoroughly in cold water until the water runs clear. When the rice is quite clean carefully strain away all the water.

Fry the onions in a large, heavy-bottomed saucepan in hot *asli ghee* until they turn a mellow gold. Throw in all the spices and stir- fry them over medium to low heat for a minute or more by which time they will darken a shade and release their aroma. Immediately add the rice. Although you will have strained the rice it may still be a little moist. Do not worry about this as it is both impossible and unnecessary to remove the last drop of water from the rice. Stir-fry the rice with the onions and spices. This must be done with some care. Brisk or vigorous stirring will cause the fragile grains of rice to break. After a few minutes the rice may begin to stick to the bottom of the pan as the moisture evaporates. If this happens immediately take it off the heat. Pour in the water (see below) and salt.

The age-old method of judging the correct amount of water for *dum* rice cooking is to stick your index finger into the saucepan so that its tip is resting on the level layer of rice at the bottom of the pan. The correct water level should be halfway above the first joint. A more scientific description may be to say that the rice should be covered by approximately an inch/2·5 cm of water, or in this case 5 cups.

Place the lid on the saucepan and turn the heat up to maximum. When the temperature reaches boiling point and the steam begins escaping fast and furiously, turn the heat down just a little and keep it boiling for a couple of minutes, then turn it low and simmer until most of the visible water has either evaporated or been absorbed by the rice. The rice will not yet be sufficiently cooked and should still be moist. The most foolproof way to proceed is to place a *tava* or heat diffuser under the saucepan and, still keeping the lid tightly closed, continue to cook over low heat for a further 10 minutes. (If you do not have a *tava*, just keep the flame as low as possible and the lid tightly shut and cook for 10 minutes.) At the end of this time, whether or not you used the *tava*, lift the lid for a moment and stir the rice a couple of times. Then place a tea towel over the mouth of the open saucepan and replace the lid, pressing it down firmly. Wrap the corners of the towel over the top of the lid and leave it to *dum* or cook in the trapped steam, still over very low heat for a final 10 minutes. Have a quick check at this point to see if the rice is done. If it still has a little way to go then leave the saucepan tightly shut although the heat has been turned off, for the rice to finish cooking in the steam. The purpose of using a towel is that it both safely seals the saucepan and absorbs any extra moisture that could otherwise make the rice soggy.

Serve the finished *pullao* on an open platter garnished with crisply fried onions.

Matar Pullao
(Green Peas Pullao)

This is a favourite North Indian *pullao* which goes well with almost all dishes I can think of. I usually use frozen peas when I make this recipe. You can use them straight from the freezer which is especially convenient when you need to rustle up something a little special without any previous planning or forethought.

1 lb/450 g/2 cups Basmati rice (*basmati chawal*)
6 oz/175 g onions, peeled and finely chopped (*pyaz*)
2 large cardamoms (*bari elaichee*)
1 in./2·5 cm cinnamon stick (*dalchini*)
1 bay leaf (*tejpatta*)
½ tsp black cumin seeds (*sabut kala zeera*)
10 black peppercorns (*sabut kali mirch*)

8 oz/225 g shelled green peas, fresh or frozen (you may increase the quantity if you wish) (*mattar*)
2½ tbsp clarified butter (*asli ghee*)
salt to taste (*namak*)

For the garnish
crisply fried onions (*pyaz*)

Cook this recipe in exactly the same way as the previous recipe for plain *pullao*. Either use the index finger measuring technique to judge the amount of water, or measure 4 cups of water.

Add the green peas straight after adding the rice. Serve garnished with crisply fried onions.

Jhingay ka Pullao
(Prawn Pullao)

This recipe is almost the same as the previous one for *matar pullao* except that it is spiced even more delicately to allow the fragrance of the prawns to dominate that of the rice.

½ lb/225 g shelled prawns, fresh or frozen (*jhinga*)

1 lb/450 g/2 cups Basmati rice (*basmati chawal*)

1 medium onion, peeled and finely chopped (*pyaz*)

1 large cardamom (*bari elaichee*)

1 tsp white cumin seeds (*sabut safeid zeera*)

a pinch of black cumin seeds (optional) (*sabut kala zeera*)

½ tsp red chilli powder (*lal mirch*)

clarified butter (*asli ghee*)

salt to taste (*namak*)

Follow the method for Green Peas *Pullao*, adding the prawns at the same time as the peas.

Tehri
(Vegetable Biryani)

This is a colourful and attractive dish of spicy yellow rice studded with tiny chopped mixed vegetables such as carrots, green peas, corn and anything else that takes your fancy. The potatoes, however, are cut somewhat larger into quarters. It is differently spiced and cooked compared both to the earlier *pullaos* as well as to meat or chicken *biryanis*. I like to think of it as a time-saver because although it is a little more work than plain boiled rice it is actually easier to make than a plain *pullao*, but is much more substantial, and can be a meal in itself if served simply with a yoghurt *raita* of your choice.

1 lb/450 g/2 cups Basmati rice
   (*basmati chawal*)
4 tbsp vegetable oil (*tail*)
1 tsp turmeric (*haldi*)
1 tsp red chilli powder, or to taste
   (*lal mirch*)
1 tsp ground coriander (*dhania*)
1 tsp white cumin seeds (*sabut safeid
   zeera*)

1½ tsp salt, or to taste (*namak*)
1½ lb/700 g potatoes, peeled and
   quartered (*aloo*)
8 oz/225 g frozen mixed vegetables
   or frozen carrots and peas
   (*mukhtalif tarkaryan*)

Wash the rice thoroughly in cold water and strain. Heat the oil and fry all
the above spices and salt, keeping the flame low. In about a minute the
spices will have turned a shade darker and you should add the potatoes.
Stir the potatoes so they are lightly fried and well covered in the spices and
immediately add the rice. Stir a couple of times to mix the ingredients and
lastly add the mixed vegetables. Carry on stirring for a couple of minutes
more taking care not to break or damage the grains of rice. Immediately
pour in 4 cups of tepid water, cover the saucepan and bring to a boil over
high heat. As soon as it begins to boil and the steam is escaping fast and
furiously, turn the heat down to medium for 2–3 minutes. Take the lid off
for a moment, spread a tea towel over the open mouth of the pan and place
the lid back on tightly, folding the corners of the towel over it. Turn the
heat down to the lowest possible position and cook slowly for a further
15–20 minutes until the rice and potatoes are done. If you have a cast iron
tava or heat diffuser, place the saucepan on it at this final stage. At the end
of this time if your rice or potatoes are still not quite done, turn the heat off
but leave the lid of the saucepan on so it can finish cooking in the trapped
steam.

Jhingay ki Biryani
(Prawn Biryani)

This dish is a combination of spicy prawns with rice that has first been half cooked with cardamoms, cloves and cinnamon and then infused with the fragrance and fine colour of real saffron.

You can cook the dish using either the recipe for Prawns with Coconut and Poppy Seeds or Spicy Stir-Fried Prawns (see pages 193 and 196). Once you have decided which recipe you want to follow for making the prawns you will need the following additional ingredients.

1 × prawn recipe (see above)
1½ lb/700 g/3 cups Basmati rice
   (*basmati chawal*)
salt to taste (*namak*)
4 small cardamoms (*choti elaichee*)
2 large cardamoms (*bari elaichee*)
2 in./5 cm cinnamon stick (*dalchini*)
2 cloves (*laung*)
1 tsp saffron threads, or more if you
   can afford it (*zafran*)

4 fl. oz/120 ml milk (*doodh*)
½ oz/15 g butter (*makhan*)
4 oz/100 g onions, peeled and
   chopped (*pyaz*)
4 tbsp cooking oil (*tail*)

For the garnish
fresh coriander leaves, finely
   chopped (*hara dhania*)

First cook the prawns according to your chosen recipe, and put them aside.

Wash the rice thoroughly in several changes of water and then set it to boil in a saucepan with 3¾–4 pints/1·8–2·3 litres water, salt and the cardamoms, cinnamon and cloves. Boil it over high heat in an uncovered saucepan. As soon as the rice comes to a boil check and see whether it is half done; if it isn't it won't be long before it is. As soon as the rice is half cooked drain it into a colander. It is important to ensure that the rice is no more than half cooked at this first stage or it will be ruined when it is put on *dum* with the saffron and prawns.

Lightly dry-roast the saffron threads in an empty frying pan and then crumble them into the hot milk. Take a heavy-bottomed saucepan and put half the rice into it, and pour in half of the saffron milk. Also add a small pat of butter which should melt quickly in the hot rice. Give a quick stir to spread the saffron colour and butter. Then put the prawns on the bed of rice and cover them with a layer of the remaining rice. Pour the rest of the saffron milk on top of the rice and stir gently so as not to disturb the layer of prawns below. Fry the onions golden brown in the oil and pour them with the oil on top of the rice.

Now *dum* the rice, starting off over high heat in a tightly covered saucepan turning it down as soon as enough steam has built up inside it. Use a *tava* or heat diffuser if you have one at this stage. Serve, mixing together the rice and the prawns in a large open platter, and garnish with fresh coriander.

_____Murgh ya Gosht ki Biryani_____
(Chicken or Lamb Biryani)

The traditional ratio of rice to meat in a *biryani* is that the meat should be double the weight of the rice. You can if you like increase the proportion of rice by a third without altering the quantities of the other ingredients if you want your dish to stretch a little further.

The first step is to make a *qorma*. Follow the recipe for Lamb *Qorma* on page 62, substituting chicken for lamb if you prefer. The only difference is that you will cut the chicken into eight pieces, on the bone (page 163), and you probably will not need to add any water to help it cook.

Here I have only listed those additional ingredients you will need and have described the rest of the process.

1 × Lamb *Qorma* recipe (see page 62)

1 lb/450 g/2 cups Basmati rice (*basmati chawal*)

3–4 large cardamoms (*bari elaichee*)

1 tsp black peppercorns (*kali mirch*)

2 bay leaves (*tejpatta*)

2 cloves (*laung*)

½ tsp black cumin seeds (*sabut kala zeera*)

a pinch each of nutmeg and mace (not essential) (*jaiphul/jaivitri*)

salt to taste (*namak*)

1 medium onion, peeled and finely chopped (*pyaz*)

2–3 tbsp cooking oil or clarified butter (*tail/asli ghee*)

6 fl. oz/175 ml creamy top of milk (*doodh*)

8 oz/225 g natural yoghurt (*dahi*)

a large pinch of saffron, or whatever you can afford (*zafran*)

2–3 green chillies or to taste, finely chopped (*hari mirch*)

3–4 tbsp fresh coriander leaves, finely chopped (*hara dhania*)

For the garnish
crisply fried onions (*pyaz*)
fresh coriander leaves (*hara dhania*)

Measure about $3\frac{1}{2}$–4 cups of water for each cup of rice and after washing it well, put it on to boil with all the whole spices, nutmeg, mace and salt. When it reaches boiling point add the rice and only half cook it over high heat. This should not take much more than 5 minutes. Take care not to overcook the rice. Strain it into a well perforated colander. Spread out half the rice at the bottom of a heavy-bottomed saucepan; then place the cooked meat or chicken with its thick spicy sauce in the middle and cover it with the remainder of the rice. Set it aside for the moment.

Brown the onions in the *asli ghee* or oil, lifting them out with a slotted spoon when they are done. Pour this hot *asli ghee* or oil over the top of the rice and distribute the onions over the surface. Then pour the milk into the rice and also spread the yoghurt evenly over it. Next sprinkle on as much saffron as you are using; finally scatter the finely chopped green chillies and fresh coriander over the top of the rice and tightly close the lid of the saucepan. (If you are making a larger biryani than this recipe describes, layer the meat and rice in several layers when arranging them in the saucepan for *dum*.)

If you have a *tava* or heat diffuser, place the saucepan on it as it provides a much more even distribution of heat than if you placed the saucepan directly on the cooker; it also prevents the rice from sticking to the bottom of the pan. In any case place the saucepan over high heat until the steam has built up well inside. Then turn the heat down low and leave it to *dum* in its own steam. The *biryani* should be ready in about 20 minutes.

Serve it on a large open platter garnished with more crisply fried onions and a sprinkling of finely chopped coriander leaves.

Hyderabadi Katchey Gosht ki Biryani
(Hyderabadi Lamb Biryani)

In most *biryanis* the meat, chicken or prawns are first cooked separately and layered with the rice only at the last stage for the final *dum*. The special feature of this *biryani* is that here the rice and lamb are cooked together in the *dum* method almost from the start with outstanding results. The idea that the meat can cook in the same time as it takes to cook rice takes all those of us by surprise who have not been privy to the miracle of this recipe. The secret lies in using tender lamb, exquisitely marinated for several hours in papaya, yoghurt, fried onion paste and a selection of spices. The following three ingredients are a must.

1. *Clarified butter or* asli ghee:
You may use either pure butter *ghee* or vegetable *ghee* for stage 2 of this recipe; cooking oil is not suitable as you need to spread the clarified butter in its solid form at the bottom of the saucepan followed by a layer of meat and then top it with the rice.

2. *Spring lamb:*
I feel that you simply cannot make any compromises in the quality of meat needed for this dish because it has to cook in the same short time as the rice.

3. *Green papaya:*
This is a powerful natural tenderizer in which the lamb is well marinated before being cooked. It is normally available at Indian greengrocers.

For the lamb and marinade
3 lb/1·4 kg lean spring lamb, cubed, on or off the bone, in small pieces (*chota gosht*)
3 tbsp finely grated green papaya (*hara papita*)
1½ tbsp crushed garlic (*lehsun*)
1½ tbsp finely grated fresh ginger (*adrak*)
12 oz/350 g onions, peeled and chopped (*pyaz*)
cooking oil or clarified butter (*tail/asli ghee*)
9–10 oz/250–275 g natural yoghurt (*dahi*)
1 tbsp fresh coriander leaves, finely chopped (*hara dhania*)
1 tbsp fresh mint leaves, finely chopped (*pudeena*)
3–4 green chillies, or to taste, finely chopped (*hari mirch*)
1 tsp freshly ground *garam masala* (see page 17)
1 tsp turmeric (*haldi*)
1½ tsp red chilli powder, or to taste (*lal mirch*)
salt to taste (*namak*)

For the rice
1½ lb/700 g/3 cups Basmati rice (*basmati chawal*)

3–4 large cardamoms (*bari elaichee*)
1 tsp black peppercorns (*kali mirch*)
3 in./7·6 cm cinnamon stick (*dalchini*)
2 bay leaves (*tejpatta*)
a pinch of ground nutmeg (*jaiphul*)
¼ tsp black cumin seeds (*sabut kala zeera*)
4 cloves (*laung*)
1 tbsp each fresh coriander and mint leaves, finely chopped (*hara dhania* and *pudeena*)
2 green chillies, finely chopped (*hari mirch*)
salt to taste (*namak*)

For the Biryani
8 oz/225 g clarified butter (*asli ghee*)
lemon juice (*neeboo ka ras*)
1 tbsp fresh coriander leaves, finely chopped (*hara dhania*)
1 tbsp fresh mint leaves, finely chopped (*pudeena*)
1 tsp saffron (*zafran*)
4 fl. oz/120 ml milk (*doodh*)
12 oz/350 g onions, peeled and sliced into rings or half rings (*pyaz*)
cooking oil or clarified butter (*tail/asli ghee*)

The Lamb Marinade: Stage One

Mix the papaya, garlic and ginger together; rub this paste well into the meat and set it aside for at least an hour. During this time, brown the onions in hot oil or *asli ghee*, lifting them out with a perforated spoon when they are done. Blend them to a smooth paste. Mix together the yoghurt, coriander and mint leaves, green chillies, *garam masala*, turmeric, red chilli powder, fried onion paste and salt. Return to the meat set aside earlier and knead all these ingredients well into it, leaving it to marinate for a further 2–3 hours.

The Rice: Stage Two

Wash the rice well in several changes of cold water and strain. Put plenty of water on to boil, (at least 4 cups water to each cup rice) in a large saucepan with all the remaining listed rice ingredients. As soon as the water comes to the boil, add the rice and cook for no more than 2–3 minutes and immediately strain into a colander.

For the Biryani: Stage Three

Spread the solid but crumbled clarified butter in the bottom of the saucepan and place the lamb in all its marinade on top. Then put in the partially cooked rice, a generous squeeze of lemon juice followed by a sprinkling of coriander and mint. Very lightly roast the threads of saffron in any empty frying pan over medium to low heat. Warm the milk and crumble the saffron into it. Pour this saffron milk over the rice. Fry the onions in the oil or *ghee* until golden brown, lifting them out with a slotted spoon once they are done. Arrange these crispy fried onions on the rice.

Dum *Cooking: Stage Four*

Place a cloth or towel over the mouth of the open saucepan and then press the lid down tightly. Bring the four corners of the cloth over the top of the lid and if you can, place a heavy weight over it to seal it securely shut. Turn the heat up high. When the steam has built up turn it down to medium for 5–10 minutes and then turn it down as low as it will go. Cook without opening the saucepan for 1–1¼ hours, after which have a quick look to see if the rice has cooked and stick a fork through to test the meat. Cook for a further 15 minutes, if necessary, and serve on a large open platter.

Chapatti

This unleavened bread that is an intrinsic part of every meal is made from wholewheat flour called *ata*. It is more finely ground than the ordinary wholewheat flour available in most shops. However you can quite easily buy bags of it of different weights and sizes at Indian grocers in England, under the name of *chapatti* flour.

In order to be able to make *chapattis* you should have a *tava* although you could use a large cast-iron or other heavy frying pan as a good substitute. You will also need a pair of tongs with which to hold the chapatti directly over an open flame, at the last stage of the cooking, while it swells up with hot air.

Makes 10–12 chapattis

1 lb/450 g wholewheat *chapatti* flour (*ata*)	approx. 8–9 fl oz/225–250 ml water 1 tsp salt, or to taste (*namak*)

Put the flour with the salt into a large mixing bowl. Add a little water at a time and knead into a dough using clenched fists. (If you have an electric gadget to do the work for you then use it to spare yourself a lot of trouble.) At first the flour will seem to be rather unmanageable but persevere, collecting it together as you go along. When the dough begins to hold continue to knead it, wetting your fists continuously in a separate bowl of water. The dough should not be too soft and watery as it will be very difficult to use, neither should it be so hard as to make the *chapattis* thick and heavy. Knead for at least 10 minutes and when the dough appears to be the correct consistency – soft, firm and sufficiently pliable – allow it to rest for at least half an hour covered with a damp cloth.

When you come to make the *chapattis* knead the dough once again for a few minutes. Pull off sufficient dough at a time to roll into the size of a ping-pong ball between the palms of your hands. You will need to dust it with some dry flour before you can do this successfully. Then flatten it between the palms of your hands before laying it on a surface well dusted with flour and rolling it out with a rolling pin to a flat round shape about 5 in./12·5 cm in diameter. Heat the *tava* well.

Lift up one *chapatti* with care, and place it on the hot *tava*. In about 30 seconds it will have cooked on one side and then you must turn it over on to the other side. In about another 30 seconds or so you will see little bubbles forming in the *chapatti*. Lift it up with the tongs and hold it directly on the gas flame and cook it first on one side and then the other. You will see it puff up beautifully with air, indicating it is ready. If you have several *chapattis* to make it will probably be most convenient if you can keep the *tava* hot on one burner on the left hand of your stove and keep the flame burning on the corresponding right hand burner. You can then just lift the *chapatti* off the *tava* and on to the flame very easily. In fact, you can have the next one already being roasted on the tava while one is on the fire but that will probably take a little experience to manage efficiently.

Serve hot. For me the real pleasure of a *chapatti* is to get it on my plate piping hot only seconds after it is cooked. You could serve it plain or lightly buttered.

Paratha

Parathas may be made purely of *ata* (finely ground wholewheat flour) or with a combination of both *ata* and *maida* (white self-raising flour). I personally prefer the fuller and more wholesome flavour of *parathas* made entirely of *ata*, although it has to be said that the ones with the *maida* are a little lighter and more flaky. The flour is kneaded into a soft dough a little more firm than that used to make *chapattis*, and some clarified butter is also added to it.

There are several traditional ways in which to fold a *paratha* to create a round, square or triangular shape and to give it the many-layered texture that is its characteristic feature. *Parathas* may be plain, as the one in this recipe, or else they may be stuffed with a whole variety of things ranging from spicy *qeema* to *Aloo Bhurta* and *Mooli Bhurta*.

Makes 4 parathas

10 oz/275 g wholewheat *chapatti* flour (*ata*)
1 oz/25 g self-raising flour (*maida*)
½ tsp salt, or to taste (*namak*)

8 fl oz/225 ml water
1 oz/25 g pure melted clarified butter (*asli ghee*) or vegetable cooking oil (*tail*)

Put the flour, butter or *asli ghee* and salt into a large mixing bowl. Add a little water at a time and knead the flour into a firm but pliable dough. Let it rest for half an hour covered with a damp cloth. When you are ready to cook the *parathas* first knead the dough again for a few minutes. Then break off a small piece and roll it out as described in the method for *chapattis*.

At this next step you have a choice of what shape to make the *paratha*. First brush some of the melted *asli ghee* on its rolled-out surface. To make a round *paratha*, roll it up tightly into a long sausage shape; smear with some more *asli ghee* then make a spiral with this rolled sausage, dusting it generously with flour to prevent it from sticking. Now flatten the spiral ball between the palms of your hands and roll it out once again into a round with a few deft strokes of your rolling pin. To make a triangular *paratha* fold the rolled-out dough in half, brush again with *asli ghee* and fold over once more to make a triangle. Use a rolling pin and, after dusting generously with flour, roll it out into a triangular-shaped *paratha*. To make a *square paratha*, fold one side of the rolled-out circle about a third of the way over and brush the folded portion with some *asli ghee*. Then fold over the other side of the circle to cover the first fold and make a rectangular shape. Lightly spread some *asli ghee* over this surface as well, and then fold one end of the rectangle over the other, brushing each layer with *asli ghee*. Roll out into a square shape, dusting with flour to prevent it from sticking.

Heat your *tava* or large cast-iron frying pan, and put the *paratha* on to cook. As it cooks the butter *asli ghee* you have folded into it will begin to come to the surface. You may like to touch it with a little more *asli ghee* as it cooks, but it will make it a lot richer if you do so. Press down the corners of the *paratha* with a spoon as it cooks. After a few minutes turn it over and do the other side. The *paratha* will be a beautiful golden brown colour when it is ready. You should neither cook it on a very high heat as it will brown before being cooked through, nor should you keep the flame too low. Find the right level somewhere in the middle.

Poori

Pooris are a kind of deep-fried bread that go particularly well with vegetable dishes, *daals* and pickles. They are also delicious when eaten for breakfast with *Sooji ka Halwa*.

They may be made of *ata*, (finely ground wholewheat flour), a combination of *ata* and *maida* (self-raising flour), or just with *maida* on its own. I have a weakness for the rich taste of wholewheat flour, and it is those *pooris* that I love best. However, unless you are planning to serve them straight away I would recommend adding 1 cup of *maida* to 4 cups of *ata*, to ensure that the *pooris* are soft and pliable even when cold.

This recipe is for a plain *poori* without any spices. Gujerati people frequently add a pinch of turmeric and some red chilli powder to give their *pooris* more of a flavour which is well worth trying. *Kalonj* or *safeid zeera* can also be added to the flour in small quantities if you feel so inclined.

The dough for *pooris* is basically kneaded in the same way as that for *chapattis*, except that it needs to be stiffer and a small amount of oil or clarified butter is added to it. *Pooris* can be made immediately the dough is ready as it does not need to rest for any length of time.

Serves 4

10 oz/275 g wholewheat *chapatti* flour (*ata*)	salt to taste (*namak*)
	8–9 fl oz/225–250 ml water (*pani*)
2 oz/50 g self-raising flour (*maida*)	cooking oil (*tail*)

Put the flours and a pinch of salt into a mixing bowl and add 1 tablespoon vegetable oil. Work this in with your fingers. Then, adding a little water at a time, make a stiff dough but one which is smooth and pliable. Break off small pieces of this dough and roll them into small balls between the palms of your hands. Dust well with some dry flour and roll them out into flat round shapes about 3–4 in./7·5–10 cm in diameter. If you find it difficult to roll them into perfect rounds with a rolling pin then take a large amount of dough and, using a dry, well-oiled surface, roll it out evenly flat. Then using a pastry cutter or other improvised round-shaped object, cut out rounds of dough and lay them to one side until all the dough has been exhausted.

Heat some oil in a *karhai* or other deep-frying utensil. When it is smoking hot, lift up one *poori* at a time and lay it in the middle of the oil. It will sink to the bottom at first and them immediately float up to the top. Now, working very quickly, use a slotted spoon to press the edges of the *poori* down under the oil. Use several quick light strokes to do this all round the edges of its circumference. This will make the *poori* balloon out. As soon as this happens, flip it over and brown the other side. In about half a minute or less the *poori* will be cooked and golden brown on both sides. Lift it out of the oil on to a plate covered with absorbent paper towel which will soak up the excess grease. Make the remaining *pooris* in the same way, one at a time. Serve hot.

· MEETHAY ·
(Sweet Things)

· Meethay ·
(Sweet Things)

In order to grasp the importance of sweets and sweet dishes in Indian cookery we must first appreciate the place of honour they occupy in Indian society and understand their intricate relationship to it. Indian *mithais*, *halwas* and *kheers* are so intimately connected to cultural habits and religious as well as social ritual that it is not possible to think of them simply as the equivalents of chocolates, cakes, desserts or puddings in western cuisines.

It all starts at birth when the new-born infant is welcomed into the world with the sweet taste of honey even before its mother's milk. *Mithai* is then distributed amongst friends and relatives by the proud parents or grandparents to announce the birth and express their joy. At weddings gifts of sweets are exchanged between the families of the bride and groom and the first ritual after the marriage vows are taken is to sweeten the mouths of both bride and groom. Every happy occasion is similarly celebrated with *mithai* – births, engagements, weddings, passing examinations, moving to a new house and so on. Equally, a guest casually dropping in may be treated as a joyous event and an excuse for *mithai* or *halwa* to be offered whatever the time of day. Sweet things are so closely linked with our social life that a simple visit to the sweet vendor or the fragrance of freshly cooking *halwa* wafting out from the kitchen can awaken powerful memories of past occasions in much the same way as old tunes.

Mithai is not properly a sweet dish like a pudding or dessert to be served after dinner – although if there was some in the house, I have no doubt that everyone with a sweet tooth would eagerly reach for a piece or more! There are some exceptions, such as *ras malai*, which would make a very suitable sweet dish. *Halwas* are more versatile in this respect and can either be eaten for dessert or served as *mithai* with tea or coffee. *Halwas* are eaten both hot as well as cold, as tastes vary according to regional differences.

If *mithais* and *halwas* are two categories of Indian sweets, then *kheer* dishes must form the third. *Kheers* such as *firni*, *gajrela*, *sivayyan* and *sheer khurma* are all made with milk and come the closest to being desserts and puddings. The basic difference between *kheer* dishes and *halwas* is that *halwas* are fried whereas *kheers* are not. Since *halwas* are much richer and heavier to digest, they are eaten in much smaller quantities. For the same reason it is also traditional to think of winters as being for *halwa* eating and summer for *kheers*.

I think it is important to mention at this point that there are very few Indian homes in which a sweet dish is cooked with every meal. It is far more common to end with fruit than pudding. In our home those with a sweet tooth would eat some home-made yoghurt with grated *jaggery* sprinkled on it to satisfy their craving at the end of a meal. However it is customary at weddings, feasts, dinner parties and other special occasions always to serve a sweet dish.

In this chapter I have not included even a single *mithai* recipe. I have always eaten shop-bought, professionally-made *mithai* whether in India, Pakistan or London, as does everyone else I know. Most people who are fond of sweets will have discovered a favourite *mithai* shop and do not mind at all if they have to travel some distance to reach it. *Halwas* can also be bought at *mithai* shops or from *halwais*, but with a few exceptions, are more traditionally made at home. All the dishes in the *kheer* family are normally home-made and are generally not available over the counter.

It is only fair to draw your attention right from the beginning to the unkind reality that most *halwas* and *kheers* take quite a long time and considerable effort to make. I have therefore sought to include a few well-known exceptions to this general rule, *sooji ka halwa* and *sheer khurma*, for instance. *Halwas* at least keep for a long time in the fridge or in cold weather, and also freeze extremely well. Traditionally *halwas* are made in fairly substantial quantities because it really does not take that much longer to make a large pot than it does a small one. It is far from being my intention to dissuade you, for even one moment, from a single recipe in this section as to do so would be to deprive you of such tastes as are guaranteed to delight your palates. Just choose the right time and give yourself the peace in which to cook, and you ought not to find it too great a hardship.

Finally, there are a couple of terms in particular that I should perhaps say a little about for those of you who may be unfamiliar with them and which you are likely to hear again and again in relation to Indian sweet cookery. The first is *khoya* which is the base of several Indian sweet dishes.

It is the name given to a creamy concentrated milk paste which is obtained by cooking milk slowly for a long time until its entire water content has been evaporated. In the subcontinent you can quite easily buy a lump of this ready made, and save yourself a lot of time. Those of us who live in the West do not have such a handy solution to fall back upon. None of the recipes that follow require you to actually dry out the milk completely, but simply to cook it and keep scraping this *khoya* off the sides and bottom of the pan as soon as it forms and mix it back in with the progressively thickening milk. Once the milk has been sufficiently reduced in this manner and the *khoya* stirred back in, not only does its colour and texture change to a thick, heavy, yellowish, cream-like substance but its flavour is also transformed into something sensationally delicious.

The second word I want to draw your attention to is *varq*. Pure silver is beaten into sheets more delicate than the finest gossamer and used for garnishing mainly sweet dishes, but on a very grand occasion it may also be used to embellish a special *biryani*. These feather-light sheets of silver *varq* are edible and can be purchased with each one carefully placed between two other ordinary pieces of paper to protect it and save it from tarnishing. You cannot touch or lift it with your fingers without damaging it and getting the silver dust on your fingers. The only way to handle it is to hold the paper on which it lies and gently invert it on to the sweets or other foods you wish to decorate. Its apparent weightless quality will make it cling to and become an inseparable part of such a dish. In the olden days it was also possible to buy real gold *varq*, but not surprisingly its prohibitive price has driven it out of the market today. I am aware that you can buy silver *varq* from several Indian shops in London and, although I mention it in my recipes where it is traditional to use it, it is entirely optional and unimportant as its presence is merely decorative and adds nothing to the flavour of the dish. I try and stock up whenever I visit my parents in Pakistan and have never paid London prices for the luxury of using it.

Unday ka Halwa
(Egg Halwa)

In the subcontinent eggs are prized very highly as a strength-giving food, a must for someone who is ill or convalescing. An egg *halwa* is therefore considered quite a treat, and could be a celebration of many things. Its sunny yellow colour and light granular texture produces a striking contrast with other Indian *halwas* which usually come in dark rich tones. Living in England I have found it very useful to know this recipe as the ingredients needed here are normally present in the house or are very easily bought.

4 eggs (*unday*)
½ lb/225 g white sugar (*shakar*)
a pinch of saffron (*zafran*)
1⅓ pints/800 ml fresh milk (*doodh*)
4 oz/100 g unsalted butter (*makhan*)
varq (optional)

8–10 blanched almonds, cut into slivers (*badam*)
8–10 unsalted pistachio nuts, blanched and cut into slivers (*pistay*)

Break the eggs into a bowl and add the sugar. Whisk well either by hand or with an electric whisk. Using a non-stick frying pan or cast-iron skillet, lightly dry-roast the saffron for just 1 minute. Heat 4 fl. oz/120 ml of the milk and crumble the roasted threads of saffron between your thumb and forefinger into the warm milk. Melt the butter in a heavy-bottomed saucepan over very low heat. Add the whisked eggs and sugar and both the saffron-flavoured as well as ordinary milk and cook over low heat stirring intermittently. Continue to cook for almost an hour, stirring more or less all the time.

When the milk has been condensed so there is no liquid left, the butter will also separate and the mixture will acquire the consistency of cottage cheese. This is when you know that your *halwa* is ready. At the end when the cooking *halwa* begins to thicken and bubble energetically its colour also turns a brighter yellow. Before taking it off the stove turn up the heat and briskly stir-fry it for a minute or two.

Transfer to a shallow open serving dish lightly greased with unsalted butter. Spread the *halwa* into it and decorate with *varq*, almonds and pistachios. Cool to room temperature before serving.

Sooji ka Halwa
(Semolina Halwa)

This *halwa* is traditionally eaten for breakfast with hot *parathas* or *pooris*. It is quickly made and is one of the less labour-intensive *halwas*, useful for unexpected guests. It is also an extremely economic way of serving a delicious home-made sweet dish at a large dinner.

1 lb/450 g semolina (*sooji*)
2½ lb/1·1 kg white sugar (*shakar*)
3 pints/1·8 litres water (*pani*)
1 tsp saffron (optional) (*zafran*)
2 oz/50 g *gram* flour (*besan*)
1 lb/450 g clarified butter (*asli ghee*)
12 small cardamoms, crudely ground (*choti elaichee*)

2 oz/50 g desiccated coconut (optional) (*naryal*)
a handful of sultanas or raisins (*kish mish*)
1 tbsp blanched chopped almonds (*badam*)
1 tbsp chopped unsalted pistachio nuts (*pistay*)

Put the sugar and water in a saucepan, add the saffron, bring it to a boil and set it to one side. In a small cast-iron or non-stick pan, lightly dry-roast the *gram* flour so it turns barely a shade darker. Melt the clarified butter in another large heavy-bottomed saucepan and fry the crushed cardamoms for a few minutes. Then add the semolina and stir vigorously over medium to high heat. After approximately 10–15 minutes the semolina will change colour from yellow to a pale almond. Do not allow it to get too brown. Add the roasted *gram* flour and stir to mix. After a few minutes also add the coconut if you are using it. (Using the coconut will give the *halwa* a stiffer consistency than its normal soft, almost fluffy, texture.)

Stir for another minute and then, very carefully, add the sugar water. Turn the heat off under the saucepan while you do this and pour the water in very slowly as it will spit and bubble up furiously on making contact with the hot *asli ghee* and fried semolina. Stir it in as you go along until all the water has been poured in. Turn the heat back on to low and cook for a few short minutes. Put aside a few of the sultanas, almonds and pistachios for decorating the dish with and stir in the rest.

You should take the *halwa* off the heat while it is still reasonably watery as it will thicken a little as it cools and sets. At this stage it will have a rich golden brown colour. Pour the *halwa* into a large serving dish, and decorate it with the almonds, pistachios and sultanas. This *halwa* may be eaten hot or at room temperature.

Gajar ka Halwa
(Carrot Halwa)

This is one of the seasonal *halwas* as carrots are only available in the winter months in most parts of the subcontinent. I believe that there is a general consensus of opinion that *gajar ka halwa* occupies pride of place amongst the top-ranking Indian *halwas* and sweets. Although you will find *gajar ka halwa* being sold in Indian sweet shops, the tastiest ones I have eaten have always been home-made.

The most time-consuming aspect of cooking this dish is the process of reducing the milk which can be made into slightly less of a chore if you allow it to cook extremely slowly over the tinest possible flame in a covered saucepan. This technique undoubtedly increases the cooking time as it reduces the speed of evaporation, but it relieves the cook from the arduous task of constantly stirring the milk.

2 lb/900 g carrots, peeled and grated (*gajar*)

1⅓ pints/800 ml milk (*doodh*)

4 oz/100 g unsalted butter (*makhan*)

8 oz/225 g white sugar (*shakar*)

10–12 small cardamoms, crudely ground (*choti elaichee*)

8–10 blanched almonds, cut into slivers (*badam*)

8–10 unsalted pistachio nuts, cut into slivers (*pistay*)

Put the grated carrots into a large heavy-bottomed cooking pot with the milk and bring it to the boil. Immediately turn the heat down extremely low, stir to mix the carrots well with the milk, cover and cook slowly until the milk has been completely condensed so that there is no liquid left. This process may take up to 2½ hours during which time you should check every now and again to make sure that the milk and carrots are not sticking to the bottom of the pan. Towards the end of this time, when there is just a small quantity of milk left, you should take off the lid and stir more or less continuously to ensure that the last drop evaporates without sticking to the bottom or burning.

When the milk has all dried off into *khoya*, add the butter and fry over medium to high heat stirring vigorously for about 10 minutes. Then add the sugar and crushed cardamoms and continue to stir briskly until the carrots become a burnished orange colour and the *halwa* begins to glisten as the butter separates and comes to the surface. This should take another 10–15 minutes.

Transfer to a serving dish and decorate with almonds and pistachios. (If the occasion is special you may want to use *varq*.) This dish may be served hot with fresh cream, at room temperature or cold straight from the fridge.

Pumpkin *halwa* is made in exactly the same way.

Kheer

In many rural areas of the subcontinent the making and eating of *kheer* is closely associated with the festivities and celebrations that seasonally accompany the harvesting of the rice crop. Although such *kheer* is similar in many respects to its urban counterpart, described here, it is made with new rice and sweetened with *jaggery* derived from sugar cane or date palm which gives it a totally different taste to this *kheer*.

My *kheer* recipe is for a dish which would be recognized as fairly typical of North Indian Muslim cookery. To explain this dish to you as being a kind of rice pudding would be both erroneous and misleading. The addition of cardamoms, ground almonds, pistachios and rosewater to flavour milk that is cooked and cooked until it is reduced by more than half, creates a dish that is dramatically different and far more delicious.

This is a simple recipe but a tiring one to make. Even though I have recommended using some canned evaporated milk as a partial but well-camouflaged short-cut, it is a slow business and can take up to several hours. It is extremely important to stir almost constantly as the *kheer* cooks, and to scrape off the *khoya* as it forms and sticks to the sides and bottom of your pan, because it can so easily burn. It is true that some people deliberately allow it to burn just a little as they enjoy the smoky flavour that is instantly absorbed by the milk. However, it is a very delicate operation to get it just right and is not to everyone's liking. I must admit not to being a fan of smoked *kheer* myself.

1½ pints/900 ml fresh milk (*taza doodh*)

1 tbsp rice (*chawal*)

7 fl. oz/200 ml canned full cream evaporated milk, unsweetened

3–4 tbsp ground almonds (*badam*)

10–12 small cardamoms, crudely ground (*choti elaichee*)

8 oz/225 g white sugar, or to taste (*shakar*)

1 tsp saffron, or as much as you can afford (optional) (*zafran*)

4 tbsp *kewra* or rosewater

slivers of blanched almonds and pistachios for garnishing (*badam/pistay*)

1 piece *varq* for decoration (optional)

Cook the tablespoon of rice in boiling water until it becomes completely soft and mushy. Strain. Put this rice and the fresh milk in a heavy-bottomed saucepan and bring it to a boil. Once the milk is boiling, turn down the heat, pour in the evaporated milk and stir well. Adjust the heat to the point where the milk is kept boiling slowly without being in any danger of boiling over. Stir frequently while the milk is being reduced and becoming thicker as during this process the *khoya* has a tendency to stick to the sides and bottom of the pan. You must keep scraping off this dried milk and mixing it back into the liquid milk.

After about 45–60 minutes, stir in the ground almonds and cardamoms. When the liquid has reduced by about half, add the sugar and saffron and carry on stirring until the *kheer* has the texture of a thick pancake mix, except that it will be bumpier on account of the grains of rice.

At the end it seems to happen all at once. One minute you are wondering whether the pudding is still too liquidy, and suddenly it's done, and you must remove it from the heat immediately. Remember that the *kheer* will thicken a little as it cools and sets so you should be careful not to let it get too thick on the stove. Stir in the *kewra* or rosewater when it has cooled a little. Garnish with almonds, pistachios and/or *varq*.

Gajreyla
(Carrot Kheer)

This dish is a sibling of *gajar ka halwa* but is simpler and quicker to make and much less heavy on the stomach. As a result it can be eaten in larger quantities and is wonderfully refreshing served cold on a summer evening.

2 lb/900 g carrots, peeled and grated (*gajar*)

1½ pints/900 ml fresh milk (*doodh*)

4 oz/100 g/½ cup rice (*chawal*)

8–10 oz/225–275 g white sugar, or to taste (*shakar*)

blanched slivered almonds to taste (*badam*)

unsalted slivered pistachios to taste (*pistay*)

a pinch of saffron (optional) (*zafran*)

1 tsp custard powder

2 tbsp *kewra* (optional)

For the garnish

slivered almonds and pistachios (*badam/pistay*)

varq

Put the carrots in a large, heavy-bottomed saucepan with the milk to cook. After bringing to a rapid boil adjust the heat so that it continues to cook briskly without any danger of boiling over.

Wash the rice and cook it in water in a separate saucepan until completely soft and then add to the carrots and milk. Continue cooking, then after 15–20 minutes add the sugar, nuts and saffron and continue to cook slowly until the carrots become soft. Add more milk at this stage if you find it too thick. Stir in the custard powder and take off the heat to cool.

When the milk has cooled, add the *kewra* if you are using it, and transfer to a serving dish. Decorate with *varq* and nuts and chill in the refrigerator before serving.

Firni

Firni is another member of the *kheer* family. Its main difference from the others is the use of ground rice or rice flour rather than whole grains of rice. This alters the consistency to such a degree that it sets beautifully when left to cool. It is served cold and makes a light and refreshing end to a rich and spice-filled meal.

Firni is a very popular choice of dessert at weddings and other large social gatherings where it is traditionally served as individual portions set in shallow bowls of unbaked clay, which have always been used in India as disposable crockery. Unfortunately that special flavour of unbaked earthenware that is so easily absorbed by the *firni* is lost to us in the West, but the delicate fragrance of rose essence and cardamoms still makes it well worth having.

4 tbsp rice (*chawal*)
1–2 tbsp unsalted pistachio nuts,
　according to taste (*pistay*)
3 pints/1·8 litres milk (*doodh*)
2 oz/50 g ground almonds (*badam*)
10–12 small green cardamoms,
　ground (*choti elaichee*)

8 oz/225 g white sugar, or to taste
　(*shakar*)
3–4 tbsp *kewra* or a few drops
　rosewater
varq (optional)

Soak the rice and pistachios in separate bowls of water for a couple of hours. Strain the rice, pat dry and grind to a fine powder. Mix with a little of the milk to make a smooth paste. When the pistachios are soft, peel and cut them into slivers.

Add the rice paste to the rest of the milk and put it on to boil in a wide-mouthed, heavy-bottomed pan. Once it reaches boiling point set the heat at a level where it continues to cook without danger of boiling over. You will need to stir continuously at this stage, scraping the milk off as it sticks to the sides of the pan, and before it has a chance to burn. The ground rice also has a tendency to stick to the bottom of the pan which makes it important to keep stirring diligently. After about 20–30 minutes, when the milk has begun to thicken, add the ground almonds and cardamoms. Carry on stirring as before until the milk thickens some more and reaches a consistency resembling pancake batter. Add the sugar and keep stirring until it has dissolved. Put in half the slivered pistachios, saving the rest for the final garnish.

Take the saucepan off the heat and leave on one side to cool. Stir occasionally while it is cooling to speed up the process and keep its texture smooth. After about 15 minutes when it is no longer so hot, add the *kewra* or rose essence and cover the pan so the aroma is absorbed by the *firni*. Pour into small individual bowls or a large serving dish, and refrigerate to set. Before serving decorate with slivers of pistachios and *varq*, if you are feeling lavish.

Muzaffer

In Indian Muslim homes all over the subcontinent, at least one sweet dish incorporating *sivayyan* is bound to be cooked on the Muslim festival of Eid, which follows Ramzan, a month of fasting. There are really only two kinds of *sivayyan* dishes most commonly seen: *doodh sivayyan* which is cooked in milk, and the other, a preparation in which the *sivayyan* are fried in clarified butter. *Muzaffer* is the third variety and is much more special than both of these and must be considered royal in comparison.

The closest western equivalent to *sivayyan* is vermicelli, although the Indian variety is much finer spun and more delicate. It is readily available at all Indian food shops and is worth trying to get if you can. If this is not possible then you could use Italian vermicelli as a substitute. A wok is the perfect utensil for this recipe because it makes handling the *sivayyan* much easier, and its wide open shape enables the excess moisture to evaporate much more efficiently than a conventionally shaped saucepan.

8 oz/225 g vermicelli broken into pieces approx. 6 in./15 cm long (*sivayyan*)

1½ lb/700 g granulated sugar (*shakar*)

¼ pint/450 ml water (*pani*)

8 oz/225 g pure clarified butter (*asli ghee*)

12–14 small cardamoms, crudely ground (*choti elaichee*)

2½ pints/1·5 litres fresh milk (*doodh*)

2 tbsp lemon juice (*neeboo ka ras*)

a generous pinch of saffron (*zafran*)

1 tbsp blanched almond slivers (*badam*)

1 tbsp unsalted pistachio slivers (*pistay*)

1 tbsp rosewater or *kewra* (preferable though not essential)

Put the sugar and water in a saucepan and bring to a boil. Turn the heat off and reserve. Melt the *asli ghee* over low heat in the wok, add the crushed cardamoms and *sivayyan*, and fry over medium to high heat stirring and turning the *sivayyan* over and around so they all brown as evenly as possible. (It is inevitable that some strands will be darker than others.) When most of the *sivayyan* are a light golden brown colour, pour in the sugar syrup made earlier, and continue to cook over low heat. It will bubble away energetically as the water evaporates. Stir occasionally to ensure that the *sivayyan* do not stick to the bottom of the pan.

As the water evaporates the *sivayyan* will stiffen a little and the *asli ghee* will separate. This is your cue to add the milk. As soon as the milk comes to a boil put in the lemon juice. The water content of the milk will immediately separate and will almost instantly be absorbed by the *sivayyan*. Continue to stir-fry for a few minutes and then add the saffron, almonds, pistachios and rosewater or *kewra*. Fry for another minute or two and then serve either warm or at room temperature.

Sheer Khurma

Since most Indian *halwas* and *kheers* can be exhausting to make, it is no great surprise that this quick and easy recipe is the one I cook most often. Like the previous recipe, this is also made with *sivayyan* (similar to dried vermicelli) but is very different in texture and taste. Here the *sivayyan* is cooked with dates, almonds and pistachios and floats in delicious saffron-flavoured milk. It is best served in a deep dish and ladled out to be eaten from small bowls. Individual preferences vary about whether it tastes best piping hot, just warm or cold. Like so many other *sivayyan* dishes, it is traditionally served on the Muslim festival of Eid.

1½–2 oz/40–50 g vermicelli (unroasted *sivayyan*)
4 oz/100–125 g dried stoned dates (*khajoor*)
4 oz/100 g almonds (*badam*)
4 oz/100 g unsalted pistachio nuts (*pistay*)
4 oz/100 g clarified butter (*asli ghee*)

10 small cardamoms, crudely ground (*choti elaichee*)
4 pints/2·4 litres fresh milk (*doodh*)
8 oz/225 g white sugar (*shakar*)
1 tsp saffron (*zafran*)
2 tbsp *kewra* or rosewater (*gulab ka pari*) (optional)

Soak the dates, almonds and pistachios overnight in water in separate bowls. The next day, when they have been well soaked, remove their skins which will already have loosened, and cut them into halves or fine slivers. Dry well. Take a large, heavy cooking utensil and fry the fruit and nuts in *asli ghee* for a minute or two and then lift them out with a slotted spoon. In this same *asli ghee* fry the crushed cardamoms for a minute before putting in the *sivayyan*, breaking them up, as you do so, into pieces approximately 3 in./7·5 cm long.

In a separate saucepan heat the milk. When the *sivayyan* are golden brown pour in the hot milk. Cook for 3–4 minutes over medium to high heat and add the sugar. Keep stirring until the sugar has dissolved, and then put in the saffron, almonds, pistachios and dates. Cook for a few more minutes, add the *kewra* or rosewater, and serve at the temperature of your choice.

Zarda

(Sweet Saffron Yellow Rice with Dried Fruit)

This is a popular dessert amongst Muslims all over India, Pakistan and Bangladesh, and is frequently seen at various festivals, weddings and religious ceremonies. The bright colour of this dish, by which it is instantly recognized and to which it owes its name, 'the yellow one', should really come from true saffron. All too often food colouring, a poor substitute lacking the flavour so vital to the recipe, is used as saffron is so exorbitantly expensive; if you do not live in a large city it can also prove hard to find. I have suggested a modest quantity of saffron which you are welcome to increase, if you want to, as it will surely improve the colour and enhance the flavour of your *zarda*.

8 oz/225 g/1 cup good quality rice (*chawal*)

½ tsp saffron (*zafran*)

8 oz/225 g white sugar, or to taste (*shakar*)

2 oz/50 g clarified butter (*asli ghee*)

8 small cardamoms, split open just a crack (*choti elaichee*)

1 in./2·5 cm cinnamon stick (*dalchini*)

4 cloves (*laung*)

15 unsalted pistachio nuts, blanched and slivered (*pistay*)

10 almonds, blanched and slivered (*badam*)

1 tbsp raisins (*kish mish*)

Wash the rice thoroughly in several changes of cold or tepid water. Add 2 pints/1·2 litres water and rapidly bring to the boil. Once the water is boiling, adjust the heat to keep it boiling without any danger of it boiling over. Cook in an uncovered pan until the rice is almost, but not quite, done and strain into a colander. To ensure that the rice does not overcook, test several times by lifting out a few grains, while it is cooking.

Put the threads of saffron in 4 fl. oz/120 ml boiling water, and leave to soak until it releases its colour into the water which will turn a bright yellow. Dissolve the sugar in 8 fl oz/225 ml of water and keep to one side.

Take a heavy saucepan and melt the clarified butter over low heat. Add the cardamoms, cinnamon and cloves and fry for a few minutes. Add the pistachios, almonds and raisins. Take the pan off the heat for a moment while you carefully pour in the sugar water. Cook over high heat for a minute or longer to allow about half this water to evaporate. Pour in the saffron water and continue to cook over high heat until you have no more than 4 fl. oz/120 ml water left in the pan. Now put in the cooked rice and stir gently to mix, taking care not to break the grains. Cook over high heat until most of the liquid has evaporated, then turn the heat down low, close with a tightly fitting lid and let it finish cooking and absorb the flavours in the trapped steam for about 5 minutes.

QULFI
(Indian Ice Cream)

This is Indian ice cream which is typically flavoured with mangoes, pistachios and almonds, or sometimes may be left just 'plain', which means it is simply flavoured with cardamoms and perhaps a little rosewater. The reason for its tasting so different from European and American ice creams is that the milk is cooked for a long time until it is transformed to a thick creamy consistency. This process is similar to that used for making *kheers* or certain other sweet dishes in which *khoya* is made from fresh milk.

In the subcontinent, *qulfi* is usually frozen in conical shaped moulds about 6 in./15 cm in length, and each person is served with their own cone of *qulfi* cut into ½ in./1·2 cm slices for convenience. It is unlikely, even if you wanted to, that you would find these traditional metal cones outside the subcontinent. It is probably best to improvise and set the ice cream in any attractive large or small individual sized moulds you may have. A fluted jelly mould or ring mould is good for this purpose although you would need to leave it outside the freezer for a while or dip it into hot water, to get the *qulfi* out. Another possibility is to use paper cups filling them up with as much or as little *qulfi* as you like and sealing them off with foil before placing them in the freezer. When it's time to serve them, you simply tear off the cup and serve individual portions that look as similar to the Indian *qualfi* as possible. Decorate the *qulfi*, whether frozen in individual portions or in a larger mould, with slivers of almonds or pistachios and slice it for your guests as you would a cake.

Aam ki Qulfi
(Mango Qulfi)

I have recommended using canned mangoes for this recipe to free you from dependence on the availability of fresh mangoes. I strongly recommend that you buy Alphonso mangoes if at all possible as there is no other that can match the fullness of its flavour and the non-fibrous quality of its flesh. Canned mangoes are available both as pulp or sliced. It does not really matter which you use except that you should remember that the proportions in my recipe refer to sliced canned mangoes and I suspect that the cans containing pulp may carry a higher proportion of mango as no weight is lost to syrup.

2 pints/1·2 litres fresh milk (*doodh*)	1 cup white sugar, or to taste (*shakar*)
14 fl. oz/425 ml canned full cream evaporated milk, unsweetened	14 oz/400 g canned mango slices, or to taste (*aam*)

Take a large heavy-bottomed saucepan or a wok. The wider the mouth of the cooking utensil you use, the quicker it is to evaporate the milk. Bring the fresh milk to a boil and adjust the heat so that it continues to boil briskly without boiling over. Stir frequently, scraping the cream off the sides and bottom of the cooking pot as it forms, and before it burns. After about half an hour add the canned evaporated milk and continue to stir more or less continuously. As the milk begins to thicken it tends to stick more and more to the pan and you must continue to scrape it off quickly and mix it back in with the milk.

When the milk has thickened considerably take it off the stove and add the sugar a little at a time and stir it in. (If you add the sugar all at once while the milk is cooking it can curdle.) Cook the milk until it is the consistency of a thick cream soup. By this stage the milk will be spitting and bubbling away frantically and sticking eagerly and uncontrollably to the bottom and sides of the pan. Allow the milk to cool.

Take the mango slices and throw out any syrup there may be in the tin. Purée the mango in an electric blender and add the pulp to the cooled milk. Whisk with a fork to blend smoothly. Pour the liquid *qulfi* into any mould you have chosen and place it in the freezer. After an hour open the mould(s), whisk the *qulfi* with a fork to ensure that it sets smoothly, and return to the freezer.

Pistay ki Qulfi
(Pistachio Qulfi)

There is no artificial colouring here as is so often seen nowadays in place of real pistachios. This is a wonderful genuine green pistachio *qulfi*.

2 pints/1·2 litres fresh milk (*doodh*)
14 fl. oz/425 ml canned full cream evaporated milk, unsweetened
1 cup white sugar, or to taste (*shakar*)
3 oz/75 g blanched unsalted pistachio nuts, finely ground (*pistay*)

6 small cardamoms, finely ground (*choti elaichee*)
2 tbsp *kewra* or rosewater (*gulab ka pani*)

This is cooked in exactly the same way as the mango *qulfi* except that you add the ground cardamoms and pistachio just as soon as the sugar has dissolved. Add the finely ground pistachios a little at a time, and stir to blend evenly with the milk. If the powdered pistachio goes lumpy use the back of a wooden spoon to mash it into a paste against the sides of the saucepan and mix it in.

Allow it to cool, add the *kewra* or rosewater, whisk well with a fork and pour into air-tight moulds to freeze. As in the case of mango *qulfi* you could give it a thorough whisking after an hour and perhaps once again yet another hour later and leave it to set.

RELISHES, RAITAS AND CHUTNEYS

· Relishes, Raitas and Chutneys ·

Here you will find some of those customary home-made chutneys and *raitas* that are a familiar and particularly tempting sight on an Indian table. While pickles, whether home or commercially made, are a popular accompaniment to an Indian meal, I personally prefer to serve freshly made chutneys, relishes and interesting yoghurt preparations, called *raitas*. Some of these yoghurt *raitas* are in fact much more than simply relishes, and could well be considered complete dishes in their own right. In Indian food, *raitas* probably occupy a similar place to salads but are eaten together with the main course and not reserved especially for the beginning or end of a meal. Chutneys and other relishes whet our appetites beautifully; at times they can have the dangerous effect of encouraging us to over-eat terribly! Most of the recipes in this section are simple and quick to make, especially so if you have an electric blender or food processor at your disposal.

Hot and cold drinks

On the question of what you should drink with an Indian meal, my answer would be that you should follow your own inclination. Strict orthodoxy in this matter teaches us that nothing at all should really be drunk with food and that if you so much as raised a glass of plain water to your lips, in certain company, it might be taken to signify that you have finished your meal. My mother warned us as children that by disregarding this rule we were hurting our metabolisms, causing the food to swim unnaturally around in our bodies and making it much harder for the stomach to fulfil its digestive function. I, for one, was never convinced by this argument which seemed to me to be characteristically based on some unscientific notion of hers.

Yet all rules have exceptions, often quite contradictory ones, and a cool tall glass of *lassi* on a hot summer day is both traditional and extremely popular. Of course in our home it tasted doubly good because for some reason it never seemed to occur to my mother that the food in our stomachs might just as easily swill or slosh around in cold *lassi* as in water.

Lassi is a drink made from diluted, strongly whisked yoghurt, the authentic version of which is lightly salted, probably to replace the large quantities of salt that are lost from our bodies through perspiration on a hot day. It can also be drunk sweetened, and is by all those who are not able to develop a taste for the salty drink, although by doing so they risk being thought of, amongst millions of *lassi* devotees, as lacking a certain sophistication.

To make *lassi*, dilute a cup of thick set natural yoghurt with 6 fl. oz/175 ml water and whisk it well in an electric blender, together with some ice, adding either salt or sugar. Serve it with extra crushed ice on the side for those who might enjoy crunching the ice through their drink. Sometimes *lassi* is diluted with milk rather than water which makes it a richer, more filling drink. There are no hard or fast rules about how much or little you should dilute the yoghurt, or when to make it with water and when with milk. For instance, if you were planning on drinking several glasses of *lassi* to get you through a hot afternoon you might dilute it a little more and would probably use water rather than milk.

Milk flavoured with cardamoms and rosewater, *kewra* or saffron, containing ground or delicate slivers of almonds and/or pistachios, perhaps also decorated with a few petals and served with crushed ice, makes a very unusual, refreshing and healthy drink. Mango and banana milk shakes are universal favourites when the fruit is in season.

Cold *sharbats* of lemon or lime, pomegranate, melon, pineapple, mango and grapes make delicious summer drinks and could be served with Indian meals if you are wanting to prepare something fresh and non-alcoholic. Freshly squeezed orange juice is generally seasoned with a little salt and a pinch of red chillies. Watermelons are diced and then crushed to extract some of their juice and served in long cocktail-style glasses along with a spoon, with which to eat the pulp of the fruit once its juice has been drunk.

A whole variety of fine Indian teas such as Assam, Darjeeling and Nilgiri are suitable for serving at the end of a meal. Indeed, they are also drunk with relish during the day, starting early in the morning, then perhaps again at mid morning, at teatime, after lunch or dinner, and in fact at every opportunity that presents itself additional pots of *chai* are brewed. The tragedy in England is that even those who wish to avoid tea bags and want to enjoy a cup of real tea are likely to find it hard to come by quality tea leaves, as most commercially packaged teas contain the poorest quality dust under the guise of real tea.

If making tea in a pot, always heat the pot first with hot water. Using only freshly boiled water, pour it over the tea leaves as soon as it comes to the boil. Immediately cover with a tea–cosy and allow it to brew for at least 5 minutes. I usually estimate a teaspoon for each cup and one for the pot as I like my tea quite strong, but this does vary as some tea leaves are naturally stronger and more full bodied than others. Use as much or as little as you wish, to suit your own taste. In many Indian homes, making tea involves cooking the leaves in a saucepan of water on top of the stove. Milk is added to the brew as soon as it comes to its first boil. After the milky tea has been rapidly brought to the boil once again, it is allowed to simmer for a while before being poured either directly into cups or mugs through a strainer or else into a teapot. Sometimes tea may be flavoured with a touch of ground, green cardamom seeds or a few mint leaves, both of which add a pleasant aroma and flavour to the drink.

Qehva or green tea is excellent for the digestion and is also quite a suitable hot drink with which to finish an Indian meal. Since it is less common than regular tea it is enjoyed as something of a treat and may be taken as showing greater than usual hospitality.

Kashmiri chai is a salty tea of a dusty pink colour and is something of an acquired taste. To make a *standard* pot of Kashmiri tea, first cook some green tea leaves very thoroughly in a saucepan on the stove, using the minimum amount of water. Add a little salt and a $\frac{1}{2}$ teaspoon baking soda. When the leaves separate and are completely soft, add 8 fl. oz/250 ml/1 cup cold water and an equal quantity of milk, and cook for a further period of time until the fullness of its colour has properly developed. You can also add a few cardamoms and cloves for additional flavour if you want to.

Drinking coffee is not a particularly Indian habit and since all coffee is imported it remains quite an expensive luxury for most people. Yet, for this very reason, it will frequently be offered to guests as the most special treat of all.

Kachoomar
(Onion, Tomato and Green Chilli Relish)

This is a recipe for a very ordinary and well-known North Indian relish that goes well with just about every meal. It is the one I have chosen to be the first in this section as it was the relish best loved by my father and one which he never seemed to tire of no matter how often it appeared on our table. You may alter the proportion of onions to tomatoes if you wish.

8 oz/225 g onions, peeled and very finely chopped (*pyaz*)

8 oz/225 g tomatoes, very finely chopped (*timatar*)

2–3 green chillies, or to taste, very finely chopped (*hari mirch*)

1 cup fresh coriander leaves, finely chopped (*hara dhania*)

½ tsp salt, or to taste (*namak*)

3–4 tbsp lemon juice (*neeboo ka ras*)

a sprinkling of freshly ground black pepper to taste (*kali mirch*)

Simply mix all the ingredients together very well.

Hara Kachoomar
(Green Salad Relish)

I improvised on the previous traditional *Kachoomar* recipe to create this relish. This provided me with a way in which to serve and eat green salads that is compatible with the style of Indian food.

8–10 lettuce leaves (*salad ka patta*)

4–5 spring onions (*hari pyaz*)

1–1½ cup/s finely diced cucumber (*kheera*)

1 small green pepper, seeded and finely diced (*simla ki mirch*)

1–2 green chillies, finely diced (*hari mirch*)

½ tsp salt, or to taste (*namak*)

freshly ground black pepper to taste (*kali mirch*)

lemon juice (*neeboo ka ras*)

Wash the lettuce leaves, then roll them up loosely and shred them into fine strips. Remove the outer wilted leaves of the spring onions, slice off any hairy root tufts on their heads, and chop them up finely using the fresh green stalk and leaves as well as the onion bulb.

Mix the lettuce, spring onions, cucumber and green chillies together and season with salt and pepper. Douse liberally with lemon juice, mix well together again, and serve.

GREEN CHUTNEYS

There are several kinds of green chutney which are popular for everyday use, and make a welcome addition to just about any meal. They all need to be freshly prepared on the day they are meant to be eaten. Green chutneys are sensationally good as fillings in sandwiches which are always a favourite whether served with afternoon tea or taken to school or work for lunch.

Dhaniyay ki Chutney
(Fresh Coriander Chutney)

This chutney can be made using either lemon juice or yoghurt as its base. Here are recipes for both.

With Lemon

2 cups tightly packed fresh coriander leaves, roughly chopped (*hara dhania*)
1–2 green chillies, or to taste (*hari mirch*)
1–2 tbsp lemon juice (*neeboo ka ras*)
salt to taste (*namak*)

With Yoghurt

1 cup tightly packed fresh coriander leaves, roughly chopped (*hara dhania*)
$\frac{1}{2}$ tsp red chilli powder (*lal mirch*)
1 garlic clove, peeled (*lehsun*)
3–4 tbsp natural yoghurt (*dahi*)
$\frac{1}{4}$–$\frac{1}{2}$ tsp salt (*namak*)

For both types, put all the ingredients in an electric blender or liquidizer and make a smooth paste. Serve in a small shallow dish as an appetizer to accompany any meal.

Dhaniyay-Pudeenay ki Chutney
(Fresh Coriander and Mint Chutney)

This is made in exactly the same way as the previous recipes for coriander chutneys except that you would use equal quantities of fresh coriander and mint leaves.

Pudeenay ki Chutney I
(Fresh Mint Chutney)

2 cups tightly packed with chopped
  fresh mint leaves (*pudeena*)
2–3 green chillies (*hari mirch*)

salt to taste (*namak*)
4 tbsp lemon juice (*neeboo ka ras*)

Blend all the ingredients together to make a smooth paste.

Pudeenay ki Chutney II
(Fresh Mint Chutney)

2 cups tightly packed with chopped
  fresh mint leaves (*pudeena*)
2–3 green chillies (*hari mirch*)
1–2 garlic cloves, peeled (*lehsun*)

salt to taste (*namak*)
tamarind juice (see page 29) (*imli ka
  pani*)

Take an electric liquidizer and blend all the ingredients together, using as much tamarind water as you need to obtain a smooth paste. Cool and serve.

Hara Dhaniyay aur Naryal ki Chutney
(Fresh Coriander and Coconut Chutney)

2 tbsp desiccated coconut (*naryal*)
1 cup tightly packed fresh coriander
  leaves (*hara dhania*)

1 green chilli (*hari mirch*)
¼ tsp salt, or to taste (*namak*)
3–4 tsbp lemon juice (*neeboo ka ras*)

Blend all the ingredients together to make a smooth paste.

Timatar ki Chutney
(Hot Tomato Chutney)

This is a Hyderabadi recipe for quite a hot chutney, though it's by no means lethal, not by Indian standards, at least. It is eaten in fairly small quantities, in much the same way as pickles are, to add some extra zest to food.

1½ lb/700 g ripe tomatoes, finely chopped (*timatar*)
2½ tsp red chilli powder (*lal mirch*)
½ tsp turmeric (*haldi*)
1 tsp finely grated fresh ginger (*adrak*)
1 tsp crushed garlic (*lehsun*)

1½ tbsp ground coriander (*dhania*)
cooking oil (*tail*)
¼ tsp mustard seeds (*rai*)
¼ tsp nigella seeds (*kalonji*)
¼ tsp white cumin seeds (*sabut safeid zeera*)
4–5 *karri* leaves (*karri patta*)

Mix the tomatoes with the red chilli powder, turmeric, ginger, garlic and coriander.

Heat some oil and add the whole spices and *karri* leaves. In less than a minute they should begin to pop and darken a little at which point you add the tomatoes with the other spices and a little water to help them cook and soften. Cook over medium heat until the water evaporates and the oil appears on the surface, which will tell you that your chutney is ready. This won't take more than half an hour.

Imli ki Chutney
(Tamarind Chutney)

Tamarind chutney is extremely popular as a dip when served to accompany *seekh kababs*, *boti kababs* and chicken *tikkas*. It also goes particularly well with *samosas* and other tea-time savouries. Tastes differ as to how chilli hot it should be, as well as in the matter of its sweetness. This recipe is fairly restrained in the use of sugar as I adore the tart, sour flavour of the tamarind. You may alter the proportions of chilli and sugar if you wish.

4 oz/100 g tamarind from a
  compressed slab (*imli*)
1 pint/600 ml water (*pani*)
2 oz/50 g soft dark brown sugar (*gur*)
3–4 whole dried red chillies, freshly
  ground (*sabut lal mirch*), or 1 tsp
  red chilli powder (*lal mirch*)

¼ tsp dried ground ginger (*sonth*)
½ tsp salt (*namak*)
1 tbsp raisins (optional) (*kish mish*)

Break off the required weight of tamarind from the compressed slab and cook it over high heat, in the water, for about 10 minutes. As the tamarind begins to soften, break it up so that the pulp and seeds separate. When it is completely soft, strain through a sieve into another pan, pushing through as much of the soft tamarind as you can so you have a rich juice. Discard the seeds and other residue in the sieve.

Add the sugar, ground spices and salt to the tamarind juice and continue cooking, over medium to high heat, for about 15–20 minutes by which time the chutney should have thickened. Add the raisins just shortly before removing the pan from the heat. Serve cold or at room temperature.

Aloochay ki Chutney
(Plum Chutney)

This is a gorgeously rich-coloured chutney, valued as much for its luxuriant good looks as its clear, full-bodied, spicy sweet flavour.

2 lb/900 g plums (*aloochay*)
8 fl. oz/250 ml water (*pani*)
1 lb/450 g granulated sugar (*shakar*)
4 fl. oz/120 ml vinegar (*sirka*)
1 tsp red chilli powder (*lal mirch*)
1 in./2·5 cm cube fresh ginger,
  peeled and cut into fine strips
  (*adrak*)

½ tsp white cumin seeds (*sabut safeid
  zeera*)
1 tsp dried mint (*sookha pudeena*)
juice of 1 lemon (*neeboo ka ras*)
½ tsp salt (*namak*)

Blanch the plums in boiling water for a brief minute, then drain them into a colander and peel. Cut the peeled plums into slices and discard their stones. Using an aluminium or stainless steel pan, cook the sliced plums in the 8 fl. oz/250 ml water, with all the remaining ingredients. After bringing to a rapid boil over high heat, continue to cook briskly until enough moisture evaporates so the mixture thickens sufficiently to reach setting point. This may take about half an hour. Cool to room temperature before serving.

Khajoor ki Chutney
(Date Chutney)

Although I have suggested fresh dates for making this chutney, dried dates, called *chhuarey*, can also be used extremely successfully. What matters most is that the dates are of good quality and fully ripe; which can be harder to judge in the case of dried ones. However, if you do decide to use them, remember that they must be pre-soaked overnight.

8 oz/225 g good quality, ripe, fresh Tunisian dates (*khajoor*)

4 oz/100 g green unripe mango, weighed without seed (*aam ki keri*)

10 oz/275 g jaggery (*gur*) or soft brown cane sugar

1 in./2·5 cm cube fresh ginger, peeled and cut into fine strips (*adrak*)

4 medium garlic cloves, thinly sliced into rounds (*lehsun*)

1 tsp red chilli powder (*lal mirch*)

½ tsp salt, or to taste (*namak*)

1 dsp vinegar (*sirka*)

Cut the dates in half lengthwise and discard the seed. Peel and coarsely grate the unripe green mango.

Put 16 fl. oz/475 ml water in a saucepan, add the *gur* or brown sugar and cook until it dissolves. Then add the dates and all the other ingredients, except the vinegar. After bringing to a rapid boil, turn the heat down very low and simmer slowly. In about 30–40 minutes much of the water will have evaporated and the mixture will have thickened sufficiently to reach setting point.

When this happens add the vinegar, remove from the heat and cool.

Aam ki Chutney
(Mango Chutney)

This chutney can be made using any variety of mango just so long as it is still green and unripe. The recipe works best if the mangoes are at the stage where they are no longer rock hard, which is a sign that they are just beginning to ripen. Take care, though, that they haven't already ripened too much when you buy them; far better that they are completely unripe than the other way around.

1½ lb/700 g green mangoes (*aam ki keri*)
1 tsp salt (*namak*)
1 oz/25 g almonds (*badam*)
1 oz/25 g pistachio nuts (*pistay*)
1–2 oz/25–50 g raisins (*kish mish*)
10–14 whole dried red chillies (*sabut lal mirch*)
2 pints/1·2 litres water (*pani*)

2 lb/900 g granulated sugar (*shakar*)
1 in./2·5 cm cube fresh ginger, peeled and cut into fine strips (*adrak*)
6 small garlic cloves, finely sliced into rounds (*lehsun*)
1 tsp nigella seeds (*kalonji*)
4 fl. oz/120 ml white vinegar (*sirka*)

Peel the mangoes, cut them in half and remove the soft seed. Coarsely grate the flesh, sprinkle with salt and set aside for half an hour. This will encourage the fruit to release its moisture so do not leave it too long. Soak the almonds, pistachios, raisins and dried red chillies, all separately in hot water. Once they have softened, drain and peel the almonds and pistachios and cut them into slivers. Slice the drained chillies into small rounds.

Put the grated salty mango and all the other ingredients, with the exception of the raisins, into an aluminium or stainless steel saucepan containing 2 pints of water. Cook over high heat until it comes to a boil. At this point turn the heat down a little and simmer briskly until the mangoes are tender and the syrup has thickened sufficiently to reach setting point. Watch the consistency of the chutney at the last stages and take care to remove it from the heat before the syrup hardens as it will thicken and set some more once it cools down. You will probably need to cook the chutney for about 30–40 minutes in all.

Stir in the raisins only a minute or so before you take it off the heat. Set the chutney aside to cool to room temperature before serving.

Kheeray ka Raita
(Grated Cucumber in Seasoned Yoghurt)

This easily prepared cucumber *raita* serves well in place of a fresh salad with the additional happy advantage that it has a pleasantly cooling and soothing effect on the palate when eaten together with more heavily spiced dishes.

8 oz/225 g natural yoghurt (*dahi*)
½ tsp ground white cumin (*safeid zeera*)
½ tsp freshly ground black pepper (*kali mirch*)
1 tsp dried mint (*pudeena*)
½ tsp salt (*namak*)

1 small to medium cucumber, grated (*kheera*)
a pinch of red chilli powder (*lal mirch*)
½ tsp white cumin seeds (*sabut safeid zeera*)

Lightly whisk the yoghurt with a fork until it acquires a smooth texture, adding a few drops of water if you find it is too thickly set. Season it with ground cumin, pepper, mint and salt before adding the grated cucumber. Transfer to the dish in which you intend to serve it and garnish the surface with a sprinkling of red chilli powder and a few cumin seeds.

If you are preparing the *raita* well ahead of time then it's probably wise to delay adding the salt until shortly before it is due to be eaten, as the salt encourages the cucumber to release its moisture and the *raita* may become a little too watery.

Baingan ka Raita
(Spicy Aubergine in Yoghurt)

This is a very special sort of *raita* that stands out perhaps as being the most unusual of all. Its dramatic taste and good looks are created by the cleverly contrasting flavours and colours of the fried spicy aubergine and the fresh white yoghurt. Bear in mind that for this dish you need to buy really tender young aubergines in which the seeds have not begun to develop.

For the yoghurt
8–10 oz/225–275 g natural yoghurt
   (*dahi*)
2 medium garlic cloves, crushed
   (*lehsun*)
¼–½ tsp red chilli powder (*lal mirch*)
½ tsp salt (*namak*)

For the aubergines
1 or 2 Dutch aubergines approx.
   12 oz/350 g (*baingan*)

cooking oil (*tail*)
2 medium garlic cloves, crushed
   (*lehsun*)
½ tsp turmeric (*haldi*)
1 tsp ground coriander (*dhania*)
¼ tsp red chilli powder (*lal mirch*)
½ tsp salt (*namak*)

For the garnish
fresh coriander leaves (*hara dhania*)

To prepare the yoghurt, lightly whisk it with a fork, mixing in the crushed garlic, red chilli powder and salt, and then transfer to a shallow open dish, spreading the yoghurt out evenly at the bottom.

Now tackle the aubergine. Cut the aubergine into slim long slices or slim rounds according to preference and the shape of the dish. In a large frying pan, heat enough oil to be able to comfortably shallow-fry the aubergine slices, bearing in mind that this vegetable tends to absorb oil. Fry them over high heat until the slices are a deep golden brown on both sides, and then lift out of the oil with a slotted spoon. Using the small quantity of oil left in the pan, now fry the remaining spice ingredients for no more than a minute over low to medium heat. Put the fried aubergine into the spicy mixture, turning them over and around for a couple of minutes so that they are well covered in it.

Lay the spicy aubergines over the yoghurt and pour over them the oil and spices from the pan. Garnish with a few coriander leaves and serve either immediately while still hot or a little later at room temperature.

Turai ka Raita
(Courgette and Yoghurt Relish)

The combination of courgettes and yoghurt is an excellent one for a *raita*. The gentle flavour and light consistency of the courgette is set off beautifully by the spiced yoghurt. Buy very tender baby courgettes.

12 oz/350 g courgettes (*turai*)

8–10 oz/225–275 g natural yoghurt (*dahi*)

½ tsp salt (*namak*)

½ tsp ground white cumin (*safeid zeera*)

½ tsp red chilli powder, or to taste (*lal mirch*)

1 tbsp fresh mint or coriander leaves, finely chopped (*pudeena/hara dhania*)

1–2 small green chillies, finely chopped (*hari mirch*)

2 tbsp cooking oil (*tail*)

1 tsp white cumin seeds (*sabut safeid zeera*)

Trim the courgettes at both ends and boil them in water for about 15 minutes. Immediately rinse them in cold water and without peeling them, mash up with a fork. Set aside to cool.

Lightly whisk the yoghurt and mix in the salt, cumin, red chilli powder, fresh mint or coriander, and green chillies. Add the mashed courgettes and transfer this *raita* to your serving dish.

Now heat the oil in a frying pan and after briefly frying the cumin seeds, for no more than a minute until they darken a little and begin to pop, pour the hot oil and cumin over the *raita* as seasoning and garnish. Do not stir to mix. Serve chilled or at room temperature.

Palak ka Raita
(Spinach and Yoghurt Relish)

10 oz/275 g fresh spinach leaves, weighed without stalks (*palak ka saag*)

10–14 oz/275–400 g natural yoghurt (*dahi*)

1–2 garlic cloves, crushed (*lehsun*)

½ in./1·2 cm cube fresh ginger, peeled and finely grated (*adrak*)

½ tsp red chilli powder (*lal mirch*)

salt to taste (*namak*)

Wash the spinach leaves thoroughly to remove all grit. Without drying the leaves place them in a pan, cover, and cook gently for about 10 minutes until tender. Squeeze out any excess moisture and once the spinach is cool enough to handle, chop it up quite small. Lightly whisk the yoghurt and season it with all the remaining ingredients. Finally add the chopped spinach. Refrigerate and serve chilled.

Salad ka Raita
(Yoghurt Salad)

15 oz/425 g natural yoghurt (*dahi*)

1 tsp concentrated, bottled fresh
   garden mint in vinegar (*pudeena*)

1 tsp white cumin seeds (*sabut safeid
   zeera*)

½ tsp red chilli powder (*lal mirch*)

½ tsp salt (*namak*)

4 spring onions (*hari pyaz*)

For the garnish
red chilli powder (*lal mirch*)
preferably roasted white cumin
   seeds, freshly ground (*sabut safeid
   zeera*)

Lightly whisk the yoghurt with a fork to achieve a smooth consistency, and blend in the mint sauce, cumin seeds, red chilli powder and salt. Remove the blemished leaves from the spring onions, slice off their roots on top, and trim their tails. Dice the spring onions, cucumbers and tomatoes into tiny pieces. Add them to the yoghurt and transfer to a serving dish. Garnish with a sprinkling of red chilli powder and ground cumin seeds.

· INDEX ·